SETTING NATIONAL PRIORITIES
The 1980 Budget

JOSEPH A. PECHMAN *Editor*

SETTING NATIONAL PRIORITIES
The 1980 Budget

Henry Aaron
Thomas A. Dine and others
Robert W. Hartman
Bruce K. MacLaury
Daniel J. B. Mitchell
Joseph A. Pechman

THE BROOKINGS INSTITUTION
Washington, D.C.

THE BROOKINGS INSTITUTION is an independent organization devoted to nonpartisan research, education, and publication in economics, government, foreign policy, and the social sciences generally. Its principal purposes are to aid in the development of sound public policies and to promote public understanding of issues of national importance.

The Institution was founded on December 8, 1927, to merge the activities of the Institute for Government Research, founded in 1916, the Institute of Economics, founded in 1922, and the Robert Brookings Graduate School of Economics and Government, founded in 1924.

The Board of Trustees is responsible for the general administration of the Institution, while the immediate direction of the policies, program, and staff is vested in the President, assisted by an advisory committee of the officers and staff. The by-laws of the Institution state: "It is the function of the Trustees to make possible the conduct of scientific research, and publication, under the most favorable conditions, and to safeguard the independence of the research staff in the pursuit of their studies and in the publication of the results of such studies. It is not a part of their function to determine, control, or influence the conduct of particular investigations or the conclusions reached."

The President bears final responsibility for the decision to publish a manuscript as a Brookings book. In reaching his judgment on the competence, accuracy, and objectivity of each study, the President is advised by the director of the appropriate research program and weighs the views of a panel of expert outside readers who report to him in confidence on the quality of the work. Publication of a work signifies that it is deemed a competent treatment worthy of public consideration but does not imply endorsement of conclusions or recommendations.

The Institution maintains its position of neutrality on issues of public policy in order to safeguard the intellectual freedom of the staff. Hence interpretations or conclusions in Brookings publications should be understood to be solely those of the authors and should not be attributed to the Institution, to its trustees, officers, or other staff members, or to the organizations that support its research.

Foreword

THE BUDGET submitted by President Carter for fiscal year 1980 reflects the pressure on political leaders at all levels to reduce government spending and deficits. During the first two years of the Carter administration, federal budget outlays rose sharply and taxes were cut to promote economic recovery and reduce unemployment. Now that the economy is close to its potential, curbing inflation has become the overriding economic challenge. The 1980 budget is the administration's response both to the political pressure for reduced federal spending and to the change in the economic climate.

The annual budget is the basic planning document of the federal government. In it, the President sets forth his spending and taxing proposals for the coming year and estimates of the costs of the programs he recommends. Since it is a political document, the budget does not discuss alternative ways of achieving the proposed objectives or the reasons for which other means were discarded. The volumes in this annual series, of which this is the tenth, are intended to explain the budget choices made by the President, to examine alternatives, and to evaluate the budgetary implications of the various options.

Although the budget plays a central role in shaping the economy, other aspects of government activity have become increasingly important in the nation's economic affairs. Thus explanations of the worsening of inflation can hardly ignore recent regulatory actions of federal agencies and the administration's anti-inflation efforts through wage-price guidelines. This book devotes considerable attention to these nonbudgetary policies.

The contributors to this volume first discuss the 1980 budget and the budget outlook. They then turn to an analysis of the policies proposed by the administration to control inflation, including fiscal and monetary policies, regulatory policies, and direct intervention into wage and price decisions. Separate chapters are devoted to the domestic and defense budgets. The two appendixes discuss proposals to limit federal spending and the deficit and the use of tax expenditures instead of direct federal expenditures to achieve social and economic objectives.

Preparation of this volume was undertaken jointly by the Brookings Economic Studies and Foreign Policy Studies programs. Joseph A. Pechman is director, and Henry Aaron, Robert W. Hartman, and Daniel J. B. Mitchell are members of the staff, of the Economic Studies program. Thomas A. Dine, John C. Baker, Robert P. Berman, G. Philip Hughes, and William P. Mako are members of the defense analysis staff of the Foreign Policy Studies program, which is under the direction of John D. Steinbruner. Elizabeth H. Cross, Tadd Fisher, Diane Hammond, and Caroline Lalire edited the manuscript.

The Brookings Institution is grateful to Carnegie Corporation of New York and the Ford Foundation for financial support of this project. The views expressed here are those of the authors and should not be attributed to the trustees, officers, or other staff members of the Brookings Institution, Carnegie Corporation, or the Ford Foundation.

BRUCE K. MACLAURY
President

May 1979
Washington, D.C.

Contents

Text Tables

Contents

Appendix Tables

SETTING NATIONAL PRIORITIES
The 1980 Budget

CHAPTER ONE

Introduction and Summary

JOSEPH A. PECHMAN

This budget for fiscal year 1980 is lean and austere. It recommends a spending level well below that suggested by the recent momentum of Federal spending. It will disappoint those who seek expanded Federal efforts across the board. It meets my commitment to a deficit of $30 billion or less.

JIMMY CARTER, *The Budget of the United States Government, Fiscal Year 1980*, p. 3.

PRESIDENT CARTER'S "lean and austere" budget for 1980 was prepared at a time when the economy was expanding rapidly, inflation was running at an unacceptable rate, and politicians at all levels of government were still reacting to the approval of constitutional property tax limitations in California and other states. During its first two years in office, the administration pursued a policy of stimulating the economy in order to reduce the rate of unemployment. By the end of 1978, unemployment had in fact been reduced from 8 percent of the labor force to 5.8 percent and real gross national product was less than 2 percent below its potential. But the basic rate of inflation was rising—inflation, as measured by the consumer price index, rose 9 percent in 1978—and there was a clear need for a program to slow the economy. Thus economic and political objectives coincided. The President responded by making the reduction of inflation his top economic priority for 1979 and publicly committed himself both to sharply reducing the rate of growth of federal spending and to holding the 1980 budget deficit to $30 billion or less.

1

Coping with Inflation

Inflation has persisted for well over a decade, and there is universal agreement that steps must be taken to curb it. Inflation hurts those who must live on fixed or low incomes. It erodes the value of all fixed-value assets and interferes with the long-term planning of individuals and businesses. Proposition 13 and the proposed constitutional amendment to balance the budget are by-products of the social tension resulting from inflation.

The administration's anti-inflation strategy is to slow the rate of economic growth through tight fiscal and monetary policies so as to avoid placing excessive demands on the nation's resources. In addition, business and labor have been asked to voluntarily moderate the growth of prices and wages, and measures are planned to reduce the inflationary effects of government regulation.

The 1980 Budget

In beginning his planning for the 1980 budget, the President was faced with a rapid upward movement in federal spending. From fiscal 1976, the last full fiscal year before he assumed office, to fiscal 1979, total outlays have risen at an annual rate of about 11 percent. An increase of 8.7 percent would be needed in 1980 merely to maintain current service and activity levels without change; with such an increase in outlays, the deficit would exceed $30 billion if there were no change in the tax laws (table 1-1). Furthermore, the administration had made strong commitments to its NATO partners to participate fully in military weapons modernization and the improved combat-readiness of their armed forces. This meant that the President could meet his budget goals only by sharply reducing the rate of growth of nondefense spending.

The President's response to this tight situation was to hold the line on existing nondefense programs and on taxes. He kept his promise to raise real defense outlays by 3 percent but limited the annual pay increase of federal employees to 5.5 percent, repeated his 1978 proposal to contain the rise in hospital costs, cut spending for countercyclical programs, and recommended a number of reductions in low-priority social security benefits. The net effect of these decisions would be to hold the outlay increase in fiscal 1980 to 7.7 percent.

Table 1-1. Comparison of the Proposed Budget with the Current Service Budget, Fiscal Years 1978–80

Billions of dollars

Item	1978[a]	1979[b]	1980[b]
Outlays			
Current services	450.8	491.3	536.1
Proposed increases	...	1.9	7.0
Proposed decreases	...	0.1	−11.6
Proposed outlays	**450.8**	**493.4**	**531.6**
Receipts			
Current services	402.0	456.0	504.5
Proposed increases	...	...	−2.3
Proposed decreases	...	...	0.3
Proposed receipts	**402.0**	**456.0**	**502.6**
Deficit			
Current services	−48.8	−35.4	−31.6
Proposed	−48.8	−37.4	−29.0

Source: *The Budget of the United States Government, Fiscal Year 1980*, p. 16. Figures are rounded.
a. Actual.
b. Estimated.

On the receipts side of the budget, all general tax cuts for individuals and businesses were ruled out. The only major proposal was to provide real wage insurance for workers who are members of a group that conforms with the administration's 7 percent wage guideline for 1979. The estimated cost of the proposal is $2.5 billion, on the assumption that inflation will not exceed 7.5 percent during 1979. Tax increases were proposed to augment some existing trust fund receipts and to establish a new fund to clean up oil spills, but the amounts involved are small (roughly $200 million in 1980). With these changes, total receipts are estimated to increase 10.2 percent in fiscal 1980.

The 7.7 percent increase would bring outlays in 1980 to $531.6 billion and the 10.2 percent increase would raise receipts to $502.6 billion, leaving a deficit of $29.0 billion—one billion dollars below the President's ceiling (table 1-1).[1]

1. The analysis of the budget in this volume is based on the budget document transmitted to Congress in January 1979 (*The Budget of the United States Government, Fiscal Year 1980*). A revision of the estimates was released by the Office of Management and Budget in March ("Current Budget Estimates," March 1979), but

These estimates are based on a set of economic assumptions that are optimistic about both the growth of the economy and the rate of inflation. The administration expected the economy to slow down in 1979 but to avoid an actual recession (which is defined by many economists as at least two quarters of declining real output). It also forecast a reduction in the inflation rate from 9 percent in 1978 to 7.4 percent in 1979 and 6.3 percent in 1980. Prices in early 1979 were rising at a much faster rate than is consistent with the administration's projections, and many private forecasters believe that a recession will begin before the end of fiscal 1980.

An alternative set of budget estimates, based on a more pessimistic set of economic assumptions, has been prepared by the Congressional Budget Office. The CBO expects the economy to slow significantly in 1979, with a downturn beginning in the second half of the year and a mild recovery in 1980. It also projects higher inflation in both 1979 and 1980 than does the administration. On these assumptions, the CBO estimates that receipts in fiscal 1980 would be $499.4 billion, outlays would be $540.0 billion, and the deficit would be $40.6 billion—$11.6 billion higher than the President's proposed goal.

These figures are based on the budget program proposed by the President. But Congress is unlikely to approve the budget without making its usual substantial modifications. It may reject the hospital cost containment program, has already deferred action on most of the social security benefit reductions, and was being importuned by governors and mayors to restore at least some of the cuts in the grants-in-aid programs for state and local governments. Shortly after the budget was submitted, the administration withdrew its proposal to establish a national development bank, but at most this action will save only $200 million. On balance, after Congress gets through with the 1980 budget, outlays may be as much as $4 billion higher than the President's proposal unless defense spending is cut to make

---

the revised estimates are not incorporated in this volume because they did not change the budget outlook for fiscal years 1980–84 significantly and did not provide the detail needed to make a careful review of the budget. For fiscal 1979 the March estimates raised receipts by $5.8 billion and expenditures by $1.6 billion, thus reducing the estimated deficit by $4.2 billion (from $37.4 billion to $33.2 billion). For fiscal 1980 the estimated deficit was revised downward from $29.0 billion to $28.4 billion. None of the estimates in this volume reflect the President's April 1979 energy proposals.

up the difference. This means that the 1980 deficit would amount to $33 billion with the administration's assumptions and about $45 billion with the CBO's less optimistic assumptions. Without real wage insurance, the deficits would be $30.5 billion and $42.5 billion.

In either case, the 1980 budget would represent a tighter federal fiscal policy than those of the last few years. If there were no change in the unemployment rate between fiscal 1979 and 1980, outlays would rise by 7.5 percent and receipts would rise by over 11 percent.[2] Even if Congress raised outlays $4 billion above those in the President's budget, the increase in outlays would be only 8.3 percent, making the budget less expansionary in 1980 than in 1979.

Monetary Policy

Monetary policy is also expected to contribute to the economic slowdown sought by the administration for 1979 and 1980. During 1978 private credit demands increased rapidly as the economy continued to expand. The money supply rose rapidly during the first nine months of the year, but interest rates went up as the Federal Reserve Board acted to restrain its growth.

A dramatic policy change was made on November 1, 1978, when it became apparent that foreign exchange traders were not satisfied with the steps that were being taken to control inflation in the United States. The new policy included a substantial tightening of monetary policy and a variety of special measures to support the dollar in foreign exchange markets. The growth of the money supply slowed significantly and interest rates reached their highest levels since their previous peaks in 1974. As a result, the federal funds rate (the rate at which banks borrow from one another to meet their reserve requirements) rose from 6.5 percent at the beginning of 1978 to 10 percent at the end of the year. The rate paid by the Treasury on three-month bills climbed from 6 percent to over 9 percent, and long-term federal bond yields rose from slightly less than 8 percent to about 9 percent.

Three major changes in financial markets have made the response

2. These calculations are based on an assumed unemployment rate of 5.1 percent, which currently represents the level defined as "full employment" by the Council of Economic Advisers. (For an explanation of the full employment budget, see chapter 2.) The conclusion that planned receipts will rise much faster than planned outlays is valid regardless of the assumed level of unemployment.

of the economy to monetary policy uncertain. First, the regulations were changed to let commercial banks and other savings institutions issue new money market certificates of six-month maturity in minimum denominations of $10,000. Commercial banks were permitted to provide approximately the same yield on these certificates as the discount on Treasury bills, and the nonbank thrift institutions were allowed to pay an additional one-fourth of 1 percent. (In March 1979, the regulations were changed to prevent the compounding of interest rates during each six-month period and to limit the interest paid by the thrift institutions to the commercial bank rate when that is over 9 percent.) Second, commercial banks were permitted to transfer funds from a customer's saving account to cover a shortage in his checking account. Third, money market mutual funds, which started in the early 1970s, became attractive alternatives for holding short-term funds, and they grew rapidly in 1978. These innovations have significantly affected the forms in which people hold their liquid assets and hence growth rates of the monetary aggregates. But the rate of growth of the money supply in the last quarter of 1978 and in early 1979 remains low even after corrections are made for their estimated effects.

The new money market certificates played a critical role in cushioning the effect of tightening monetary policy on credit availability for home buying in 1978. In the past, when interest rates increased sharply, funds would flow out of the thrift institutions into direct purchases of high-yielding securities because comparable yields were not available on deposits. This "disintermediation" would greatly restrict the supply of mortgage funds and lead to a reduction in residential construction. With the advent of the money market certificates, the thrift institutions held a major share of their deposits, and mortgage lending declined much less than in previous periods of high interest rates. The adjustment to credit restraint was much smoother in the home-building industry during this expansion, but the result is that interest rates must rise to even higher levels to achieve a given degree of restraint on aggregate demand.

The administration is prepared to accept high interest rates in order to "create a favorable climate for unwinding inflation," but it is impossible to predict how high they will have to go to meet this objective. If the economy slows down soon, the interest rates prevailing in early 1979 may turn out to be the peak for this cycle. On the other hand, further increases in interest rates could take place if the economy does not respond to the tighter monetary and fiscal policies already in effect.

Wage-Price Guidelines

In addition to restraining demand through monetary and fiscal policies, the administration is seeking to influence price and wage decisions directly. The mechanism is a system of voluntary price-wage guidelines. On the price side, the rules request that price setters decelerate their rate of price increases by half a percentage point relative to the increase they experienced in the base period 1976–77. Under this rule, a maximum increase of 9.5 percent is allowed and a minimum increase of 1.5 percent is accepted without challenge. Firms with cost increases that would push their prices above the 9.5 percent ceiling are permitted to apply a cost-justification rule involving profit markups.

The wage rules provide for a basic 7 percent increase (8 percent for the first year of union contracts, averaging 7 percent over the entire contract) with special rules for escalator clauses, fringe benefits, and other aspects of compensation.

As the program is voluntary, there are no court-enforced penalties for noncompliance. However, the government has stated that government contractors—especially large ones—may lose their existing contracts or the right to bid on new ones if they do not comply. The legal authority for such contract denials is questionable, and there has already been some litigation on the issue. In general, enforcement of the guidelines depends on moral suasion and public opinion. The harmful publicity—especially for large firms, which are the most visible—that would result from being branded a noncooperator is a strong incentive to comply.

As with previous efforts at direct intervention, the major focus of the guideline program is on the wage side, even though some of the most complicated rules involve prices. Wages are a major element of total costs; the premise of the program is that, if wage increases can be held to 7 percent, price increases will eventually fall below 7 percent because of rising productivity.

In theory, it is possible to imagine a guideline focused on prices and based on the assumption that wages would eventually follow prices. The problem is that, from an administrative point of view, controlling prices (or even setting rules for voluntary price restraint) is much more complicated than controlling wages because it is difficult to allow for the introduction of new products, changes in quality, changes in the prices of internationally traded goods and agricultural products, and differences in product mix. This is not to say that there are not many technical problems on the wage side, but the price side is much more complex.

Apart from the administrative aspect, a system of rules for wages is less likely to cause dislocations than rules geared to the absolute prices charged by a firm. Employers and workers tend to be tied together in long-term relationships. Within limits, wage restraints are unlikely to provoke labor shortages and the loss of valued workers. But product markets are more prone to shortages and distortions, because buyers and sellers are not often tightly linked.

The difficulty with a wage-centered program is that, even if prices are geared to wages over the long run, there are periods in which price movements reflect external influences. In early 1979, for example, upward pressure on prices came partly from the agricultural sector—where labor costs are only a minor factor—and partly from foreign oil prices. Bad news about prices makes it difficult for union leaders to sell wage restraint to their members. The Carter administration's initial solution to this dilemma was to propose real wage insurance, a potential tax rebate to workers in groups that accepted wage increases of 7 percent or less. Under this plan, workers in complying firms would receive a tax rebate proportional to the excess of price inflation above 7 percent, up to 10 percent.

While real wage insurance is a novel method of reconciling short spurts of price inflation with wage restraint, the plan had a number of drawbacks. It required the approval of Congress as a tax measure, a potentially prolonged process. Yet the plan needed to be put into effect quickly if it was to provide the desired incentive. Moreover, it is difficult to write guideline-type rules into the tax code and administer them. As a result, the actual plan did not include the details of the guidelines in such areas as fringe-benefit calculations, promotions, and low-wage workers. Congress was also concerned about the budgetary costs and the possibility of a large federal payout in a period of inflation. If the plan promoted wage restraint, the inflationary effects of the payout could be offset or more than offset by the reduced pressure on costs. There was no simple way of estimating the incentive effects, but it is clear that as time passed and the program was not adopted its incentive effects for the period it covered (October 1, 1978, to September 30, 1979) diminished. Wage setters had to make their decisions without knowing whether a tax rebate plan would be approved by Congress.

Apart from real wage insurance, a number of other problems will have to be resolved if the guideline program is to continue for an extended period. Nominally, the guidelines apply to firms and other units of all sizes, including governmental units. Yet the Council on Wage and Price Stability has a small staff and cannot monitor the entire economy. In principle, the council has established a system of appeals for exceptions from the wage and price standards, but it is not clear who will make such decisions or how timely access to the process can be provided. A price-wage program—especially a voluntary one—needs flexibility to adapt to changes in economic circumstances, such as a higher-than-expected level of inflationary pressure. In early 1979 it was unclear how such flexibility would be injected into the guidelines.

Regulatory Reform

The federal government affects costs and prices in many industries through its regulatory powers. Traditionally, regulation has been confined mainly to transportation, communications, energy, banking and finance, and agriculture. More recently, there has been an increase in health, safety, and environmental regulations, which affect a wide variety of businesses across the entire spectrum of industry and commerce.

The costs of regulation are reflected in the federal budget to only a small degree. Most of the costs are borne by business enterprises and are usually included in the prices paid by consumers. The benefits of regulation are significant, but they are difficult to measure. The unmeasured benefits of regulation must be balanced against the measured cost increases they may generate, but in a period of inflation it is particularly important to avoid adding to costs and prices unnecessarily.

The biggest success story in reducing prices through changes in regulation concerns the airline industry. The Civil Aeronautics Board permitted the airlines to charge lower fares and eased the restrictions on the use of air routes by the carriers. These actions markedly reduced fares, increased air travel, and raised airline earnings. In 1978 Congress enacted legislation to phase out entry and price regulation for domestic airlines by 1983. The new legislation should lower air fares even more (though fuel and other cost increases may affect them) and may also broaden the variety of services offered customers. Similar reforms in surface transportation have been proposed, but progress is likely to be slow because of the potential real income losses of truckers.

Regulatory reform in some of the newer agencies, such as the Occupational Safety and Health Administration and the Environmental Protection Agency, will also be difficult. While these agencies do not explicitly set prices, their decisions do affect costs and are therefore important for anti-inflation policy. Regulatory budgets that would limit the costs an agency could impose on the private sector have been suggested. However, measuring the costs of regulation is almost as complicated as measuring its benefits, and some agencies are not currently required to consider costs in many of their decisions. Thus though regulatory reform is vital, it will be slow in coming. In the meantime, the Carter administration has formed a regulatory analysis review group to encourage economic analysis of major regulations and a regulatory council to prepare a centralized calendar of proposed regulations.

Standard-setting regulation is not the only mechanism by which the government adds to costs without making budgetary outlays. Agricultural price supports and acreage set-asides are designed to increase the incomes of farmers by increasing cash prices for farm products. The principal beneficiaries of these policies are the most affluent farmers, not the poorest. Trade protection—especially for textiles, consumer electronics, steel, shoes, and sugar—is intended, without a visible government outlay, to raise the incomes of workers and businesses in industries subject to intense foreign competition. Minimum wages raise the incomes of some low-paid workers while reducing the employment prospects of others (often teenagers and members of minority groups). In each of these cases, the government could transfer income directly to alleviate hardship, but direct budget outlays would call attention to the irrational consequences of these policies; indirect, price-increasing methods are chosen because they are less conspicuous. Modification of any one of these policies would have only a slight effect on inflation in the near future, but a combination of several changes would help reduce the rate of price increases in the long run.

The Outlook for Inflation and Growth

The rate of inflation is likely to decline in the latter part of 1979, especially if a recession occurs. In that sense, there are grounds for optimism about inflation. However, since it is perpetuated by the price-wage spiral, a rapid reduction in the inflation rate should not be anticipated. The administration's wage guidelines may have to be relaxed to accommodate recent price developments, but it is important to retain a framework to encourage responsible behavior on the part of business and labor. Mandatory price and wage controls are another possibility, but controls lead to cumulative distortions of the economy, impose heavy burdens of compliance on business, and are expensive to administer.

The economy has been more buoyant despite monetary tightness and high interest rates than most forecasters expected. The pace slowed in the first quarter of 1979, but output was still growing. It is thus possible that the administration's relatively optimistic real growth assumptions will be realized and that the federal deficit in fiscal 1980 can be held in the vicinity of $30 billion. If a recession develops, the automatic stabilizers in the budget (unemployment compensation payments and reduced taxes) will raise the deficit. Efforts to prevent this, either through cuts in expenditures or increases in taxes, would exacerbate the recession.

The Humphrey-Hawkins Act passed in 1978 specified a goal of 3 percent inflation and 4 percent unemployment by the end of calendar year 1983. Thereafter, the inflation rate is supposed to be brought down to zero. However, the growth and employment objectives of the legislation cannot be reconciled with the need to reduce inflation. It would be self-defeating to overstimulate the economy just to reach the employment goals of the act in the time stipulated; the result would be an acceleration of inflation, which would then require measures to restrain the economy, and these, in turn, would lead to higher unemployment. In theory, it is possible to develop special programs for the structurally unemployed that could lower the measured rate of unemployment without intensifying inflationary pressure. But most employment programs have had mixed results; while they have provided temporary employment and income for some disadvantaged groups, they have not succeeded in training many workers for active participation in the economy at regular wages. The goals of the Humphrey-Hawkins Act are therefore unattainable with the present tools of economic policy.

The Domestic Budget

Nondefense outlays are scheduled to increase from $378.9 billion in fiscal 1979 to $405.7 billion in 1980. This 7.1 percent increase is only just enough to offset the rise in prices projected in the budget; in real terms, nondefense outlays will be virtually the same in 1980 as they were in 1979 and 1978. The composition of the nondefense budget does not remain the same, however. Despite proposed reductions in health care outlays and social security benefits, payments for individuals—social security benefits, federal employee retirement benefits, veterans' benefits, food stamps, public assistance, medicare, and medicaid—will continue to rise rapidly as the number of beneficiaries increases and medical prices rise. To keep the nondefense totals the same in real terms, it was necessary to cut outlays elsewhere, most notably in grants-in-aid to state and local governments. The major issues in the nondefense budget are the proposed reductions in health outlays, social security benefits, and grants-in-aid.

Health

The rise in health costs has become a large drain on the federal budget. Federal health outlays have more than doubled in the last five years and are expected to almost double again over the next five years if current policies continue. This is partly the result of the increasing demand for health care as incomes rise and the population ages, but it can also be attributed to the nation's health care financing system, which relies heavily on third-party reimbursement by private insurers and the federal government to pay doctors and hospital bills. Under this system, each health care decision is insulated from its financial consequences, with the result that there is little incentive for doctors or patients to economize in the prescription and use of medical services.

The Carter administration's ultimate objective in the health field is a comprehensive national health insurance system, but it recognizes that something must be done to slow the growth of hospital costs before such a system can be enacted. In 1977 it proposed to limit the annual increase in hospital revenues, but the proposal was rejected by Congress because of the determined opposition of the hospital lobby. The new budget contains an even more stringent version of hospital cost containment than the 1978 version. The average saving in federal outlays would amount to $1.7 billion in fiscal 1980, $4.9 billion in 1982, and $9.2 billion in 1984.

If Congress fails to enact any form of hospital cost containment, the administration may be forced to use the power it now has under the law to limit medicare and medicaid reimbursements. This would reduce the rate of growth of federal expenditures, but nothing would prevent hospitals from segregating medicare and medicaid patients and charging other patients more. The result would be a shift in costs from the federal government to private payers and a reduction in the quality of health care for the poor and the aged.

Social Security

The social security system, which will pay $115 billion in benefits to retired and disabled people and their dependents in fiscal 1980, is being examined carefully by at least four governmental commissions. This scrutiny of what is widely acknowledged to be the most successful federal program was undertaken partly because of the large increases in payroll taxes enacted in 1977 to put the system on a sound financial basis and partly because the character of the system has not changed even though basic economic and social changes have occurred since it was adopted. The administration is awaiting the results of the four studies before proposing fundamental changes in the system, but it feels that some reductions in low-priority benefits are called for in a period of budget stringency.

The administration proposes to set a limit on family disability benefits of 80 percent of predisability earnings; phase out benefits to students over the age of eighteen; terminate the $255 lump-sum death benefit; repeal the $122 minimum benefit (but retain the special minimum benefit of $11.50 a month for each year of covered employment above ten); and eliminate the widow's benefit for mothers after the youngest child reaches sixteen (instead of eighteen, as under present law). These changes would apply only to future beneficiaries, so that the immediate reduction in federal outlays would be small—only $700 million in fiscal 1980—but by 1984 the savings would amount to $4.4 billion.

Although the proposals are modest and leave the basic benefits intact, long-time supporters of social security have interpreted the administration's action as the beginning of an attack on the very structure of the system. In response to this pressure, the House Ways and Means Committee decided to consider early in 1979 only the suggested changes in disability benefits (which account for about 20 percent of the long-term savings from all the administration's proposals) and to defer action on the remainder of the program until late 1979.

Grants-in-Aid

Federal grants to state and local governments have risen sharply in the last decade—from $20.3 billion in fiscal 1969 to an estimated $82.1 billion in 1979. They rose from 17.4 percent of total state-local expenditures in fiscal 1969 to a peak of 26.7 percent in 1978, but they are now beginning to decline relative to both the size of the federal budget and state-local expenditures. The 1980 budget calls for $82.9 billion in federal grants-in-aid. This increase of $0.8 billion over 1979 outlays would amount to a reduction of more than 5 percent in real terms, even under the administration's optimistic inflation projections.

The largest proposed reductions in federal grants are in three programs that were introduced or expanded to speed economic recovery from the 1974–75 recession—local public works, public service employment, and countercyclical revenue sharing. Although these programs were intended to be temporary, the recipients have come to rely on them and the cutback is being resisted by representatives of the states, cities, and counties. Even if the grants enacted for purposes of economic stimulus are excluded, federal assistance to state and local governments will decline in 1980 by about 3 percent in real terms.

The allocation of federal budget funds in fiscal 1980 for grants-in-aid reflects no overall theme or principle other than the judgment that countercyclical aid should disappear when the economy reaches high levels of employment. The administration is putting the states and local governments on notice that the heyday of federal assistance has passed. The particular cuts proposed in the budget may not reflect congressional priorities, however, and a heated battle is likely to develop over the size and allocation of the cuts.

Prospects for Nondefense Spending

With defense outlays rising rapidly (see below), President Carter has responded to the public clamor for reducing the growth of federal spending by cutting the growth of nondefense outlays. The proposed cuts are being strongly resisted by the groups that benefit from the threatened programs. Other cuts are possible, but these would require even more unpalatable changes than those already proposed. The only other possibility is to offset increases in the nondefense budget by reductions in defense outlays, but this would also encounter strong opposition inside and outside Congress. Congress thus has little room to maneuver and will find it difficult to deviate very much from the President's proposed nondefense budget.

The Defense Budget

The President's budget proposes to raise national defense outlays from $114.5 billion in fiscal 1979 to $125.8 billion in 1980, an increase of $11.3 billion, or almost 10 percent. In real terms, this amounts to an increase of 3.1 percent, which corresponds to the commitment made by the President at the May 1977 meeting of NATO. Budget authority rises by 1.7 percent in real terms. The sharp increase in defense spending comes at a time when the growth in nondefense spending is being restrained. This reordering of priorities is in response to the widely shared perception that the Soviet Union is building up its military capability to dangerous levels and that U.S. leadership in world affairs is eroding.

The most significant issues in defense policy are to define the military purposes of U.S. forces and to allocate defense resources in a manner that will best achieve these purposes. The dispute over these issues raises serious questions about the effectiveness of current defense policy and may lead to basic changes that would alter the course of the current five-year defense plan.

The Strategic Force Mission

The principal purposes of U.S. strategic forces are to deter a nuclear attack on the United States and its allies and to help deter a nonnuclear attack and coercion by adversaries. These forces now consist of land-based intercontinental ballistic missiles, sea-launched missiles, and bombers carrying nuclear bombs or air-launched missiles. This year's budget calls for $10.8 billion in budget authority to fund additional strategic forces and represents about a 17 percent real increase over last year. Based on current program plans, the total acquisition cost of the new strategic systems now under development would be about $88 billion over the next fifteen years.

The major problem for American strategic force policy is whether the United States should merely offset the Soviet Union's capability to threaten its strategic forces or also acquire a matching capability to destroy the Soviet land-based missiles. The Defense Department's response suggests that the answer may lie in adopting a "countervailing strategy"—U.S. strategic nuclear forces must be able to respond to a Soviet first strike in such a way that "the enemy could have no expectation of achieving any rational objective, no illusion of making any gain without offsetting losses." In essence, countervailing strategy implies a "second-strike counterforce" capability.

The specific implications of this strategy have not been clarified by the Carter administration. The composition of the strategic forces continues to be determined in a piecemeal way. For example, the 1980 budget proposes full development of a new land-based ballistic missile, the MX, which would be mobile and thus less vulnerable than the current fixed missiles. The MX would be capable of attacking Soviet missile sites. Proponents see the MX system as the only solution to the growing vulnerability of the U.S. land-based force. They argue that the MX would also prevent the USSR from attaining superiority with large numbers of highly accurate land-based missiles.

There are many uncertainties about the MX. The MX mobile basing system would be very expensive. Because it would create serious verification problems for the prospective strategic arms limitation agreement, critics contend that the MX system could be destabilizing to the strategic balance. Instead of deploying this system, they would place greater reliance on more survivable bomber and sea-launched missile forces.

The United States is continuing to build large, expensive Trident submarines and is starting development of the new, more capable Trident II missile for these vessels. However, the cost increases and delays of the Trident program have led the Defense Department to consider alternatives. One of these is to build smaller, less expensive submarines. Another is to build fewer Trident submarines but equip them with the Trident II missile. But there will not be enough Tridents to replace the existing Poseidon submarines, whose retirement is projected in the next ten or fifteen years. The solution will probably be to postpone the retirement of the Poseidon submarines, adopting more flexible deployment practices in order to extend their service.

The final question concerns the strategic penetrating bomber now being developed for use in the 1990s. Proponents argue that Soviet defenses would be most vulnerable to a force consisting of aircraft equipped with long-range cruise missiles and penetrating bombers armed with bombs and short-range missiles. To maintain the effectiveness of this mixed force they believe that the United States must have an advanced penetrating bomber by the 1990s. Opponents argue that the United States should rely on larger numbers of advanced cruise missiles to offset improving Soviet defenses.

Theater Nuclear Mission

Like strategic forces, theater nuclear forces—an important item on the NATO agenda—are going through a period of modernization. The administration proposes in 1980 to procure new warheads, develop more capable artillery shells and accurate, longer-range ground-launched missiles, and improve present theater nuclear systems.

Recent modernization of Soviet nuclear aircraft and missiles capable of attacking Europe has increased their flexibility and capability to mount a nuclear or a conventional attack. However, the administration's response is a modernization program that replicates and adds to the current stockpile of tactical nuclear weapons and delivery systems. This stockpile, which has been accumulated over two decades, was assembled without a strategy of theater nuclear deterrence. Since the administration has not proposed a coherent strategic concept, it is difficult to see how duplicating the stockpile will produce an optimal deterrent to the Soviet Union.

Besides its conceptual weakness, the theater nuclear modernization program impinges on the strategic nuclear program. By 1985 the United States is scheduled to increase the number of strategic warheads by an estimated 40 percent. Since there are limits on the amount of nuclear material, it may not be possible to build all the planned strategic weapons unless the old tactical weapons are replaced by equally efficient weapons using less nuclear material.

NATO Ground and Air Mission

The budget proposes outlays of $51.4 billion in 1980 for ground and air forces intended for the defense of NATO. The U.S. Army plans to procure fifteen new systems for ground combat, which will quintuple annual expenditures between fiscal years 1980 and 1984. In contrast, the U.S. Air Force's annual outlays for new tactical aircraft should decrease by about 60 percent in the same period. In view of the improvements in the ground and air forces of the Warsaw Pact countries in the past decade, this level of expenditures may be reasonable, but the administration's plans for allocating the funds deserve scrutiny.

The primary threat from the Warsaw Pact countries is of a short and intense conflict, with little warning and perhaps accompanied by a nuclear attack. This raises questions about the administration's plans for placing enough equipment in Europe for five divisions, for retaining large reserve ground forces, and for continuing to emphasize the qualitative rather than the quantitative superiority of its ground combat weapons.

There are also questions about the future relationship between the army and the air force. First, given the substantial increases in the Soviet threat to U.S. air bases and in the air defense capabilities of Warsaw Pact ground forces, some redistribution of funds from air force ground attack programs to army fire support capabilities might be in order. Second, a close look should be taken to see whether the air defense program of the two services can be more closely integrated.

Naval Mission

The budget requests $4.8 billion in funding for general purpose naval shipbuilding in fiscal 1980. This is an increase of 60 percent over 1979, mainly the result of spending for a new diesel-powered aircraft carrier and the continuation of the patrol frigate program. In fiscal 1980 to 1984 the navy will acquire 61 new general purpose ships and 13 conversions at a cost of nearly $30 billion. This is three fewer ships than planned for 1979. It also plans to request another

$12 billion to purchase 525 naval aircraft for use on aircraft carriers. The new carrier claims one-third of this year's general purpose shipbuilding resources, the patrol frigate program another 26 percent, and new destroyers equipped with advanced radar 17 percent.

The threat that impels much of the navy's general purpose construction derives from the view that the Soviet Union's maritime posture is similar to that of the United States, allowing it to control the open ocean and to project its power against the opponent's land and sea defenses. But another view is that the Soviet navy has been designed to wage a general strategic war, involving strikes against the United States and U.S. aircraft carriers while protecting its own strategic submarines.

The U.S. shipbuilding program is divided between sea control forces to protect the sea-lanes in the Atlantic and the Pacific and to conduct strike operations against the USSR. These are the same purposes for which ships have been built for the past thirty years. The U.S. Navy, built around aircraft carriers with surface ships and submarines as escorts, is designed for both peacetime and wartime operations. In peacetime, it gives the United States an overseas presence that can be used for a quick response in a political crisis. In wartime, the carriers would defend NATO's northern and southern flanks, and the patrol frigates and attack submarines would be available for escort duty in the open ocean.

Because of the high cost of shipbuilding and a limited budget, the navy is becoming a smaller, less flexible fighting force than it was in the 1960s, when it decided to construct fewer but far more sophisticated vessels. Without adjustments, the navy may be unable to carry out its NATO assignment or to play a role in dealing with the strategic threat posed by the Soviet navy. If the U.S. Navy's role is to control the oceans during a major conflict, smaller, more capable naval vessels could be substituted for the big carrier task forces it now seeks.

The Budget Outlook

The budget outlook depends not only on spending and tax decisions but also on the state of the economy. The official five-year budget projections are based on the economic goals of the Humphrey-Hawkins Act. Under these unrealistic assumptions, federal spending would be reduced to 21 percent of GNP in fiscal 1981 and the budget would be nearly in balance that year. Thereafter, expenditures would decline to 19.3 percent of GNP and the margin of receipts over expenditures would increase rapidly until it reached $106.5 billion in fiscal 1984. This reflects the relatively austere spending program proposed by the President and the response of receipts to the assumed rapid growth of the economy.

An alternative set of projections based on more realistic economic assumptions has been prepared by the Congressional Budget Office. In these projections, the unemployment rate declines to 5.5 percent and the inflation rate to 6.0 percent in 1984. Receipts would not overtake outlays until 1982, but by 1984 the margin of receipts over outlays would amount to $126 billion (in a $3.9 trillion economy). The margin is greater in these alternative projections because receipts respond faster than outlays to the growth of nominal incomes at the higher inflation rate.

The $126 billion margin of receipts over expenditures also assumes that no new programs would be enacted and that there would be no tax reductions to offset the inflation-induced increases in receipts. In the past, Congress has not allowed individual income tax receipts to exceed 11 percent of personal income for very long. Without any changes in the tax law, individual income tax receipts in the five-year projections would rise to more than 14 percent of personal income in 1984. Reducing this percentage to 11 would require using up $103 billion of the 1984 margin.

Another claimant for part of the budget margin is the corporation income tax. In the past, when individual income taxes have been reduced, business taxes were also cut roughly in the ratio of 1:3. A cut of $103 billion in individual income taxes would thus generate a business tax cut of $34 billion if past practices were followed. In combination, the individual and corporation income tax cuts would amount to $137 billion, which is more than the estimated margin of receipts over expenditures in fiscal 1984. There is also pressure to roll back at least part of the payroll tax increases enacted in 1977, but any such action would reduce the margin available for income tax cuts.

One way of increasing the margin is to make cuts in existing programs beyond those proposed by the President in submitting the 1980 budget. For example, one proposal would restrict annual federal expenditure increases to the rate of inflation plus 1 percent. This limit would reduce federal spending to 18.5 percent of GNP, the lowest level since 1965, and would add $13 billion to the $126 billion margin, permitting some further tax cuts. To accomplish this objective, it would be necessary to reduce projected 1984 spending by about 2 percent, avoid all new spending, and confine inflation adjustments to the federal programs that have mandatory inflation adjustment features. Such large reductions in spending would require a political consensus that has not yet emerged.

Proposals are being made to adopt a constitutional amendment reducing the rate of growth of federal spending substantially below currently projected levels. One group of proposals would require a balanced budget every year; another would directly limit the growth of federal spending. Adding an amendment of either type to the Constitution would reduce fiscal flexibility and make it extremely difficult to use the federal budget to help stabilize the economy. A more appropriate method would be to require Congress to use its annual budget resolutions to limit spending and taxing. The amendment route would clutter up the Constitution and invite the use of techniques to circumvent the constitutional language.

CHAPTER TWO

The 1980 Budget
and the Budget Outlook

JOSEPH A. PECHMAN *and* ROBERT W. HARTMAN

THE BUDGET submitted by President Carter for fiscal year 1980 is a crucial step toward achieving the budgetary objectives he developed during his presidential campaign and has repeated frequently since he took office. The objectives are, first, to reduce federal spending to 21 percent of the gross national product, and second, to balance the budget. The 1980 budget is also a response to the growing public demand for a reduction in the rate of growth of federal spending. This chapter traces the recent budget trends that led to this year's decisions, reviews the choices made by the President in putting together the 1980 budget, and analyzes the future budget outlook in light of current policies, proposed legislative changes, and prospective economic developments.

Recent Budget Trends

President Carter came into office at a time when federal outlays were increasing sharply both in dollars and in relation to the size of the economy. These increases were the result partly of decisions that had been made during the late 1960s and early 1970s and partly of the countercyclical programs enacted by Congress to bring the country out of the deep recession of 1974–75. Trends in the composition of the budget were also beginning to change. Defense expendi-

The authors thank Darwin G. Johnson for helpful comments on early drafts of this chapter and Andrew Winokur for research assistance.

23

tures had fallen in real terms in the early 1970s as the Vietnam War wound down. In fiscal 1976 real defense expenditures were lower than they had been in more than two decades while nondefense expenditures were going up sharply. President Ford made the decision —and Congress approved it—to turn the defense budget around before he left office, and President Carter accepted this policy. During the first two years of the new administration, federal spending for both nondefense and defense programs increased rapidly.

The Size of the Budget

Federal budget outlays were $451 billion in fiscal 1978, the last full fiscal year, and are projected to rise to $493 billion in fiscal 1979, the current fiscal year. The 1979 estimate is 83 percent higher in current dollars than the level five years earlier, an annual growth of 12 percent at a time when the gross national product was rising only 11 percent. The increase in spending was the result of five factors.

First, there was a substantial increase in outlays on domestic social programs, particularly in transfer payments for individuals and federal grants-in-aid to state and local governments. Many of these programs were initiated in the mid-1960s just before the Vietnam War, but the largest increases were in the social security and unemployment insurance programs that date back to the 1930s.

Second, the sharp decline in real defense spending in the early 1970s, which had provided room for growth in spending on domestic programs, was turned around and by 1979 was rising as fast as the rest of the budget.

Third, beginning in 1975, the federal government made large outlays to lift the economy out of recession. Some of these outlays are being phased out, but most of them were still running at or near peak levels in 1978.

Fourth, although the economy was recovering from the recession, unemployment was still high by past standards. It averaged 6.2 percent of the labor force in fiscal 1978 and 6.0 percent in the last quarter of that year. Unemployment compensation and, to a lesser extent, social security benefits and welfare payments were therefore higher than usual at that stage of the business cycle.

Fifth, inflation has had a major impact on federal spending. Some federal programs are automatically adjusted for inflation, and many others are adjusted by Congress on a discretionary basis. For instance, the adjustments in medicare and medicaid are both automatic and tied to the unusually high rate of inflation in the health sector.

As a result of these influences, outlays in fiscal 1978 were 22.1 percent of GNP, close to the highest percentage they had reached since the end of the Second World War—even including the years in which Vietnam War expenditures were at their highest levels. Federal spending amounted to about 19 percent of GNP in the early 1960s, rose to 21.5 percent at the height of the Vietnam War in 1968, declined to slightly below 20 percent in 1974, and then rose again to a new peak of 22.6 percent in 1976 (table 2-1). In 1977 and 1978 it was about 22 percent of GNP and is expected to decline further, to 21.6 percent, in 1979.

Since federal spending is heavily influenced by the business cycle and price developments, these figures obscure the underlying budget trends. To see the trends, the official budget figures must be adjusted for the shortfall of economic activity below its potential and for the effect of relative price changes in the government sector and in the rest of the economy. Both adjustments put recent budget developments in a somewhat different perspective.

The correction for the business cycle is made by calculating what outlays and GNP would be if the economy were operating at full employment.[1] On this basis, federal spending as a share of GNP peaks at 22.1 percent during the Vietnam War. From this peak, spending falls to 19.7 percent of GNP in 1974; it rises to 21.3 percent in 1978 and is expected to fall again in 1979, to 21.0 percent (table 2-1, column 2).

Inflation has had a pronounced effect on the trend of the federal spending share because the prices paid by government have risen faster than the general price level. Prices of services, which account for a large part of government budgets, tend to rise more rapidly than prices of goods. This is because productivity rises more rapidly in industries that produce goods, but wages in both goods and service industries—including the wages of federal employees—rise at about the same rate. There were also special factors in the 1970s that raised

1. The only adjustment in outlays made here is to exclude the higher unemployment benefits when the economy is operating below its potential. Outlays for other countercyclical programs are not adjusted. The full-employment GNP estimates used here are the official estimates prepared by the Council of Economic Advisers; see *Economic Report of the President, January 1979*, pp. 74–75.

Table 2-1. Relation of Federal Budget Outlays to the Gross National Product,
in Current and Constant Dollars, Fiscal Years 1960–79

| | Budget outlays as percent of GNP | | | |
| | Current dollars | | Constant dollars[c] | |
Fiscal year[a]	Actual (1)	Full employment[b] (2)	Actual (3)	Full employment[b] (4)
1960	18.5	17.6	20.6	19.6
1961	19.2	17.7	21.3	19.6
1962	19.5	18.5	21.6	20.4
1963	19.3	18.4	21.0	20.0
1964	19.2	18.7	20.8	20.2
1965	18.0	17.8	19.3	19.1
1966	18.7	19.0	19.6	20.0
1967	20.4	21.0	21.3	21.9
1968	21.5	22.1	22.3	22.9
1969	20.4	21.1	20.8	21.6
1970	20.5	20.3	20.5	20.3
1971	20.7	19.9	20.5	19.7
1972	20.9	20.1	20.5	19.7
1973	20.0	20.0	19.3	19.3
1974	19.8	19.7	18.8	18.6
1975	22.4	20.5	21.2	19.5
1976	22.6	20.9	21.5	19.9
1977	22.0	20.8	20.5	19.6
1978	22.1	21.3	20.5	19.9
1979[d]	21.6	21.0	19.9	19.5

Sources: *The Budget of the United States Government, Fiscal Year 1980*, pp. 577–78. Full-employment
figures are from the Office of Management and Budget.
  a. Ending June 30 for 1960–76 and September 30 for 1977–79.
  b. Full-employment outlays as a percentage of full-employment GNP.
  c. Calculated in fiscal 1972 prices.
  d. Estimated.

the prices paid by the federal government more than prices in the
rest of the economy: a catch-up of federal pay scales to private pay
levels; increases in pay to attract military personnel when the draft
was eliminated; and the large relative price increases in construction.
Consequently, when budget outlays and GNP are both expressed in
constant prices, the federal spending percentages in recent years are
no higher than they were in the early 1960s.[2] In relation to full-

2. The constant-price estimates follow the convention used in the national income
accounts that there is no productivity growth in government. This means that wage
and salary increases of government employees are counted as price increases, even
though some part of these increases may be associated with more output. As a result,

employment GNP at constant prices, real federal spending rose from an average of 20 percent in 1960–64 to a peak of 22.9 in the Vietnam War year 1968 and then declined to below 20 percent in every year after 1970 (table 2-1, column 4).

Thus while the federal spending ratio in nominal terms is relatively high by past standards, the federal government's use of economic resources in relation to the resources available has not been growing.[3] The rise in the spending ratio has been mainly the result of the failure of the economy to reach full employment and the increase in prices paid by the government relative to prices in the rest of the economy. Even if full employment were reached and general inflation were arrested, the ratio of federal spending to GNP wou.a ̮reep up because the prices of services tend to rise more than the prices of commodities over the long run.

The Composition of the Budget

There has been a fairly steady decline in the portion of the federal budget allocated to defense since the end of the Korean War and a corresponding increase in the share of nondefense programs. Between fiscal years 1960 and 1976, the share of total outlays devoted to defense was cut in half, from 49.0 percent to 24.4 percent (with a temporary interruption during the Vietnam War), and the nondefense share rose from 51.0 percent to 75.6 percent (table 2-2). Even though real defense spending began to increase in 1977, the defense share has continued to decline. The low point is projected to be in 1979, when defense outlays are expected to account for 23.2 percent of total outlays. Thereafter, the budget calls for faster increases in defense spending than in nondefense spending.

---

the trend in the federal spending share is biased downward when it is measured in constant prices, but there is no way of knowing how much. The declining real federal share in the past decade is completely accounted for by a shrinking measured defense budget, which is accounted for in turn by reduced numbers of military and civilian employees in the Defense Department. Whether fewer people are really producing fewer services is the kind of question that must be answered to determine to what degree the constant-dollar ratios understate the federal share.

3. It should be noted that the direct use of resources—purchases of goods and services by the federal government—has been steadily declining in recent years and the indirect use—through transfers and grants-in-aid—has been growing rapidly. In terms of state control over production, therefore, federal budget activity is low by historical standards. However, the federal government's regulatory effects on production have increased (see chapter 3), as has its influence on credit markets through devices such as guarantees and lending by off-budget agencies. None of these are reflected in budget outlays.

Table 2-2. Federal Budget Outlays as a Percentage of Total Outlays,
by Major Category, Fiscal Years 1960–79

		Nondefense				Grants-in-aid to state and local governments[c]
Fiscal year[a]	Defense	Total	Payments for individuals[b]	Net interest	Other	
1960	49.0	51.0	24.8	7.5	18.7	7.6
1961	47.7	52.3	26.5	6.9	18.9	7.3
1962	45.9	54.1	25.4	6.4	22.3	7.4
1963	45.0	55.0	25.7	6.9	22.4	7.7
1964	43.5	56.5	25.1	6.9	24.5	8.6
1965	40.1	59.9	25.7	7.2	27.0	9.2
1966	40.7	59.3	25.5	7.0	26.8	9.6
1967	43.1	56.9	25.3	6.5	25.1	9.6
1968	44.0	56.0	25.7	6.2	24.1	10.4
1969	43.0	57.0	28.6	6.9	21.5	11.0
1970	40.0	60.0	30.4	7.3	22.3	12.2
1971	35.9	64.1	35.3	7.0	21.8	13.3
1972	33.0	67.0	36.8	6.7	23.5	14.8
1973	30.2	69.8	38.8	7.0	24.0	16.9
1974	28.8	71.2	41.2	8.0	22.0	16.1
1975	26.2	73.8	43.7	7.1	23.0	15.3
1976	24.4	75.6	45.7	7.3	22.6	16.1
1977	24.2	75.8	45.3	7.4	23.1	17.0
1978	23.3	76.7	43.3	7.9	25.5	17.3
1979[d]	23.2	76.8	43.2	8.7	24.9	16.6

Sources: Office of Management and Budget, "Federal Government Finances" (January 1979), pp. 40–42, 65–67.

a. Ending June 30 for 1960–76 and September 30 for 1977–79.

b. Payments for retirement, disability, and unemployment (principally social security, medicare, veterans' pensions and compensation, and unemployment insurance) and low-income assistance (principally welfare, food stamps, housing, and medicaid). Includes grants-in-aid to state and local governments that subsequently result in payments for individuals.

c. Total grants-in-aid, including grants for payments for individuals.

d. Estimated.

The major developments in the nondefense budget have been increases in transfer payments for individuals and in grants-in-aid by the federal government to state and local governments. Nondefense payments for individuals—mainly for social security, veterans' benefits, medicare, and unemployment compensation, and grants for public assistance and medicaid that result in state payments to individuals—increased from 24.8 percent of total outlays in 1960 to 45.7 percent in 1976. These outlays rose especially rapidly in the early 1970s, but the rate of increase tapered off after that, and their share of the total budget began to decline in 1977.

The new federal initiatives in the late 1960s and the outlays to promote economic recovery in 1975 and 1976 were to a large extent funneled through grants to state and local governments. The result was that grants, which accounted for 7.6 percent of federal spending in 1960, increased steadily and reached 17.3 percent in 1978. The share of these grants is projected to decline in 1979.

The only categories of expenditures with rising shares of the budget in recent years are interest payments and "other" programs. The latter category, which accounts for about a quarter of total outlays, includes such programs as energy, development of natural resources, housing, and personnel compensation in civilian agencies.

The Budget Deficits

Since 1961 the federal budget has been in surplus only once—in 1969, when there was a surplus of $3.2 billion. Between fiscal years 1961 and 1967, the deficits never exceeded $10 billion, but they have fluctuated over a much wider range since 1968, when the deficit amounted to $25.2 billion. The largest deficit ever in nominal terms occurred in 1976, when it reached $66.4 billion, or 4.1 percent of GNP.

The deficits have been so much larger in recent years because 1974–75 brought the deepest and longest recession of the postwar period. Taxes were reduced in 1975, 1976, and 1977, and another tax cut was enacted in 1978, generally to be effective at the beginning of 1979. These cuts were made to offset the increases in the effective income tax rates caused by inflation, as well as to stimulate the economy. Federal outlays also were increased sharply to stimulate the economy. While these actions enlarged the deficit, they also helped reduce the unemployment rate from a peak of almost 9 percent in early 1975 to 5.8 percent in the last quarter of calendar year 1978.[4] The recovery from the recession would have been even slower if fiscal (and monetary) policies had been less stimulating.

4. This rate was still almost three-quarters of a percentage point higher than the officially estimated unemployment rate at full employment, which crept up from 4 percent in the early 1960s to 5.1 percent in 1978 as the percentage of adult women and teenagers in the labor force rose. Increased participation of these groups raises the unemployment rate because their unemployment rates are typically higher than those of adult men. See George L. Perry, "Changing Labor Markets and Inflation," *Brookings Papers on Economic Activity, 3:1970*, pp. 411–41. Although the 5.1 percent rate corrects for demographic changes in the labor force, inflation may acceler-

Table 2-3. Federal Budget Surplus or Deficit (−), Fiscal Years 1960–79
Amounts in billions of dollars

Fiscal year[a]	Actual		Full-employment basis	
	Amount (1)	Percent of GNP (2)	Amount (3)	Percent of GNP (4)
1960	0.3	0.1	−1.1	−0.3
1961	−3.4	−0.7	3.9	1.0
1962	−7.1	−1.3	4.8	1.1
1963	−4.8	−0.8	2.7	0.6
1964	−5.9	−1.0	−8.2	−1.7
1965	−1.6	−0.2	7.7	1.5
1966	−3.8	−0.5	9.8	1.8
1967	−8.7	−1.1	3.1	0.5
1968	−25.2	−3.0	4.6	0.8
1969	3.2	0.4	1.5	0.2
1970	−2.8	−0.3	−1.0	−0.1
1971	−23.0	−2.3	−13.0	−1.2
1972	−23.4	−2.1	−13.0	−1.1
1973	−14.8	−1.2	−15.0	−1.2
1974	−4.7	−0.3	−2.0	−0.1
1975	−45.2	−3.1	−14.0	−0.9
1976	−66.4	−4.1	−35.0	−2.0
1977	−45.0	−2.5	−20.0	−1.0
1978	−44.8	−2.4	−31.0	−1.5
1979[b]	−37.4	−1.6	−23.0	−1.0

Sources: *The Budget of the United States Government, Fiscal Year 1980*, pp. 577, 579. Full-employment estimates are from the Office of Management and Budget.
a. Ending June 30 for 1960–76 and September 30 for 1977–79.
b. Estimated.

The effect of recent departures from full employment on the federal deficit can be seen by comparing columns 2 and 4 of table 2-3. Over the past decade, the actual federal deficit has averaged about 2 percent of GNP; about half of this represents deficits solely attributable to the failure of the economy to reach full employment. In fiscal 1976, when the actual deficit was 4.1 percent of GNP, the full-employment deficit was 2.0 percent of full-employment GNP. As the economy has recovered, the actual and full-employment deficits

ate before full employment, so defined, is reached. The Council of Economic Advisers points out that "under current labor market conditions the danger of accelerating wages begins to mount as the rate of unemployment falls significantly below 6 percent." *Economic Report of the President, January 1979*, p. 65.

have both declined, but the full-employment deficit has remained high by past standards. In 1979 the actual deficit is projected to be 1.6 percent of GNP and the full-employment deficit to be 1.0 percent of full-employment GNP. This indicates that the deficit is not the result primarily of underemployment but of the spending and tax decisions in the budget itself. President Carter's objective of eliminating the deficit depends not only on the economy staying close to full employment, but also on what decisions Congress makes on the 1980 spending and tax proposals.

The 1980 Budget

The budget for 1980 calls for outlays of $531.6 billion and receipts of $502.6 billion, leaving a deficit of $29.0 billion (shown in table 1-1).

The President's planning for this budget began with two sets of constraints: first, there was a public demand for a reduction in the rate of growth of government expenditures; and second, the President himself made a public commitment in the fall of 1978 to hold the fiscal 1980 deficit to $30 billion or less. The outlays needed merely to maintain current service and activity levels without change were estimated to be 8.7 percent higher in fiscal 1980 than in 1979, with an estimated deficit of more than $30 billion if there were no changes in the tax laws. Thus it was clear at a very early stage that there was little elbow room if the President was to meet his $30 billion deficit goal. He met it by making only minor modifications on the receipts side of the budget and by proposing numerous changes on the outlay side, which netted out to a reduction of $4.5 billion below current service outlays.

The Current Services Budget

The current services budget, which was introduced in the Congressional Budget Act of 1974, provides a base against which the President's budget proposals and congressional decisions on these proposals can be evaluated. Current service outlays are defined as the estimated outlays for the budget year assuming all federal programs and activities are carried out without any changes in policies. In effect, the current services budget is intended to answer the question: "How would the budget come out if the federal government were left to operate on automatic pilot through next year?"[5]

The 1980 budget projects a rise in current service outlays from $491.3 billion in 1979 to $536.1 billion in 1980 (table 2-4). Over two-thirds of the increase is accounted for by the rise in costs of social security, unemployment compensation, and other income security programs and defense. The remaining one-third is made up mainly of increased costs of medicare and medicaid, interest payments on the national debt, and pay increases for employees of civilian agencies. Reductions in outlays were expected as a result of the termination of the local public works program enacted in 1976 and 1977, lower payments for farm income stabilization because of the continuing rise in farm prices, and slower additions to the strategic petroleum reserves. The net costs of all other programs were estimated to rise.

Current service receipts were expected to rise in 1980 more than current service outlays (table 2-4). Almost all of the increased receipts are from individual income taxes and payroll taxes to finance social insurance programs. These estimates take into account the considerable tax legislative activity in recent years, carried out in part to offset the increasing real income tax burdens caused by inflation. The income tax legislation approved by Congress in 1977 and 1978 will reduce receipts by $29.7 billion in fiscal 1980 (table 2-5). On the other hand, social security legislation enacted in 1977 and earlier years increased payroll tax rates and the amount of earnings subject to these rates significantly between 1978 and 1986. These increases will make payroll tax receipts $20.4 billion higher in 1980 (with an even greater spread in later years) than receipts from the payroll tax rates and earnings base in effect in 1977. Other

5. *Special Analyses, Budget of the United States Government, Fiscal Year 1980,* p. 8. The current services budget takes into account mandatory inflation adjustments, previously legislated changes in the benefit base, and the anticipated number of beneficiaries for entitlement programs such as social security and unemployment compensation; formula increases or legislative commitments for grants to state and local governments; and continuation of procurement and construction activities at approved levels. Estimates for entitlement programs not linked to the cost of living take into account changes in the benefit base and the number of those eligible, but inflation adjustments are not included for these programs or for grants-in-aid programs unless explicitly indexed to prices by law. The estimates assume no change in federal employment levels, and the salaries of federal employees are assumed to rise so that they will be comparable to those earned in similar private sector jobs.

Table 2-4. Changes in the Current Services Budget from Fiscal Year 1979 to Fiscal Year 1980

Billions of dollars

Item	Amount
Outlays	
Current services, 1979	**491.3**
Changes, 1979–80	**44.8**
Income security	20.7
Social security	13.5
Unemployment compensation	2.1
Federal civilian employee retirement	1.7
Housing assistance	0.9
Other	2.5
National defense	11.9
Other	12.2
Medicare and medicaid	4.9
Net interest	3.4
Pay raises for employees of civilian agencies	2.1
Local public works	−1.7
Farm income stabilization	−0.9
Strategic petroleum reserves	−0.4
All other, net	4.8
Current services, 1980	**536.1**
Receipts	
Current services, 1979	**456.0**
Changes, 1979–80	**48.5**
Individual income taxes	26.0
Social insurance taxes and contributions	19.4
Other	3.1
Current services, 1980	**504.5**

Source: *Special Analyses, Budget of the United States Government, Fiscal Year 1980*, pp. 12, 15. Figures are rounded.

increases in receipts amount to $2.6 billion.[6] The net effect of the changes in tax rates and structure since January 1977 has been to reduce receipts by $6.8 billion (table 2-5).

With receipts rising $48.5 billion and outlays only $44.8 billion, the current services deficit narrows by $3.7 billion—from $35.4 billion in 1979 to $31.6 billion in 1980—which suggests that the

6. These include $2.2 billion from a speed-up (through changes in regulations) of deposits of social security taxes by state and local governments and $0.4 billion from higher taxes to pay for the regulation of surface mining and for black lung benefits.

Table 2-5. Effect of Recent Tax Legislation on Budget Receipts in Fiscal Year 1980
Billions of dollars

Item	Receipts, 1980
Tax rates and structure in effect on January 1, 1977	511.3
Income tax reductions[a]	−29.7
Social security tax increases[b]	20.4
Other tax increases[c]	2.6
Tax legislation in effect on January 1, 1979	504.5

Source: *The Budget of the United States Government, Fiscal Year 1980*, p. 75. Figures are rounded.
a. Includes the effects of the Tax Reduction and Simplification Act of 1977, the Revenue Act of 1978, the Energy Tax Act of 1978, and the Foreign Earned Income Act of 1978.
b. Includes the effects of scheduled increases in tax rates and taxable earnings under the Social Security Amendments of 1977 and prior law.
c. Includes the effects of the Surface Mining Control and Reclamation Act of 1977, the Black Lung Benefits Revenue Act of 1977, and accelerated state and local government deposits of social security taxes.

goal of a deficit of $30 billion or less could be reached only if proposed outlays were reduced below the amounts required to maintain current services levels.

The President's Budget

In view of the constraints under which he was operating, it is not surprising that the President did not propose any major new initiatives for 1980 and generally followed a "hold-the-line" policy on existing programs and on taxes. He kept his promise to NATO to increase real defense spending by 3 percent, maintained a tight lid on the annual pay increases of federal employees, repeated his proposals for containing the rise in hospital costs, cut the outlays of some countercyclical programs, and recommended a number of reductions in social security benefits. Otherwise, the changes were minor.

OUTLAYS. The major proposals affecting outlays in 1980 are given below (see table 2-6).

• To strengthen the NATO deterrent against the Warsaw Pact countries, the fifteen member governments of NATO in May 1977 agreed to increase their defense spending by 3 percent a year in real terms over the period 1979–83. Real defense spending in the United States is projected to rise only 1.5 percent in fiscal 1979, but the 1980 budget provides for a full 3 percent increase. To meet this goal, 1980 defense outlays would have to exceed the current services level by $2.2 billion.

Table 2-6. Differences between Current Services and Proposed Budget Outlays and Receipts, Fiscal Year 1980
Billions of dollars

Item	Amount
Outlays	
Current services	536.1
Major increases	
Defense (excluding pay)[a]	2.2
Veterans' compensation	0.5
Major reductions	
Pay restraint[b]	−3.0
Health care[c]	−3.1
Countercyclical programs[d]	−1.3
Social security and railroad retirement	−0.7
Agricultural price supports	−0.7
Rail transportation	−0.5
Other changes, net	2.1
Proposed outlays	531.6
Receipts	
Current services	504.5
Major increases	
Increases in railroad retirement payroll tax	0.2
Other increases	0.1
Major reductions	
Real wage insurance	−2.3
Proposed receipts	502.6

Sources: *The Budget of the United States Government, Fiscal Year 1980*, pp. 16, 20; and *Special Analyses, Budget of the United States Government, Fiscal Year 1980*, pp. 21, 214. Figures are rounded.

a. Includes atomic energy.

b. Includes employees of civilian and defense agencies.

c. Includes savings in medicare and medicaid resulting from proposed hospital cost containment legislation ($1.7 billion) and other health financing proposals ($1.4 billion).

d. Includes reductions in the public service employment program ($0.6 billion), the summer youth program ($0.3 billion), and countercyclical revenue sharing ($0.4 billion). Local public works reductions ($1.8 billion) were included in the current services budget.

- The 1980 budget proposes automatic annual cost-of-living increases in veterans' compensation benefits, beginning in October 1979. This legislation, which would put veterans' compensation on a par with social security and railroad retirement benefits and veterans' pensions, would increase 1980 outlays by $0.5 billion.
- The largest single reduction in 1980 outlays is the result of the administration's general policy of reducing wage and price increases. Pay increases of federal employees were held to 5.5 percent in the

year beginning October 1, 1978—almost 3 percentage points lower than was needed to maintain parity with wages elsewhere in the economy. The President proposed that the percentage increase in October 1979 be held to the same figure. This one decision, which would widen the gap between federal pay scales and so-called comparability to about 5 percentage points, reduces 1980 outlays by $3 billion.

• Private and public health care expenditures have been rising sharply in the past decade, and the drain on the federal budget has been large. Outlays for federal health care programs in 1979 are expected to be more than twice the outlays of five years earlier; without a change in policy, these outlays will continue to increase rapidly and contribute to unacceptably high rates of inflation. In 1978 the administration proposed that the annual hospital cost increases under the medicare and medicaid programs be limited. Congress did not enact the legislation, but this year the administration has introduced an even more stringent version of its 1978 plan. Federal saving from this legislation would amount to $1.7 billion in 1980; other measures to control federal health care spending would raise the total saving to $3.1 billion.

• Since the administration expects the business expansion to continue into 1980, there is less need for special countercyclical federal programs. The public works program received no new funds in 1978, with the result that outlays for public works in the current services budget for 1980 decline by $1.7 billion from those of 1979 (table 2-4). In addition, the President proposed a reduction in the number of countercyclical public service jobs (title VI of the Comprehensive Employment and Training Act) from 358,000 at the end of fiscal 1979 to 200,000 at the end of 1980. Public service jobs designated for the structurally unemployed are held constant at 267,000 in 1980. The administration also proposed a reduction in the number of part-time jobs under the summer youth employment program from 1 million to 750,000 and removal of fourteen-year-olds from eligibility for the program. Finally, standby legislation will be proposed to replace the countercyclical revenue sharing grants that expired in 1978. The new program will start at a higher unemployment level and will reach fewer cities than the program it replaces. The reduction in outlays for these countercyclical programs will amount to $1.3 billion in 1980.

• Except for a revision of the formula to eliminate overadjustments for inflation, the basic structure of social security benefits was left unchanged by the 1977 amendments. A number of committees and task forces were organized to recommend changes that would improve the long-run structure of the social security and related retirement systems.[7] These groups will complete their studies late in 1979, but the administration felt that, in a period of budget stringency, some proposals to eliminate low-priority benefits need not await the results of the studies. The major proposals were to eliminate the $120-a-month minimum benefit for new recipients, replace the $255 lump-sum payment with a new death benefit based on need under the supplemental security income program, phase out benefits for post–secondary school students, and reform the disability program. Similar changes were proposed for railroad retirement benefits. These changes would reduce outlays by $0.7 billion in fiscal 1980, $1.8 billion in 1981, and $3.1 billion in 1982.

• Outlays for agricultural price supports are expected to go down by $0.9 billion in 1980 as a result of recent increases in farm prices (table 2-4). The President proposed the establishment of an international emergency food reserve, which would permit a further reduction of $0.7 billion.

• The administration intends to follow its success in deregulating airlines with a similar program in rail transportation and to assist the railroads only as they make the transition to competitive operation. Legislation to modify federal assistance to achieve this objective will be proposed. This would reduce outlays by $0.5 billion in 1980.

The net effect of the President's proposals on the size and composition of the budget is shown in table 2-7. Total outlays are estimated to increase from $493.4 billion in 1979 to $531.6 billion in 1980, a rise of $38.2 billion, or 7.7 percent. Defense spending and nondefense payments for individuals will increase at a much faster rate than the budget as a whole—9.9 percent and 11.5 percent respec-

7. These include the quadrennial Advisory Council on Social Security and the congressionally mandated National Commission on Social Security. Special studies on universal coverage and the treatment of women under social security were also authorized by Congress. The report on the treatment of women, "Social Security and the Changing Roles of Men and Women," was transmitted to Congress by the Department of Health, Education, and Welfare on February 15, 1979.

Table 2-7. Proposed Budget Outlays by Major Category, Fiscal Years 1979 and 1980
Billions of dollars

Category	1979	1980	Change, 1979–80 (percent)
Defense	114.5	125.8	9.9
Payments for individuals (nondefense)	213.2	237.7	11.5
Net interest	43.0	46.1	7.2
All other	122.6	122.0	−0.5
Total	**493.4**	**531.6**	**7.7**
Addendum: Grants to state and local governments[a]	82.1	82.9	1.0
Stimulus grants[b]	5.2	2.9	−44.2
Other	76.9	80.0	4.9

Sources: Office of Management and Budget, "Federal Government Finance," January 1979 edition, p. 42; and *Special Analyses, Budget of the United States Government, Fiscal Year 1980*, p. 214.
a. Total grants-in-aid, including grants for payments for individuals.
b. Grant programs enacted in 1977 and 1978 to reduce unemployment and promote economic recovery.

tively—and interest payments on the national debt will rise at about the same rate as total spending. Outlays for the remaining federal programs, which account for only a little more than a fifth of the entire budget, will be about the same in 1980 as in 1979—roughly $122 billion. This means that they are projected to decline in real terms by about 7 percent, the rate of inflation assumed in the budget.

A major part of the President's decision to slow down the growth of federal spending will fall on the grant programs for state and local governments. The economic stimulus programs enacted during the first two years of the Carter administration resulted in a 14 percent increase in grant outlays from fiscal 1977 to 1978. These stimulus programs were designed to be temporary, and the plan is to phase them out rapidly. As a result, total grant outlays are expected to increase by about 5 percent in 1979 and by only 1 percent in 1980. Grant outlays, excluding the stimulus programs, rise somewhat more in 1980—5 percent—but still at a substantially lower rate than the rate of inflation (table 2-7). This part of the budget has provoked criticism from representatives of state and local governments and will probably be a major battleground in the annual congressional budget struggle.[8]

RECEIPTS. The President's budget includes a proposal to provide real wage insurance for workers who are members of a group that

8. See chapter 4 for a discussion of the issues.

conforms with the administration's anti-inflation guidelines. Such workers would be eligible for an income tax credit if inflation in fiscal 1979 should exceed 7 percent. The rate of the credit would be the difference between the percentage increase in the consumer price index and 7 percent, up to a maximum of 3 percentage points, and it would apply to wages up to $20,000.[9] If enacted, real wage insurance would reduce fiscal 1980 receipts by $2.3 billion on the assumption that consumer prices will have increased 7.5 percent between October-November 1978 and October-November 1979. Another $0.2 billion, which would be paid to people who do not have a large enough income tax liability to use up the credit, is included in the budget as an outlay. The budget costs would be higher, of course, if inflation should rise faster than the 7.5 percent assumed in the budget.

Tax increases are proposed to shore up the railroad retirement trust fund, to add to the receipts of the airport and airway trust fund, and to establish a $200 million fund to clean up oil spills.[10] Employers would also be required to pay social security taxes on all tips.[11] These tax changes would increase receipts by $300 million in 1980.

Several modifications in tax payment and collection procedures are proposed to bring payments during the tax year closer to taxpayers' final liabilities and to require taxes withheld by employers to be deposited with the federal government more quickly.[12] These proposals have no effect on 1980 receipts but would raise receipts by $3.3 billion in 1981 and $4.5 billion in 1982.

All told, the President's proposals would cut receipts in the 1980

9. See chapter 3 for a discussion of real wage insurance.

10. The proposals are to eliminate the taxable earnings maximum (currently $1,700 a month) on the employer portion of the railroad retirement tax, to convert the current tax of 7 cents a gallon on aviation fuel to an ad valorem tax of 10 percent and to enact a 6 percent tax on new aircraft and aircraft equipment, and to impose a fee of up to 3 cents on each barrel of oil received in U.S. refineries and terminals.

11. Currently, only the part of income from tips necessary to bring employee earnings up to the minimum wage level is subject to the employer tax, though all cash tips are subject to the employee tax.

12. One major change would be to require large corporations to make estimated income tax payments that are at least 60 percent of the current year's tax liability, even if they base the estimate on the prior year's tax liability. In addition, for both individuals and corporations who base their estimated tax payments on the current year's tax liability, the minimum percentage that must be met (to avoid penalties) through current withholding and estimated payments would be increased from 80 percent to 85 percent. Deposits of withheld taxes by large employers would also be accelerated.

current services budget by $2 billion, reducing total receipts from $504.5 billion to $502.6 billion (table 2-6).

THE DEFICIT. The effects of all the changes proposed by the President in the 1980 budget were shown in table 1-1. Proposed outlays of $531.6 billion and proposed receipts of $502.6 billion leave a deficit of $29 billion—$1 billion below the ceiling announced by the President last fall.

Alternative Assumptions

The official budget estimates for 1980 are based on a set of economic assumptions that are generally regarded as optimistic about both inflation and real growth. Prices in early 1979 were rising faster than originally projected, and many forecasters now believe that a recession before the end of 1980 cannot be averted. Even if inflation slows down in late 1979 and 1980 to the rates projected by the administration, the mandatory inflation adjustments for social security and other government programs will be higher than the official budget estimates because of the higher-than-projected price increases early in 1979. These sources of higher spending, together with the automatic increases in unemployment benefits that would result if the economy were to turn in a weaker performance than the administration assumes, would make it difficult to hold outlays to the administration's proposed level of $531.6 billion. Furthermore, it is already clear that a number of the proposed spending cutbacks (such as the reductions in social security benefits) will not be accepted by Congress.

The higher inflation rate and lower real growth move receipts in opposite directions and the effects tend to offset one another. If Congress should reject the administration's real wage insurance proposal, the estimate of receipts would be raised by $2.3 billion and there would be a little room for increasing spending above the level proposed by the President without increasing the deficit.

An alternative set of budget estimates for 1980, based on the President's own program, has been prepared by the Congressional Budget Office.[13] The CBO expects real output to slow significantly in 1979, with the downturn beginning in the second half of the year. For 1980 they forecast a mild recovery with real growth of 4 percent.

13. *An Analysis of the President's Budgetary Proposals for Fiscal Year 1980* (Government Printing Office, 1979), pp. xvii–xviii, 30–33.

Table 2-8. Comparison of Administration and Congressional Budget Office Economic
Assumptions, Calendar Years 1979 and 1980

	Fourth quarter		Calendar year	
Item	1979	1980	1979	1980
Real GNP (percent change[a])				
Administration	2.2	3.2	3.3	2.5
CBO	1.0	4.0	2.9	2.4
Consumer price index (percent change[a])				
Administration	7.5	6.4	8.2	6.7
CBO	8.0	7.5	8.4	7.8
Unemployment rate (percent)				
Administration	6.2	6.2	6.0	6.2
CBO	6.7	6.7	6.2	6.8

Sources: *The Budget of the United States Government, Fiscal Year 1980*, p. 35; and "Statement of Alice Rivlin, Director, Congressional Budget Office, Before the Committee on the Budget, U.S. Senate," February 6, 1979.

a. For year ending in period shown.

Unemployment is projected to climb to 6.7 percent in the fourth quarter of 1979 and to remain close to that level in 1980. The CBO also projects significantly higher inflation rates during 1979 and 1980 than does the administration (table 2-8). With these assumptions, the CBO estimates that the President's proposals for fiscal 1980 would result in receipts of $499.4 billion and outlays of $540.0 billion, making the deficit $40.6 billion—$11.6 billion higher than the President's goal (table 2-9).[14]

The deficit will be even higher if Congress restores or modifies some of the spending cuts proposed by the administration. Hospital cost containment was not enacted in 1978 and it will have tough sledding in Congress again in 1979. Early in the year the House Ways and Means Committee announced that it will defer until 1980

14. Part of the difference between the CBO's estimates and those of the administration appears to be caused by tight administration estimates of spending rates in continuing programs. In recent years administration estimates of outlays have been too high, resulting in spending "shortfalls." The 1979 and 1980 estimates were apparently corrected for the bias; if the CBO is right, it was an overcorrection. For a discussion of the shortfall, see Robert W. Hartman, "The Spending Shortfall," in Joseph A. Pechman, ed., *Setting National Priorities: The 1979 Budget* (Brookings Institution, 1978), pp. 301–05; and Congressional Budget Office, *Analysis of the Shortfall in Federal Budget Outlays for Fiscal Year 1978* (GPO, 1979).

Table 2-9. Effect of Congressional Budget Office Economic Assumptions on the Administration's Budget Estimates, Fiscal Year 1980

Billions of dollars

Item	Amount
Outlays	
Administration's estimate	531.6
Changes due to CBO economic assumptions	
Unemployment insurance	2.3
Social security	0.9
Medicare and medicaid	0.6
Food stamps and other	0.8
Changes due to other estimating differences	3.8
CBO estimate	540.0
Receipts	
Administration's estimate	502.6
Changes due to CBO economic assumptions	
Real wage insurance	−0.9
Other	−2.3
CBO estimate	499.4

Source: Congressional Budget Office, *An Analysis of the President's Budgetary Proposals for Fiscal Year 1980* (Government Printing Office, 1979), p. xviii.

consideration of the proposed cuts in social security benefits, except for the reforms in the disability program. The administration proposes to provide "impact aid" to school districts only on behalf of children whose parents both live and work on federal property, but Congress has regularly rejected such proposals in the past and may do so again. The administration's proposal to reduce school lunch and breakfast subsidies and to restrict the subsidies to needy children is also unpopular. Outlays for the new program of federal fiscal assistance for cities with the greatest need may be increased and some of the cutbacks in other grant programs may be restored. On the other hand, shortly after the budget was submitted, the administration withdrew its proposal to establish a national development bank to promote community and regional development because it did not have enough support in Congress. On balance, these changes would increase spending in 1980 by $4.4 billion (table 2-10), which would raise the CBO's estimate of the budget deficit to $45 billion.

Even this figure gives too bright a picture of the budget for the coming fiscal year. In the first place, the administration has proposed

Table 2-10. Possible Congressional Modifications of the Administration's Proposed
Outlays, Fiscal Year 1980

Billions of dollars

Source of change	Change in outlays
Inaction on health cost reductions	2.4
Deferral of social security benefit changes (other than disability)	0.6
Rejection of reforms in impact aid program	0.2
Maintenance of school lunch subsidies	0.4
Increases in grant programs	1.0
Inaction on proposed national development bank	−0.2
Total additional outlays	**4.4**

Source: Authors' estimates based on *The Budget of the United States Government, Fiscal Year 1980*, p. 16.

virtually no inflation adjustment in the nondefense budget except where it is mandatory. Estimates of how much it would cost to adjust the rest of the budget for inflation range from $4 billion to $8 billion.[15] If only a small fraction of the grants to state and local governments were restored to maintain their real value, the increase in outlays could be much larger than the amount shown in table 2-10. On the other hand, congressional opposition to the fact that nondefense spending is treated less favorably than defense spending may result in the rejection of some of the defense expansion, although it is difficult to cut outlays in the defense budget quickly. While it is true that Congress is in a budget-cutting mood, its will to translate this mood into specific program reductions is yet to be tested and the President's estimate of outlays may well be too low.

Second, except for real wage insurance, the budget assumes changes in the tax laws that would have only minor effects on 1980 receipts. Pressure for tax cuts is always heavy, but it is particularly severe when the real burden of individual income taxes rises during periods of inflation. Recent experience suggests that Congress acts to offset these inflation-induced tax increases. Congress is also considering modifications in the social security tax increases scheduled for the next several years, particularly 1981.

In brief, the President has presented Congress with a tight budget

15. The higher estimate is from the Office of Management and Budget and the lower estimate is from the Congressional Budget Office. See *Special Analyses, Budget of the United States Government, Fiscal Year 1980*, p. 13; and Congressional Budget Office, *Analysis of the President's Budgetary Proposals for Fiscal Year 1980*, p. 40.

that leaves little room for maneuvering. Congress is acutely aware of the pressure for more spending and for tax cuts, yet in present circumstances it cannot approve a budget resolution calling for higher spending or a larger deficit than those proposed by the President. Resolving the conflicting pressures will be the most difficult challenge yet faced by the relatively new congressional budget process. To a considerable extent, however, the lack of flexibility is self-imposed. The emphasis on the budget deficit as a target will haunt both the President and Congress if a recession does develop late in 1979 or in 1980. In such circumstances, the built-in stabilizers in the budget (lower tax receipts and higher unemployment compensation payments), which will help sustain incomes and moderate the fall in employment, will generate a higher budget deficit. The crucial question is whether the size of the budget and of the budget deficit will be under control later when the economy is operating at or close to full employment.

The Outlook for 1981–84

Along with his proposals for the 1980 budget, President Carter sent Congress projections for 1981–84. The estimates of 1981 and 1982 outlays received "explicit policy review, and represent tentative planning bases for executive branch agencies." In principle, the budget estimates for these years reflect the administration's tentative multiyear plan for federal programs, subject to revisions as the economic picture changes. The estimates for 1983 and 1984 are described as "simple extrapolations for 2 years beyond the planning base."

The Macroeconomic Plan

To make even a tentative budget plan, some assumptions must be made about the level of real activity and the rate of inflation. For this purpose, the administration was required to follow the provisions of the Humphrey-Hawkins Act, which stipulates that the economic goals for the end of 1983 should be to reduce overall unemployment to 4 percent of the labor force and inflation to an annual rate of 3 percent.[16] To meet these goals, the budget assumes

16. The President is authorized to change the timetable for reaching these goals, but not until the 1981 budget is submitted. For an analysis of the goals, see chapter 3.

that, after the slowdown in calendar years 1979 and 1980, the economy will grow rapidly enough to reduce the unemployment rate to 4.9 percent in 1982 and to reach the 4 percent goal by the end of 1983.[17] At the same time, the rate of inflation would decline steadily over the planning period, averaging about 4 percent in 1982 and 2.7 percent in 1984.

With these unrealistic assumptions, the budget presented by the administration shows what would happen to federal spending over the next five years if the 1980 budget proposals (and proposed future initiatives) were accepted and if nothing else happened. In these circumstances, the President would meet his objective of reducing federal spending to 21 percent of GNP by 1981 and the budget would be nearly in balance that year. Thereafter, the projections show that the margin of receipts over expenditures would rise to $106.5 billion in 1984 (table 2-11).[18] This occurs for two major reasons. First, the outlay estimates reflect the relatively austere program proposed by the President and are conservative in several respects. Not only are there cutbacks in many programs, but there are also few new spending initiatives. Many programs that are not indexed are held constant in nominal terms; by 1984, with prices assumed to be almost 20 percent above the 1980 level, the implied cut in real services would be unprecedented. Moreover, the projections assume that pay raises for federal employees would be held below pay increases in the private sector for five consecutive years; this would be a major reversal of the pay policies of the past decade. Second, receipts rise rapidly, both in dollars and as a share of GNP. This is caused by legislative increases in social security taxes and substantially increased individual income tax burdens as inflation and real growth move taxpayers into higher tax brackets. By 1984 receipts would have grown to 22.3 percent of GNP, which would be the highest in history except in wartime—in times of peace this ratio has never exceeded 20 percent.

17. The 4.9 percent average unemployment rate for 1982 would be "full employment" as currently defined by the Council of Economic Advisers and the gross national product would then equal its potential level. See chapter 3 for a discussion of these concepts.
18. This estimate does not include the costs in fiscal 1984 of the possible congressional modifications of the administration's 1980 budget shown in table 2-10. If these modifications were made, outlays in 1984 would be $15.7 billion higher than the amounts shown and the budget margin would be reduced to $90.8 billion under the administration's economic assumptions.

Table 2-11. Relation of Budget Projections to the Gross National Product, Fiscal Years 1978–84

Fiscal year	Amount (billions of dollars)				As percent of GNP		
	GNP	Receipts	Outlays	Margin	Receipts	Outlays	Margin
	Administration estimates						
1978[a]	2,043	402.0	450.8	−48.8	19.7	22.1	−2.4
1979	2,289	456.0	493.4	−37.4	19.9	21.6	−1.6
1980	2,506	502.6	531.6	−29.0	20.1	21.2	−1.2
1981	2,759	576.8	578.0	−1.2	20.9	21.0	*
1982	3,025	652.6	614.9	37.8	21.6	20.3	1.2
1983	3,277	718.3	645.6	72.7	21.9	19.7	2.2
1984	3,496	780.2	673.7	106.5	22.3	19.3	3.0
	Congressional Budget Office assumptions						
1978[a]	2,043	402.0	450.8	−48.8	19.7	22.1	−2.4
1979	2,300	454.6	493.5	−38.9	19.8	21.5	−1.7
1980	2,524	499.4	540.0	−40.6	19.8	21.4	−1.6
1981	2,814	582.0	590.6	−8.6	20.7	21.0	−0.3
1982	3,142	674.7	641.5	33.2	21.5	20.4	1.1
1983	3,501	761.7	688.5	73.2	21.8	19.7	2.1
1984	3,888	860.4	734.1	126.3	22.1	18.9	3.2

Sources: *The Budget of the United States Government, Fiscal Year 1980*, pp. 35–36, and authors' estimates.
* Less than 0.05 percent.
a. Actual.

An alternative set of long-term economic projections based on assumptions that are closer to the current expectations of private forecasters has also been prepared by the Congressional Budget Office. Real GNP growth is slower in 1979 and faster in 1980, but it is not as vigorous thereafter. The unemployment rate is assumed to average 6.8 percent in 1980, 6.2 percent in 1982, and 5.5 percent in 1984. Inflation is assumed to remain high in 1979 and 1980 and then to taper off to an average of 6.7 percent in 1982 and 6.0 percent in 1984, still much higher than the administration's estimate.

With the CBO's assumptions, receipts would not overtake outlays until 1982 (table 2-11). By 1984 the margin of receipts over outlays would amount to $126 billion.[19] The bigger margin in these alternative projections is the result of the assumed higher rate of inflation: receipts rise more rapidly than outlays because they are more responsive to the growth of nominal incomes.

19. The modifications to the budget in table 2-10 would grow to $15.7 billion in 1984. With these modifications, the budget margin would be reduced to $107.3 billion under the CBO economic assumptions.

This kind of increasing fiscal restraint (less spending and more taxing in relation to the size of the economy) would not be compatible with the real economic growth paths incorporated in either set of assumptions. The recent increases in employment and incomes have been due in large measure to the stimulus provided by the federal budget. The slowdown now expected in 1979 and 1980 is intended to exercise a depressing influence on the rate of growth in prices. It is conceivable that the economy could ride out the degree of restraint implied by the budget projections and reach the levels of real activity projected for 1982 and 1984, but most forecasters believe that this is not possible.

The Council of Economic Advisers concedes that strong growth "would be virtually impossible" under the fiscal program implied by the budget projections. Accordingly, the Council notes:

Adjustments of fiscal policy . . . would be needed to keep the economy moving forward steadily and strongly. In principle, a lessening of restraint through fiscal policy adjustments could be accomplished either by increasing federal outlays above the [planning] base or by cutting tax rates. Relying mainly on reductions in taxes to promote growth in the private sector would be consistent . . . with the goals of this administration. It would also prevent tax burdens from reaching an unprecedented level.[20]

The administration's macroeconomic plan beyond the immediate future is thus to maintain a policy of steady restraint on the spending side of the budget. Fiscal stimulus of the economy would come primarily from tax reductions.

The Composition of Increases in Outlays

The administration's resolution to hold down expenditures makes it all the more important to look at the composition of the proposed expenditure changes. Since the estimates for fiscal 1981 and 1982 are firmer than those for 1983 and 1984, the changes through 1982 will be examined here.

Spending is projected to increase by $83.3 billion from 1980 to 1982. The rate of growth over this period averages about 7.5 percent a year, very close to the increase in 1980 but higher than the 5.5 percent average inflation rate assumed for 1980–82. Over half of the dollar increase in outlays in the administration's budget plan is

20. *Economic Report of the President, January 1979*, p. 115.

Table 2-12. Current Services and Proposed Outlays in Fiscal Year 1982 Compared
with Proposed Outlays in Fiscal Year 1980
Billions of dollars

Category	1980, proposed	1982 Current services	1982 Proposed
Payments for individuals	249.2	296.6	290.4
Social security and railroad retirement	119.8	145.8	142.8
Medicare and medicaid	44.5	59.3	54.6
Other	84.9	91.5	93.0
Welfare reform	...	...	5.5
National defense (excluding pay and military retirement)	66.8	75.7	82.1
Federal personnel costs (military and civilian)	78.8	93.1	87.1
Grants-in-aid (excluding grants included in payments for individuals)	54.9	58.9	59.1
Interest	46.2	45.0	45.0
Other	35.7	41.3	45.7
Total	531.6	610.6	614.9
Addendum: Grants to state and local governments	82.9	92.8	91.8
Grants included in payments for individuals	28.0	33.9	32.7
Other	54.9	58.9	59.1

Sources: The Budget of the United States Government, Fiscal Year 1980, pp. 40–52, and authors' estimates.

for programs providing payments for individuals (table 2-12). These outlays will increase annually between 1980 and 1982 about 3.7 percentage points faster than the expected general inflation rate. This growth is the result not of any proposals to liberalize benefits, but rather of the growing number of beneficiaries, the automatic adjustments of the benefits resulting from inflation and growth, and relatively high inflation in health services. The only significant departures from current law proposed by the administration turn out to be offsetting. Reductions in social security benefits, savings from hospital cost containment, and some small reductions in other entitlement programs amount to $6 billion; these savings are invested back in a modest ($5.5 billion) welfare reform package.

Defense represents a second large component of expenditure growth between 1980 and 1982. To show the President's commitments to NATO, total defense outlays are scheduled to rise 3 percent a year in real terms. If total personnel costs and outlays for military retirement are removed from the defense budget, the real increase is even greater. These nonpersonnel defense outlays are expected to be $15.3 billion higher in 1982 than in 1980, which is an average nominal increase of 11 percent a year and a real increase of almost 6 percent a year (table 2-12).

Federal employee compensation will be held down by a combination of restraint on employment and the abandonment, at least temporarily, of the policy of setting federal pay at levels that are comparable to pay for similar jobs in the private sector. Federal civilian employment (excluding the postal service) is expected to decline from 2,195,000 at the end of fiscal 1979 to 2,184,900 at the end of 1980 and then to be held at that level through 1982. At the same time, pay increases will be constrained both to conserve budget funds and to demonstrate the administration's commitment to reducing the rate of growth of wages as part of the anti-inflation program. Under the comparability formula, compensation of federal employees would rise $14.3 billion from 1980 to 1982, but this is cut by $6.0 billion, for a net increase of $8.3 billion, in the multiyear budget plan.

Finally, the administration proposes to reduce in fiscal 1980–82 the real level of federal grants to state and local governments (aside from those—like medicaid—that support payments for individuals). Most of these programs are held steady in nominal dollars, although there are some proposed shifts in priorities. For example, impact aid for education is cut, but aid for the education of the disadvantaged and handicapped is increased. On balance, however, grants are strictly controlled and become a diminishing fraction of federal outlays under the administration's plan. The 1980–82 increase in grants for programs other than payments for individuals is $4.2 billion, well below the growth needed to compensate for inflation.

The decision to restrict grants stems in part from a simple process of elimination. Committed to slow growth in total outlays, real growth in defense, and protection of the interests of the poor and the aged through transfer programs, the administration had no alternative but to apply restraint to grants-in-aid. At the same time, it supplied a more direct rationale for restraint in the grant programs. In an unprecedented discussion of "Population Change and Long

Range Effects on the Budget,"[21] the budget document notes the substantial increase over the coming decades in the number of elderly people and the corresponding decline in the school-age population. It then observes that 37 percent of the federal budget supplies the elderly with retirement and medical benefits and that "education is the largest component of most state and local budgets. . . . With a decreasing number of students to be educated, state and local governments might assume new responsibilities, run surpluses or cut taxes." The administration is putting the state and local governments on notice that federal funds must be conserved for uniquely federal activities and that they may have to shift some of their own funds into activities now partially supported by Washington or give up such activities altogether.[22] Indeed, in its discussion of high-priority uses of the gross national product, the Council of Economic Advisers puts one priority, business investment, above all the rest and projects a reduction in the government sector share to make room for rising private investment.[23]

Major Issues

The most controversial issues in the administration's multiyear plan are its approach to dealing with additional fiscal stimulus and its decision on the trend in the composition of outlays.

In the recent past, Congress has offset weakness in the private economy by establishing countercyclical federal spending programs, such as public service employment, public works, and grants-in-aid geared to the level of unemployment. The administration, which pursued this route in 1977 and 1978, now contends that, when a stimulus is warranted by economic conditions in the next five years, it will favor tax reductions. The acceptability of this method of stimulating the economy is uncertain, but antispending sentiment and antipathy to high taxes seem to support such a shift in policy.

Which taxes to cut will surely set off a fierce debate. Although the administration has not stated its position, it has broadly hinted that a partial rollback of what would otherwise be a large rise in social security payroll taxes in 1981 will be high on its agenda. If productivity continues to lag in 1979–80, there will be strong pressure to

21. *The Budget of the United States Government, Fiscal Year 1980*, pp. 52–57.
22. It is notable that the administration has taken no stand on the issue of renewing the general revenue sharing program.
23. *Economic Report of the President, January 1979*, pp. 108–12.

relieve business taxes thought to be restraining investment. At the same time, the effect of the high rate of inflation on income tax burdens and the significant political support for much larger personal income tax cuts than were finally enacted in 1978 foreshadow the development of pressure for further income tax reductions. Even if fiscal stimulus is required in the next two years—implying the abandonment of a balanced budget—the total claims for tax reduction will probably exceed any prudent tax cut. Hard choices will therefore be necessary on the tax side.

The administration's push toward strong upward growth in national defense outlays and restraint in grants to state and local governments is by no means a settled issue. Whatever the condition of overall financing of state and local governments, certain states and cities are in no financial position to withstand reduced federal support. If the economy performs more weakly than the administration projects, the financial condition of these needy jurisdictions will worsen. In principle, these difficulties could be alleviated by designating aid for areas where the need is greatest. Here again, the history of targeting aid in Congress does not make one sanguine about the outcome: proposals that limit aid usually become "something for everybody" before enactment. In any event, attempts to restore some grant funds to the administration's budget plan seem a likely feature of the fiscal 1981–82 period, with the proponents seeking to cut national defense proposals to finance the restorations.

All in all, the President's spending programs for 1981–82 will probably be changed in only marginal ways. Barring a continuation of very high inflation or the development of a deep and prolonged recession, the broad outlines of the administration's program are not likely to be revised, if only because of political forces that offset each other. Even as far ahead as 1983–84, significant departures from currently planned federal programs are unlikely.

Will There Be Room for Tax Cuts?

The margin of receipts over expenditures jumps to $126 billion in fiscal 1984 under the CBO assumptions, but this is a relatively small amount of money in a $3.9 trillion economy. It also assumes no tax reductions to offset inflation-induced increases in receipts, no new federal spending programs—such as national health insurance or a more costly welfare reform program than is now proposed—and congressional approval of the decision to cut the real growth of grants to state and local governments. Enactment of any new programs and liberalization of grants-in-aid would cut into this budget margin.

Even if the entire 1984 margin of receipts over expenditures were allocated to tax reduction, the cuts would be relatively modest. To begin with, Congress has had second thoughts about the social security tax increases enacted in 1977 and pressure is building to reduce at least part of the increases. The estimated 1984 receipts include $29 billion from these amendments. One possibility for moderating this increase is to freeze the social security tax rate at its 1980 level of 12.26 percent and to limit increases in the maximum taxable earnings to amounts necessary to compensate for inflation.[24] These changes would roll back about three-quarters of the increase approved in 1977 and reduce receipts in 1984 by about $25 billion. Another possibility is to finance part or all of the hospital insurance trust fund receipts under the medicare program out of general revenues, on the ground that a payroll tax is not the proper source of financing for benefits that bear no relation to past earnings. The employer and employee payroll tax rates for this program will be 1.35 percent each in calendar year 1984 and the hospital trust fund's receipts will amount to $42 billion in fiscal year 1984, so that it would be possible to cut each tax rate by 0.8 percentage point if the revenue loss were limited to $25 billion.

There is also pressure for cutting the individual income tax. Because tax rates are graduated and exemptions and the standard deduction are fixed in dollar amounts, individual income taxes rise faster than personal income. In the past, Congress has enacted tax

24. Under the 1977 amendments the combined employer and employee social security tax rate, the taxable earnings ceiling, and the maximum tax paid by employees are as follows:

	Calendar year					
	1979	1980	1981	1982	1983	1984
Tax rate (percent)	12.26	12.26	13.3	13.4	13.4	13.4
Taxable earnings ceiling (dollars)	22,900	25,900	29,700	32,100	34,500	36,900
Maximum employee tax (dollars)	1,404	1,588	1,975	2,151	2,312	2,472

The taxable earnings ceilings for 1982–84 in this table are based on the automatic inflation adjustment mechanism. The figures for earlier years are scheduled under present law.

cuts that have more than offset the effects of inflation on real tax burdens,[25] and individual income tax receipts have rarely been allowed to exceed 11 percent of personal income.[26] The percentages for 1979 and 1980 are now expected to be about 11 percent. Without any changes in the tax law, individual income tax receipts would exceed 14 percent of personal income in fiscal 1984 under the CBO's assumptions. If this percentage were reduced to 11, 1984 receipts would be cut by $103 billion.

A third claimant for part of the 1984 budget margin is the corporation income tax. Because it is virtually a proportional tax,[27] the ratio of corporate tax liabilities to corporate profits as measured for tax purposes does not change much. However, the real burden of the tax increases because measured profits reflect inflationary gains from inventories and allow for depreciation on a historical rather than a current cost basis. Furthermore, business tax cuts will be advocated as a device to increase investment and accelerate productivity growth. In the past, when individual income taxes were reduced, business taxes were also cut, the ratio being roughly 1:3. A cut of $103 billion in individual income tax receipts might thus generate a business tax cut of $34 billion. The combined individual and corporation tax cuts of $137 billion would amount to more than the currently estimated margin of receipts over expenditures in fiscal 1984; any payroll tax rollback would add to this excess claim on the margin.

Can Expenditures Be Restrained?

The estimates of federal spending in table 2-11 are simply projections of existing programs plus the new proposals made by the President in submitting the 1980 budget. Under the CBO's economic assumptions, outlays would fall from 21.3 percent of GNP in 1980 to 18.9 percent in 1984. Measures have been proposed that would go even further, limiting spending in various ways so as to reduce the size of the federal sector and provide more room for tax cuts.[28]

25. Individual income tax cuts were enacted in 1964, 1969, 1971, 1975, 1976, 1977, and 1978. The reductions have exceeded the effects of inflation in the aggregate but not necessarily at each income level.

26. They did exceed this percentage in fiscal 1968 and 1969, however.

27. Beginning in 1979, the corporate tax rate is 46 percent on profits above $100,000, which account for over 90 percent of total profits. On profits up to $100,000, the rate ranges from 14 to 40 percent.

28. For an analysis of proposals to limit federal spending and deficits by constitutional amendment, see appendix A.

One limit, based on a defeated amendment to the Revenue Act of 1978 introduced by Senator Sam Nunn of Georgia, would restrict annual federal expenditure increases to the rate of inflation plus 1 percent. If this limit were applied starting with the estimated outlays for the administration's 1980 program, it would generate spending of $721 billion in 1984, $13 billion below the amount currently projected. It would be necessary to pare projected 1984 spending by about 2 percent, avoid all new spending, and confine inflation adjustments to programs that have mandatory inflation adjustment features. If such reductions were achieved, federal spending would fall to 18.5 percent of GNP in 1984, the lowest level since 1965.

Although a large part of the budget for the coming year is uncontrollable,[29] over the longer run a considerable amount can be controlled. The real question is whether cuts could be made in ongoing programs through legislative action and the line held on new programs and discretionary inflation adjustments so that a reduction in spending below current program projections would be achieved.

Since two-thirds of the budget consists of defense and payments for individuals, any sizable spending cuts would have to be principally in these programs. One possibility is to reduce real growth in defense spending to 2 percent a year (instead of 3 percent) beginning in 1981. Another is to put a cap on the automatic inflation adjustments in federal income security programs; for example, inflation adjustments for social security and other benefits could be limited to 80 percent of the amount allowed under present law. A third is to cut federal grants-in-aid by eliminating the portion of general revenue sharing that goes to the states. These cuts would reduce federal spending in 1984 to more than $13 billion below current projected levels.[30]

These illustrations suggest that significant cuts in prospective outlays are possible, provided Congress is willing to make major changes in present spending policies and the legislation underlying them. But the reductions must come from programs that have been worked out over a period of years and that have substantial political support.

29. According to official estimates, 76 percent of the 1980 budget is uncontrollable. *The Budget of the United States Government, Fiscal Year 1980*, p. 561.

30. The limit on real defense spending would amount to $6.0 billion in 1984; the 80 percent cap on the automatic inflation adjustment in income security programs, to $5.1 billion; and the elimination of general revenue sharing for the states, to $2.3 billion.

And they would not cut overall spending if they were offset by out-lays for new programs or discretionary increases in current pro-grams. Any significant reduction in future spending will therefore require a political consensus that is not yet apparent despite the support given the notion that the federal deficit should be cut.

Summary

The budget submitted by the President is tight not only for 1980 but also for the entire five-year period 1980–84. For those who are looking for a balanced budget in 1981, there is no room for spending increases beyond those projected in the budget plan or for tax cuts. Even that dim hope rests on a strong economic performance despite a restrictive fiscal policy. The longer-range projections, which include extremely conservative outlay estimates, do suggest that there will be some room for additional outlays and tax cuts. But all the de-mands cannot be met. The budget will not be able to accommodate sizable increases in spending on new and existing programs, a roll-back of scheduled increases in social security taxes, reductions in individual income taxes sufficient to hold the ratio of these receipts to personal income at current levels, and corresponding reductions in business taxes. Proposals to limit federal spending even more than is now projected for fiscal 1980–84 would make more room for tax cuts but would require cutting programs that are strongly supported by Congress and the public.

CHAPTER THREE

Controlling Inflation

DANIEL J. B. MITCHELL

IN ALL BUT ONE of the previous editions of *Setting National Priorities,* the problems of inflation—and the policies established to combat them—have not been the subject of a special chapter.[1] Rather, anti-inflation policies have been subsumed in chapters on general economic policy and the budget. Last year the administration was "faulted for giving inflation control little emphasis in its various initiatives" and for not dealing with the wage-price spiral.[2] It became clear in 1978 and early 1979 that inflation had become the dominant economic issue. The tax revolt that began with California's Proposition 13 and led to strong pressures for constitutional amendments requiring balanced budgets was the product of an anti-inflation backlash as well as of concern about tax burdens per se. Responding to these pressures, the Carter administration submitted an austere budget for fiscal year 1980 and announced new voluntary wage-price guidelines; the Federal Reserve pushed up interest rates until the growth rate of the money supply was drastically reduced. This

The following persons provided helpful comments on drafts of this chapter or contributed to particular sections: Ralph C. Bryant, Robert W. Crandall, Robert W. Hartman, Lawrence B. Krause, Joseph J. Minarik, Arthur M. Okun, and George L. Perry. Cynthia M. Browning provided research assistance.

1. The exception is the chapter by George L. Perry in a special edition that provided a longer-range perspective. See "Stabilization Policy and Inflation," in Henry Owen and Charles L. Schultze, eds., *Setting National Priorities: The Next Ten Years* (Brookings Institution, 1976), pp. 271–321.

2. Joseph A. Pechman, ed., *Setting National Priorities: The 1979 Budget* (Brookings Institution, 1978), p. 20.

chapter reviews these developments and evaluates the prospects for containing inflation.

Inflation: An Overview

Inflation is a general rise in the price level, a phenomenon more easily measured than understood. Nevertheless, public opinion polls in recent years have consistently shown that inflation is perceived as a major economic problem.[3]

Since World War II the consumer price index has generally moved upward. In only two periods did the CPI actually decline slightly (1948–49 and 1954–55). From 1952 to 1967 the annual inflation rate never exceeded 4 percent. Since that period the inflation rate dropped below 4 percent only in one year (1972). But even in recent years the rate of inflation has varied considerably. On a year-over-year basis it has been as high as 11.0 percent (1973–74) and as low as 3.3 percent (1971–72). Between 1977 and 1978 the increase in the CPI was 7.6 percent. Most forecasts at the end of 1978 anticipated an inflation rate in the 7 to 8 percent range for 1979, but large price increases in early 1979 led to upward revisions of these forecasts.

The Causes of Inflation

The inflation that began in the mid-1960s has many causes. The initiating cause was excessive stimulus from monetary and fiscal policy—traditional demand pull—during the Vietnam War buildup. To the surprise of many, however, a mild recession in 1970 did not halt the inflation. During 1971–72, a period of wage-price controls, inflation was reduced, but in 1973–74 it burst out again. The 1973–74 episode was initiated by special cost-push factors, including world crop shortages, dollar devaluation, and foreign oil price hikes as well as renewed monetary-fiscal pressures.[4] This experience cannot be attributed to a domestic struggle for income shares, since much of the impetus was international. And, in particular, it cannot be attributed to domestic wage gains. The deep 1974–75 recession, which

3. "Inflation, Unemployment Dominate the Agenda of Important National Problems," *Gallup Opinion Index* (May 1977), pp. 22–24.

4. Commodity inflation was estimated to account for 45 percent of the rise in the consumer price index in 1973. See Joel Popkin, "Commodity Prices and the U.S. Price Level," *Brookings Papers on Economic Activity, 1:1974*, p. 256.

was reinforced by monetary and fiscal restraint, slowed inflation but left it at historically high rates. Thus the search for an initiating cause, though of interest, does not explain the persistence of inflation. For the late 1970s, the interesting question is not what starts inflation, but what maintains its momentum.

The Momentum of Inflation

The notion of a self-perpetuating wage-price spiral is based on the simple observation that wages are a major element of total costs and that prices determine the purchasing power of wages. Although there are various models of firm behavior, it can be safely assumed that cost increases to the firm will be reflected in price adjustments. In the labor market the impact of prices on wages is more difficult to define. It is true that the price level will determine the "real" value of nominal wages. Often it is said that workers will demand wage increases to match price increases in order to sustain real purchasing power. But only workers in the unionized sector are in a position formally to *demand* such adjustments, and even in that sector a demand does not necessarily produce acquiescence by employers.

Although there are important differences between the union and nonunion sectors, available evidence suggests that wage adjustments in response to price inflation are a common feature of both types of employment. Even in relatively depressed labor markets, nonunion employers do seem to respond to price inflation with wage increases that at least partially offset the loss of real purchasing power. Nonunion employers act as if they had some obligation to protect real wages and to insulate their workers' incomes from fluctuations in labor-market demand. In the union sector, of course, these tendencies are more pronounced, since worker demands can be backed up with strike threats.[5]

In both the union and nonunion sectors, therefore, wage behavior does not accord with simple textbook models. The labor market does not function as an auction in which workers daily sell their services to the highest bidder. Employers find turnover of labor expensive, since new employees must be screened and trained. Workers find involuntary turnover (layoffs) costly, since they must engage in

5. For more discussion on union and nonunion wage-setting practices, see Daniel J. B. Mitchell, "Union Wage Determination: Policy Implications and Outlook," *BPEA, 3:1978,* pp. 537–82.

job search, which, in a world of imperfect job information, can involve the loss of regular income. Both parties have an incentive to enter into implicit long-term relationships in which notions of equity play an important part. Workers—even nonunion ones—may view it as the employers' duty to keep wages in line with inflation, and employers hoping to retain their workers over long periods of time will take account of such perceptions.[6]

The degree to which the past rate of inflation affects current wage determination will vary with the institutional setting. Collective bargainers without cost-of-living escalators are likely to consider past inflation in formulating expectations about inflation during the lives of their contracts. Contracts with partial escalator protection will reflect both current and past inflation. Nonunion employers typically set wages annually or more frequently; they have the least need for projections of future inflation and can base wage decisions on very recent or current price inflation. In all sectors, past and current inflation becomes embodied in future wage decisions, which are eventually reflected in future price increases.

Inflation perpetuates itself not only in the interaction of the labor and product markets. In financial markets, for example, interest rates will reflect—among other influences—expected rates of inflation. Firms bidding on long-term sales contracts must include an allowance for the rising prices of materials as well as for wage inflation. The income channel is also important. Wage increases that protect purchasing power permit wage earners to continue buying products whose nominal prices have risen. Nonwage incomes are also affected. Most transfer payments, such as social security and federal employee pensions, are automatically adjusted for inflation.[7] And, as noted, inflationary expectations tend to boost interest rates, thus raising the nominal incomes of interest recipients.

At one time, inducing a recession through monetary and fiscal policy may have reminded people of the Great Depression, when prices fell and economic ruin seemed at hand. This memory may

6. Arthur M. Okun, "Inflation: Its Mechanics and Welfare Costs," *BPEA*, 2:1975, pp. 366–67.

7. The Bureau of Labor Statistics estimated in late 1977 that more than one-half of the U.S. population received some income that was subject to automatic escalation geared to the consumer price index. However, only about 15 percent of all income was subject to escalation. See Julius Shishkin, "A New Role for Economic Indicators," *Monthly Labor Review*, vol. 100 (November 1977), p. 4.

explain why the recessions just before and after the Korean War were able to produce actual price declines. Thus monetary and fiscal policy could halt the wage-price spiral in that period; inflation's tendency to perpetuate itself was less of a problem then than in the 1970s. Although a market for prophecies of doom still exists in some circles, there is now a whole generation that has no memory of severe and prolonged depression. Moreover, the social insurance programs that began in the 1930s provide cushioning in the event of economic decline.

The Costs of Inflation

In an inflationary situation, any stickiness in prices and wages will have both distributional and allocative effects. Interest rate ceilings under state usury laws provide an excellent example. If market interest rates climb above the usury ceilings, borrowers will have trouble obtaining loans and lenders will be forced to seek out new areas of investment. Wage stickiness may hold down real wage rates and thus temporarily transfer income from wages to profits and to job seekers who might otherwise have had difficulty in finding employment.

Some transfers of income may occur between taxpayers and government. To the extent that revenue is raised from progressive income taxes, rising nominal incomes will push taxpayers into higher tax brackets and lower the real value of personal exemptions and the standard deduction. On the other hand, those taxes that are assessed in absolute terms against volume measures (for example, 5 cents of tax per gallon) decline in real terms during inflation.

In the case of property taxes, inflation and speculation intertwined to produce income gains for local governments and an eventual taxpayer revolt. It has become part of the folk wisdom on inflation that homeownership is a hedge against rising prices. The belief that home buying would be a good investment helped fuel the inflation of house prices. And since property taxes are geared to assessments of house value, collections tended to rise. Homeowners began to worry about whether they could expect their incomes to keep pace with their property taxes. (This is an example of the difficulty inflation creates for all long-term planning decisions, such as saving for retirement.) In California the outcome of these fears was Proposition 13, an amendment to the state constitution that not only cut property taxes but drastically limited the rates at which they could increase. During 1978 proposals of this type were considered or adopted in other states and localities.

To the extent that political decisions are required to correct for inflation, questions of income distribution that might otherwise be suppressed come out in the open. If it becomes necessary, for example, to enact income tax cuts periodically to offset the revenue-increasing effect of inflation, political debate over the desirable degree of progressivity and the treatment of certain sources and uses of income must be renewed. This increase in the costs of political transactions is mirrored in private-sector contracts. For example, increased strike activity accompanied the inflation that built up in the late 1960s. And landlord-tenant disputes have resulted in pressures for rent control.

One of the important economic rules of thumb that inflation distorts is the aversion to reduction in wages in periods of slack demand for labor. When combined with the rule that the most senior employees are the last to be laid off in a business downturn, the aversion to wage cuts can be seen as an income-maintenance guarantee. The degree of protection provided by the guarantee grows as the employee demonstrates loyalty to the employer by remaining on the job, and can be viewed as part of the implicit labor agreement. This guarantee applies to nominal wages, not real wages, a consideration of no consequence when prices are stable.

In a period of inflation, however, an employer can cut real wages without taking any overt action against nominal wages. Thus income-security arrangements are disrupted, and worker insecurity grows. The fact that real wages can reflect downward labor-market pressures during inflationary periods may be regarded as "efficient" by economists. But it creates resentment among workers. In the early 1970s, for example, previous changes in birthrates as well as taxpayer resistance created adverse labor-market conditions for school-teachers. Real wages for secondary-school teachers fell about 6 percent from 1972 (the peak for real earnings) to 1977, despite a 36 percent increase in nominal wages.[8] Had the rate of price inflation been zero during this period, a 6 percent wage cut might have been more difficult for school boards to accomplish and, indeed, might not have occurred at all.

8. U.S. Bureau of the Census, *Statistical Abstract of the United States, 1977* (GPO, 1977), p. 147.

Inflation makes contractual relationships—explicit and implicit—more difficult to maintain, increasing the potential for disputes about economic relationships and obligations, decreasing economic security for senior members of groups for whom labor markets are weak, and forcing more open recognition of income distribution issues in the political arena. In addition, a major cost of inflation is an increase in social tensions, another cost that cannot be meaningfully reduced to a dollar equivalent. But even though its social and economic costs defy measurement, inflation is a serious problem and economic policy must deal with it. Ultimately, the political process provides the index of public unhappiness with inflation. Imperfect though that index is, the anti-inflation mood of the electorate has been demonstrated in a range of recent political developments.

Aggregate Demand Policy and the Short-Term Economic Outlook*

By the end of 1978 virtually all economic forecasters were expecting a slowdown in real economic growth during 1979. Opinions differed, however, on the timing and severity of the slowdown and on whether it would technically meet the necessary qualifications for a "recession." Table 3-1 shows a series of such forecasts. Administration estimates tended to be significantly more optimistic about real growth, but still conceded a slowdown. The range of predicted inflation rates is close to that of the third quarter of 1978, when prices increased at an annual rate of 6.9 percent. Thus the forecasters were essentially projecting a continuation of the most recent inflation experience (the third-quarter figures were the latest available when these forecasts were made), despite an expected slowdown in real growth. The administration's forecast was more pessimistic about inflation than four of the others, perhaps because it assumed a better real growth performance. All seven forecasts recognized the limitations of macroeconomic policy. That is, all expected economic policy to create economic slack, but none anticipated that the rate of inflation for 1979 would fall below 6 percent.

Evaluation of current and proposed aggregate-demand policies must be made within the context of considerable uncertainty about the economic outlook. However, it is clear that monetary policy

* Joseph J. Minarik contributed to this section.

Table 3-1. Selected Economic Forecasts, Late 1978 and Early 1979
Percent

Source	Date	Inflation rate, 1978:4 to 1979:4[a]	Growth of real GNP, 1978:4 to 1979:4	Peak unemployment rate, 1979[b]
Data Resources	January 1979	7.4	−0.5	7.1
Manufacturers Hanover Trust	Winter 1978–79	7.2	0.2	7.2
UCLA Business Forecast	December 1978	6.2	0.9	7.1
Wharton	December 1978	6.9	1.4	6.1
George L. Perry, Brookings Institution	January 1979	6.8	0.8	6.4
Goldman Sachs	January 1979	7.8	0.7	7.1
Carter administration	January 1979	7.4	2.2	6.2

Sources: "Data Resources U.S. Forecast Summary" (Data Resources, Inc., January 1979), table 7, p. 8; Irwin L. Kellner, "Economic Forecast for 1979," *Business Report* (Manufacturers Hanover Trust Co., Winter 1978–79), p. 4; "The UCLA National Business Forecast: Executive Summary" (December 1978), p. 2; "The Wharton Quarterly Model Forecast, December 28, 1978, Control Section Update" (Wharton Econometric Forecasting Associates, Inc.), p. 1; data supplied by George L. Perry, January 2, 1979; *Economic Research*, "The Pocket Chartroom" (Goldman Sachs Economic and Financial Research Group, January 1979), p. 3; *The Budget of the United States Government, Fiscal Year 1980*, p. 35.
a. Change in the GNP deflator.
b. All forecasts expect highest unemployment rate in 1979 to occur in the fourth quarter.

definitely became tighter in the second half of 1978. And the Carter administration's budgetary proposals for fiscal year 1980 also represent a tightening.[9] These shifts in direction are the consequence of fears of accelerating inflation and the related concern over the value of the dollar in international exchange markets.

Fiscal Policy

Fiscal policy could affect the rate of inflation in three ways. First, the standard analysis suggests that a decrease in spending or an increase in tax rates is contractionary. The problem in the past has been that much of the contractionary effects associated with a tightening of fiscal policy have fallen on real output rather than on inflation. In the short term, say over a period of a year, a 1 percentage point increase in unemployment might slow the inflation rate by 0.3 percentage point. At current levels of production, a loss of real GNP of over $200 billion would be required to reduce the inflation rate

9. See chapter 2.

by 1 percentage point.[10] The burden of that cost will not fall on the population in a proportional manner.

A second aspect of fiscal policy relates to taxes that have a direct influence on prices. The most obvious examples of such taxes are state and local sales and excise tax levies. A substitution of income taxes for sales and excise taxes would directly lower the price level. Since the federal government has no general sales tax and the importance of excise taxes in federal receipts is small, there is little room for such adjustments by the federal government. Unless the federal government were prepared to compensate state and local governments for lost sales or property tax revenues, the only major tax cut available for direct cost effects would be a cut in social security payroll taxes. It is often assumed that a reduction in labor costs resulting from reduced payroll taxes would be passed on in lower prices. However, such cuts would raise significant questions about social security financing, questions that Congress is unlikely to face during 1979. Thus the chance for any direct downward fiscal pressure on the price level in the near term is unlikely.

A third possible influence of fiscal policy on inflation could operate through an induced effect on monetary policy. It is sometimes argued that large budget deficits force the Federal Reserve Board to finance the deficit through monetary expansion. Were the monetary authorities to feel obligated to buy a substantial fraction of the net issues of Treasury obligations, large deficits would indeed have substantial monetary implications. However, there are no legal or institutional obligations forcing the Federal Reserve to finance the deficit. And, as table 3-2 illustrates, the statistical evidence does not show any close links between Federal Reserve purchases of Treasury obligations (column 2) and Treasury issuances of such obligations (column 1). In some years the Federal Reserve bought only a small fraction of the change in net federal debt; in others it bought more than 100 percent. Deficits do not automatically determine the policy of an independent Federal Reserve, nor should they.

The alleged monetary effect of fiscal policy is really the only channel through which the budget deficit itself—*as opposed to spending and tax decisions*—could play an important role in aggregate demand policy. Obviously, it is those tax and spending decisions that

10. See Arthur M. Okun, "Efficient Disinflationary Policies," *American Economic Review*, vol. 68 (May 1978), pp. 348–52.

Table 3-2. Changes in Federal Debt Held by the Public and by the Federal Reserve, Fiscal Years 1955–78

Amounts in billions of dollars

Fiscal year	Net change in federal debt held by public[a] (1)	Net change in federal debt held by Federal Reserve (2)	Ratio, col. 2 to col. 1 (percent) (3)
1955	2.1	−1.4	−66.2
1956	−4.3	0.2	−4.6
1957	−2.8	−0.8	28.5
1958	6.9	2.4	34.6
1959	8.6	0.6	6.9
1960	2.2	0.5	23.0
1961	1.4	0.8	56.1
1962	9.8	2.4	24.6
1963	6.1	2.3	38.2
1964	3.1	2.8	89.5
1965	4.1	4.3	106.0
1966	3.1	3.1	99.8
1967	2.8	4.6	160.3
1968	23.1	5.5	23.9
1969	−11.1	1.9	−16.7
1970	5.4	3.6	67.1
1971	19.4	7.8	40.1
1972	19.4	5.9	30.4
1973	19.3	3.8	19.5
1974	3.0	5.5	181.7
1975	50.9	4.3	8.5
1976	83.4	9.7	11.7
1977	57.2[b]	8.2[b]	14.4
1978	59.1	10.0	16.9

Sources: *Annual Report of the Secretary of the Treasury on the State of Finances*, various issues; *Economic Report of the President*, various issues.

a. "Public" includes the Federal Reserve and all other holders except federal government agencies.

b. Figures for fiscal year 1977 reflect an extra "transitional" quarter. Data have been adjusted by multiplying them by 4/5.

determine the deficit at any given level of economic activity. But the recent concentration by the public on the deficit as the source of inflation is too one-sided. Over the long term the deficit does have significance for the rate of national saving and investment. Yet even from that perspective, an expanding economy with good prospects for investors is a precondition for a high rate of investment.

For the present, federal fiscal policy is largely a matter of spending decisions. Tax policy has already been laid out. The reductions in expenditures proposed by the administration for discretionary components of the budget (see chapter 2) can have only a small effect on inflation in the short term, perhaps a reduction of one- or two-tenths of a percentage point in the inflation rate.

Monetary Policy

Monetary policy is currently in a paradoxical position. On the one hand, it is the more flexible of the two aggregate demand policies because it can be changed quickly in response to economic developments. But on the other, changes in the institutions surrounding the financial sector have made the response of the economy to monetary policy more uncertain than ever. For example, the development of money market mutual funds and payment drafts for savings accounts provided consumers with interest-bearing substitutes for checking accounts. Such developments have changed the relationships of the money supply and interest rates to economic activity.

In the past a major element in the responsiveness of the economy to monetary contractions was through the flow of funds out of the savings institutions (disintermediation), a shortage of funds to the housing industry, and a resultant construction crunch. The disintermediation occurred as market interest rates surpassed legal ceilings on interest rates paid on deposits in savings institutions, thus enticing savers to move into such assets as Treasury bills. But the introduction in June 1978 at savings institutions (and banks) of new "money-market" certificates geared to six-month Treasury bill interest rates appeared to shelter the housing industry from the impact of disintermediation. Savings institutions retained their deposits—although at considerable cost—and borrowers were able to obtain mortgage loans, except in states with restrictive usury ceilings. This development was somewhat ironic, since housing prices were clearly an area of overheated speculation. A cooling off of such speculation would have been especially desirable. In March 1979 interest rates on the new certificates were moderately restricted in order to dampen housing demand.

Whether one prefers interest rates or monetary aggregates as indicators of the financial consequences of Federal Reserve actions, it is clear that in the last quarter of 1978 a dramatic shift occurred. During the first half of 1978 the Federal Reserve appeared to be in a reactive posture allowing gradual interest rate increases, especially

Table 3-3. Indexes of Monetary Policy, 1977–79
Percent

	Annual rate of growth of money supply[a]			End-of-period federal funds rate	Discount rate (New York)
Period	M-1	M-2	M-3		
December 1976–December 1977	8.0	9.3	11.3	6.56	6.0
December 1977–June 1978	8.6	7.8	8.0	7.60	7.0
June 1978–September 1978	9.5	10.8	12.4	8.45	8.0
September 1978–December 1978	0.2	4.5	7.4	10.03	9.5

Source: *Economic Report of the President, January 1979*, pp. 251, 259.
a. M-1 = circulating currency plus demand deposits (excluding domestic interbank and U.S. government deposits); M-2 = M-1 plus bank time and savings deposits other than large negotiable certificates of deposit; M-3 = M-2 plus deposits at mutual savings banks, savings and loan associations, and credit unions.

in the second quarter. Growth in the monetary aggregates tended to exceed the goals established by the Federal Reserve for 1978, a pattern that continued into the third quarter. As table 3-3 shows, M-2 was rising at an annual rate of over 10 percent during that quarter. By that time, however, the Federal Reserve had moved toward a more restrictive position and was pushing up interest rates, partly in response to depreciation of the dollar. The interest rate on federal funds was substantially higher at the end of the third quarter than at the beginning of the year.

International considerations produced a dramatic policy reaction in the fourth quarter, when it became apparent that foreign-exchange traders were not satisfied with the prospects of the newly outlined anti-inflation program. Domestic actions included an increase in the discount rate from 8.5 to 9.5 percent and an increase in required reserves on large time deposits. (International actions are discussed below.) The Federal Reserve pushed interest rates to new peaks and continued this tighter stance into 1979. Partly because of Federal Reserve policy and partly because of unprecedented shifts out of money into other assets, growth in the conventional definitions of the money stock slowed substantially in the fourth quarter.

Given the uncertainties over monetary policy and the economic outlook, it would be unwise for the Federal Reserve to react to each month's announcement of high inflation rates with a further tightening of monetary policy. The short-term response through the housing industry and disintermediation was initially attenuated. Monetary mechanisms can be expected to work more gradually under the new institutional arrangements, mainly through the effect of interest rates on investment decisions and financial markets. Because of the lags involved in this mechanism, the Federal Reserve could easily over-shoot, pushing the economy into a deeper recession or slowdown than intended. Indeed, some monetarist economists would argue that the sudden slowdown in the growth of the monetary aggregates in late 1978 indicated an excessively tight policy.

Finally, it is important to note that the channels through which monetary policy affect inflation are much the same as those of fiscal policy. That is, monetary policy restrictions will primarily slow the growth of real output, producing only a small anti-inflation dividend, especially in the short run. The boom in agricultural prices in early 1979 and the effects of the oil price increase by the Organization of Petroleum Exporting Countries (OPEC) and of the production shortfall in Iran cannot be considered responsive to monetary policy. And, perversely, the impact of increased mortgage interest rates has a dramatic worsening effect on inflation as measured by the consumer price index.

International Aspects of Anti-Inflation Policy*

As 1978 progressed, movements in the exchange rates of the dollar vis-à-vis other currencies began to play an important role in decisions regarding monetary policy. Table 3-4 shows that the U.S. dollar declined in value relative to most other important currencies during the first ten months of 1978. By late October there were many indications of a loss of international confidence in the dollar. For the first time in the post–World War II period, domestic monetary policy was heavily influenced by international exchange markets.

The Policies of November 1, 1978

On November 1 the Federal Reserve and the Treasury announced a series of moves to reverse the decline. For the first time the Presi-dent spoke of the exchange rate as a policy goal and supported a tighter monetary policy as an instrument to pursue that goal. Swap arrangements with foreign central banks were increased by $7.6 bil-

* Lawrence B. Krause contributed to this section.

Table 3-4. Value of Foreign Currencies Relative to the U.S. Dollar, 1970–78

Indexes of value (December 1977 = 100)

Month and year	German mark	Italian lira	French franc	Swiss franc	British pound	Japanese yen	Canadian dollar	Composite average of 10 major currencies[a]
December 1970	59.0	140.5	86.9	48.1	128.9	67.4	107.8	72.5
December 1972	67.2	150.2	94.3	55.1	126.4	80.0	110.1	88.8
December 1977	100.0	100.0	100.0	100.0	100.0	100.0	100.0	100.0
March 1978	105.8	102.4	102.0	109.4	102.7	104.0	97.5	103.9
June 1978	103.2	101.9	104.8	110.1	99.1	112.7	97.8	104.0
September 1978	109.2	105.6	109.9	132.4	105.7	126.9	94.1	109.2
October 1978	117.1	107.9	114.0	135.3	108.2	131.3	92.8	113.8
November 1978	112.9	103.9	110.1	124.1	105.7	125.5	93.5	108.5
December 1978	114.4	103.9	111.2	123.9	107.1	123.0	93.0	110.2

Source: *Federal Reserve Bulletin*, various issues.

a. Index of the dollar relative to the weighted average of currencies of the other Group of Ten countries plus Switzerland, weighted by 1972–76 global trade.

lion to $15 billion. A plan was unveiled to sell abroad Treasury securities denominated in foreign currencies. Arrangements were made for drawing from the International Monetary Fund and for other borrowing. Increased U.S. gold sales were announced, presumably to attract foreign currency and lessen the attractiveness of gold as a vehicle to speculate against the dollar. All these actions, in addition to their actual or potential effects, were intended as symbolic gestures showing the resolve to defend the dollar.

Finally, the Federal Reserve raised the discount rate from 8.5 percent to 9.5 percent and lifted the goal for the federal funds rate. The latter action had the immediate effect of making returns on assets denominated in U.S. dollars higher—thus increasing the attractiveness of such assets to foreign investors and Americans thinking of investing abroad—and of signaling a willingness to fight inflation, even at a cost in U.S. real output. As a result of these various steps, the dollar showed a substantial gain in price relative to foreign currencies in November. Much of this gain was retained through the first quarter of 1979.

Foreign central banks apparently were willing to intervene to stem the dollar's decline initially. During the last quarter of 1977 and the first quarter of 1978, foreign central banks increased their dollar holdings in the United States by over $31 billion. In the second quarter, however, when the dollar appeared to stabilize, these holdings were reduced by $5.7 billion. Foreign official net acquisitions of U.S. dollar assets increased in the third quarter by $4.9 billion, which was not enough to stem the decline of the dollar. In the fourth quarter of 1978, official holdings of dollar assets rose by over $19 billion, a sign of renewed confidence.

Exchange Rates and Inflation

The post–World War II system of fixed exchange rates was officially abandoned in early 1973. The U.S. policy after that date was primarily to let the dollar float against other currencies. Domestic policy was determined largely by domestic objectives, and the exchange rate was left to adjust for any inconsistency between U.S. policy and economic conditions and those of other countries. Hence the 1978 decision to defend the dollar marked a notable change in emphasis from the prevailing direction of U.S. policy after 1973. Policymakers concluded that the level of the exchange rate was an important additional objective that acted as a constraint on overall macroeconomic policy.

The exchange rate affects the domestic price level and the internal rate of inflation and is also affected by them. It is estimated that a 10 percent devaluation of the dollar ultimately produces a 1 to 2 percent increase in the consumer price index, because of the resulting increases in import prices and the secondary effects on the prices of domestic substitutes.[11] If the dollar is maintained at a given value on the exchange markets rather than permitted to depreciate, inflation caused by internal disturbances will tend to be dampened. Internal demand pressure—if that is what is causing inflation—will spill over into increased imports and possibly into reduced exports. Less of the demand pressure will go into bidding up domestic prices. But if the demand pressure continues, the eventual surplus of imports over exports must be financed by depleting U.S. foreign assets or by U.S. borrowing abroad. Unless foreigners have an insatiable appetite for U.S. liabilities, the use of the exchange rate to dampen inflation cannot go on indefinitely. At some point the internal demand pressures must be reduced.

Exchange-rate movements may affect the speed and timing at which internal demand pressures are felt. As the economy approaches full utilization of capacity, a series of stages in the relationship of the internal price level to the exchange rate may occur. Initially, imports are stimulated relative to exports, but currency traders may be slow to perceive that a fundamental weakening of the competitiveness of U.S. exports and import-competing goods is occurring. Indeed, if internal demand pressures raise U.S. interest rates, a sufficient capital inflow from abroad may be created to maintain a balance between the demand for and the supply of dollars at existing exchange rates. Thus initially the exchange rate may act as a dampener of inflation.

As the perception of U.S. inflation becomes more widespread and expectations are created that inflation will continue, the offsetting capital flows may cease and reverse. The dollar may begin to sink in value more or less in proportion to the inflation differential between

11. *Economic Report of the President, January 1979*, p. 43; Peter Hooper and Barbara Lowrey, "Impact of Dollar Depreciation of the U.S. Price Level: An Analytical Survey of Empirical Estimates," International Finance Discussion Paper 128 (Board of Governors of the Federal Reserve System, January 1979), p. 44.

the United States and other countries. Thus the inflation-dampening effect comes to an end because foreign prices—measured in dollars—are rising at the same rate as U.S. domestic prices. Moreover, the inflation expectations of currency traders may worsen and lead to a run on the dollar, especially if monetary growth is not held down for domestic reasons. At this point the further decline in the dollar set in motion by asset-market shifts out of dollar-denominated assets can itself add to inflation, since it exceeds the difference between the inflation rate of the United States and those of other countries.

Obviously, it is easier to identify such stages of the inflation—exchange rate relationship conceptually than empirically. In recent years inflation has had components that are not directly due to internal demand pressures. These have included disturbances originating abroad (for example, foreign oil price hikes), and cost-push originating at home (for example, regulatory costs and social security tax increases). Therefore, policymakers may have difficulty determining at any given moment whether the economy is truly overheated. This uncertainty makes policy decisions about exchange rates complicated. If the exchange rate has depreciated more than is warranted by general economic conditions at home and abroad—including inflation—intervention to boost the value of the dollar in exchange markets could be justified on anti-inflation grounds. If the depreciation is occurring because of shifts in general economic conditions at home or abroad, however, attempts to prop up the dollar may simply result in a larger devaluation at a later date and capital losses to the government. It is often only in hindsight that a decision to intervene in the exchange market can be evaluated.

When anti-inflationary internal policies are followed, the exchange rate plays a similar role in affecting the timing of inflation. After a prolonged period of inflation, the exchange rate may not react fully to a change in policy. But this lag in the perception of currency traders caused by lost confidence in the dollar—which initially reduces the effectiveness of anti-inflation policy—will ultimately be made up when confidence is restored.

If policymakers are sure that they are willing to follow restrictive policies for an extended period, and if they are sure that the exchange markets are reacting to past inflation and not to the new anti-inflation resolve, deliberate actions to boost the dollar exchange rate can be justified. Boosting the exchange rate under those circumstances could dampen inflation. This was evidently the kind of analysis that supported the strong moves to boost the dollar in November 1978.

The Simultaneity Problem for Domestic Policymakers

In a textbook demand inflation, a steady state is possible in which all prices are rising at the same rate—plus or minus differences that reflect relative changes in demand and supply—and the exchange rate is depreciating at a rate determined by domestic and foreign inflation. Capital movements are not seen as playing a destabilizing role. But because the exchange market tends to move unevenly during periods of inflation, this steady state never arrives. Even if U.S. demand policies were aimed at maintaining a given rate of inflation, there would probably be periods in which exchange-rate movements either slowed that rate or caused it to accelerate. Thus a policy aimed at perpetuating a rate of inflation would nevertheless be forced to react to the exchange rate. In particular, if the dollar exchange rate began exacerbating the rate of inflation, domestic demand policy would have to become more restrictive. And vice versa.

Dollar exchange-rate movements, however, are not merely reactions to internal U.S. policies. Since each rate is the relative price of the dollar against some other currency, the policies and conditions in other countries inevitably affect the dollar. Indirectly, therefore, U.S. domestic policy must respond to events in other countries just as their domestic policies must respond to developments in the United States. The fundamental interdependence of national economies creates a need for coordination of objectives across countries and domestic macroeconomic policies.

Trends in international trade have increased the importance of the foreign sector to U.S. economic activity. In 1968 U.S. exports amounted to 5.7 percent of GNP; by 1978 the figure had reached 9.7 percent. The figures for imports are 5.5 percent and 10.3 percent respectively.[12] Corresponding interdependence has grown in capital markets. These data suggest that the United States needs to consider the foreign sector in formulating its domestic policy.

Recent events further illustrate this need. In 1976 net exports fell $13 billion below their level the previous year. Although such declines are often referred to as "deteriorations," they are not neces-

---

12. These figures are based on national income and product accounts data. Exports and imports include both goods and services.

sarily bad. It could be argued that, given the large OPEC surpluses, the large net export surplus of the United States in 1975 ($20.4 billion) was inappropriate. However, unless there were strong reasons to believe that the decline in net exports was temporary, the decline could have been viewed as a forerunner of eventual dollar decline on the exchange market. The fact that the economy of the United States was expanding more rapidly than those of its important trading partners suggested that the decline in net exports was more likely to be an ongoing process than a one-shot event. A further decline in net exports in 1977 of $18.5 billion confirmed this hypothesis.

During 1977 other countries accumulated dollar reserves in an effort to keep their own currencies from rising in value relative to the dollar. But basically the U.S. policy was to avoid intervention in the exchange markets. The result was a rapid adjustment of the exchange rate during 1978 rather than the more gradual change that might otherwise have occurred over the whole period 1976–78.

After witnessing a declining net export surplus trend, the United States had two policy choices if it acted promptly. It could have taken steps to slow down the domestic expansion, thus reducing the rate at which imports were being drawn into internal markets and having some moderating effect on the rate of inflation. Or it could have decided to continue the expansion and to discourage foreign support of the dollar, thus producing a gradual fall in the dollar's value abroad rather than a sudden one. At a minimum, however, the United States should not have ignored the foreign sector and then been surprised by the inflationary fallout and other consequences of dollar devaluation in 1978.

Foreign Price Shocks

In 1973 OPEC quadrupled the dollar price of crude petroleum. Two immediate consequences of this action are especially worth noting. First, the value of imports of crude petroleum, petroleum products, and other energy supplies was suddenly raised. Second, despite the controls imposed on prices of domestic oil, the U.S. price level rose sharply, resulting in a loss of real income for most Americans.

Since the increased value of imports had to be paid to foreigners, the United States had to increase net exports or borrow abroad.

Initially the apparent desire of the oil-producing countries to hold their increasing wealth in American assets—that is, to lend to the United States—was sufficient to sustain the exchange value of the dollar. However, the OPEC trade surplus began to decline as the oil-producing countries displayed a surprising appetite for increased imports as well as an interest in a diversified portfolio of assets not wholly confined to the dollar.

All this meant that eventually the United States would have to divert more resources into the production of exports and import substitutes. Thus there would have to be a reduction in U.S. domestic absorption of goods, relative to the level that would have been sustained at high employment, to accommodate the resource shift. That is, Americans would have to live within their reduced means. This is of course more easily said than done. For which component of absorption is going to be cut—consumption, investment, or government spending? And which groups in society will bear the burden of the reduction in real national income?

The immediate price level effects of an OPEC-type shock create a difficult issue for public policy. Clearly, a big difference exists between such an exogenous price increase and one resulting from general excess demand. In theory, the OPEC price increase could have been neutralized if other prices had been made to fall. But the ability of monetary and fiscal policy to produce absolute price declines sufficient to offset a quadrupling of oil prices is questionable. Some inflation after the OPEC increase was inevitable and simply reflected the real income loss in the face of the downward inflexibility of American wages and prices.[13]

The Dollar Overhang

Throughout the postwar period, the dollar has served as the world's primary reserve currency, that is, the currency in which foreign monetary authorities held their nations' international reserve balances. For the most part these holdings represent voluntary accumulations. At times, however, foreign central banks have sought to prevent the appreciation of the currencies through purchases of dollars in the exchange market, even in periods when the United States

13. As noted in the text, the initial loss of real income was primarily a matter of accruing liabilities to OPEC. When OPEC increased its demand for imports and transferred some of its holdings into nondollar assets, a real transfer of output was necessary.

did not wish to resist dollar devaluation. Foreign officials have therefore acquired a larger volume of dollar balances than they would ordinarily choose to hold. These balances—sometimes called the dollar overhang—constitute dollar holdings that foreign governments might not normally wish to hold for their portfolios. The overhang has been estimated at $60 billion.[14] Should these dollars be released into the currency markets rapidly, the dollar would be further devalued, thereby adding to the upward pressure on prices. Furthermore, if foreign central banks attempt to unload unwanted dollars whenever the dollar appreciates, significant appreciations will not take place. Speculators will then view the dollar as having only a downward option, and the dollar will be prone to unstable downward movements.

One option for the United States would be to squeeze domestic absorption sufficiently to be able to buy back the dollar overhang. A second would be to transfer the overhang to the International Monetary Fund in exchange for special drawing rights or some other nondollar assets. A third would be to persuade foreign central banks simply to retain the overhang until the volume of world trade became large enough to create a demand for the unwanted dollars as transactions balances. Obviously, all these options involve international cooperative arrangements.

Domestic and International Economic Policy: The Interaction

At present the objectives of domestic and international policies coincide. The United States needs to reduce its inflation rate. To make this reduction, it has adopted a series of policies aimed at inflation restraint. These include a restriction on budget expenditures, a boost in interest rates, and a reduction in monetary expansion. Also included is a policy of direct intervention in wages and prices and other supplementary programs.

To the extent that these policy actions are perceived as anti-inflationary, the exchange value of the dollar will be supported. Inflation restraint will tend to reduce relative costs of production in the United States, thus stimulating exports and reducing imports. The somewhat greater slack in the economy that will result will permit transfer of real resources into export and import-competing production.

14. Lawrence B. Krause, "The 1979 International Business Outlook," *Economic Research* (Goldman Sachs Economic and Financial Market Research Group, February 1979), p. 6.

From the standpoint of foreign and domestic asset holders, a reduction of the inflation outlook improves the dollar's usefulness as a vehicle for investment. To the extent that the value of the dollar rises on exchange markets—or at least stops declining—the inflation outlook is improved, although possibly at a cost of a greater loss of U.S. output. It is to be hoped that participants in the foreign-exchange market are under no illusions as to the speed with which the measures adopted by the United States will slow the rate of inflation. By any reckoning, the road back to price stability will be a long one.

Direct Intervention in Wage and Price Setting

Because of the limited response of inflation to demand-restraining policies, governments in all industrialized countries have sought other means to influence wage and price decisions directly. The diagnosis of a wage-price spiral suggests that inflation will perpetuate itself unless some outside force changes inflationary psychology and puts downward pressure on a large number of wage and price setters simultaneously. This type of diagnosis ultimately led to the guidelines program announced in October 1978, after a milder effort to promote deceleration of inflation through exhortation was abandoned.

The new guidelines program is nominally voluntary; it is not backed by the force of law. Pains are taken to distinguish the program from mandatory controls. Yet the distinction is one of degree. Larger government contractors are required to certify that they have complied with the standards. The legality of this aspect of the program has been challenged. But even without it, large firms and contractors would probably feel compelled to comply. Although the program is voluntary, the Council on Wage and Price Stability filled the *Federal Register* with rules of good behavior that are hard to distinguish from regulations. Larger companies were requested to send in reports to the council, just as they would be required to do under controls.

It is important to avoid dogmatism in assessing the new program. A common response to the effort has been the assertion that "controls don't work." Yet the evidence is mixed. During the Korean War, wage-price controls were accompanied by relatively stable prices and no bubble of repressed inflation escaped when the controls were lifted. Since the mid-1960s there have been episodes of controls, other forms of direct wage-price intervention, monetary restraint, and fiscal restraint. It is hard to say which policy didn't work in recent years. No policy was highly effective.

Specifics of the Wage-Price Guidelines

Under the new guidelines, firms must decelerate their annual rate of price increase by 0.5 percent relative to the increase experienced in the base period 1976–77, with a maximum increase of 9.5 percent allowed. In addition, a minimum increase of 1.5 percent is permitted without question. Firms that cannot comply with the deceleration standard because of uncontrollable cost increases are permitted cost-justified price increases. Under cost justification, firms are required to limit their profit markups to the margin experienced during the best two of the three fiscal years preceding October 2, 1978. Their profits per unit of output, however, are not to rise more than 6.5 percent. Special rules apply to certain industries and to state and local agencies.

On the wage side, pay adjustments are limited to 7 percent a year unless they were set forth in contracts or pay practices before the guidelines announcement. Union contracts can include 8 percent wage increases in the first year of multiyear contracts averaging 7 percent a year. Maintenance of benefits increased by such factors as rising insurance premiums is chargeable only up to 7 percent. Certain costs of maintaining pension benefits cannot be charged at all. And union escalator clauses must be charged as if the inflation rate were 6 percent, regardless of the actual experience.

Both the pay and price standards allow exceptions for "gross inequities." But the pay standard also provides exceptions for pre-guidelines tandem relationships, post-guidelines tandem relationships, productivity bargaining, and labor shortages. In addition, low-wage workers (those earning four dollars an hour or less) are exempt from the 7 percent standard. Special rules cover certain types of executive compensation, such as stock options. Professional fees are limited to an average annual increase of 6.5 percent.

Administration of the Guidelines

The guidelines program is very ambitious. It is apparent that the program's administrators really wish to concentrate on larger firms and wage-determining units. But the rules nominally apply to firms and units of all sizes, including governments. The Council on Wage and Price Stability (COWPS) is requesting funding for an additional 90 staff members, which would bring the total to 233. By comparison, the wage-price controls of Phase II (late 1971 to early 1973) involved a staff of about 4,000 people. And the Phase II controls exempted small businesses (in most industries) with 60 or fewer workers.

COWPS faces a dilemma under the current arrangements. Even with 233 staff members, the council will be swamped with work. And even if there were a desire to increase the staff further, there are limits to the speed at which an agency can expand. The new program does impose obligations on wage and price setters, despite its voluntary label. Therefore, COWPS must be prepared to answer questions, hear appeals, and generally regularize procedures. If regularization does not prove to be possible, a reduction in coverage of the program —given the staff size and workload—must be seriously considered.

Obvious areas for the reduction of program coverage are small businesses, public utility prices, and rents. A small business exemption would have to be carefully worded to avoid exempting small firms covered by major union contracts involving many employers. But in general, small businesses are not likely to be sources of strong, administered wage or price pressures. (If they become sources of demand-induced pressures, COWPS can do little about it.) Public utility rates are already regulated by governmental agencies on a cost-markup basis; additional regulation is superfluous. Rent coverage is virtually meaningless. There are simply too many rental housing units for COWPS to undertake meaningful rent controls. Such controls would probably have undesirable consequences, even if they were possible. Rent complaints took up an inordinate amount of time and resources during Phase II of the controls program under the Nixon administration.

Before the announcement of the guidelines, COWPS had an ongoing program of review of regulatory decisions and general research into cost problems of certain industries. A certain tension exists between the guidelines operation and the regulatory activities. For example, COWPS may find itself asking for guidelines cooperation from firms and unions with which it has a disagreement concerning regulatory policy. Therefore, it would be useful to insulate the regulatory and guidelines components of COWPS activities from each other.

Can Guidelines Help?

By itself, the guidelines program is obviously not a cure-all for inflation. But movements in real economic growth are expected to be in an anti-inflation direction by late 1979. Slower growth would reinforce the guidelines effort. It is possible, however, that economic forecasters have underestimated the momentum of expansionary forces. Output in the fourth quarter of 1978 rose at a surprisingly rapid 6.9 percent annual rate. Continued fast growth could turn 1979 into a repetition of 1966 and 1973, when strong expansionary forces destroyed efforts at direct intervention in wages and prices.

With good luck, the guidelines could reduce the inflation rate by as much as one percentage point. With moderate luck, the guidelines might at least prevent short-run inflationary impulses from food and fuel from becoming permanently embodied in the wage-price spiral. With bad luck, the guidelines could be blown apart by a food-fuel price explosion, leading to a rejection of the guidelines in a major collective bargaining situation or to simply a loss of confidence in the program by the public.

In short, whatever success occurs is likely to be modest. The public must be told not to expect miracles. The guidelines authorities should avoid the temptation to grasp at food-fuel problems that are beyond their reach. In 1973 attempts to control meat prices quickly emptied supermarket meat counters. Attempts to prevent world oil prices from being reflected at U.S. service stations led to gasoline lines and informal rationing. These mistakes should not be repeated.

Clearly, attempting to operate a wage-price program with only a limited threat of sanctions in a period of inflation requires a deft touch. A repudiation of the standards, especially by a powerful union, could so severely compromise the entire effort that it would be difficult to ask for continued compliance from other unions and firms. The surge in price inflation in early 1979 accentuated this dilemma. Inflation makes it more difficult for union leaders to sell a moderate contract to their constituents. One possibility for the guidelines authorities would be to adjust the wage standard so as to avoid such confrontations. This could involve preserving the nominal 7 percent wage standard while allowing exceptions for keeping up with inflation. Another option is simply to continue the program as it was established in late 1978, on the assumption that the inflation surge is temporary and that it will recede in the latter part of the year. Such a stance preserves credibility but makes the program more vulnerable to confrontation and possible collapse.

Real Wage Insurance

The most novel feature of the wage-price guidelines program was a proposal for real wage insurance. Under this plan, workers in employee units that negotiated within the wage standard would receive a tax rebate designed to protect the purchasing power of their wages if price inflation climbed above 7 percent. It was the view of the designers of this concept that, by limiting the risk and cost to workers of wage restraint, real wage insurance would induce more voluntary compliance than the simple announcement of a wage standard. This expectation accounts for the surprising combination of a system of tight wage restraints applicable to the entire economy but carried out by a very small staff.

Prospects for real wage insurance were dimmed by a number of factors; two are specially worth noting. First, as a piece of tax legislation, the proposal had to be submitted to a skeptical Congress that was concerned about the potential loss of tax revenue. When the concept was first proposed in October 1978, the administration's projection of the rate of inflation for 1979 was below 7 percent. Hence real wage insurance was not anticipated to involve an actual revenue loss. But by the end of 1978 it was apparent that the earlier estimate was too low and that real wage insurance would probably involve significant rebates.

Second, the implementation of real wage insurance is a complex matter. Labor compensation is received in various forms, including fringe benefits, and wage increases sometimes occur through such mechanisms as merit plans, bonuses, and promotions. Rules must be established and written into the tax code dealing with all these characteristics. Special complications also arise because taxpaying units are not identical to wage-determining units. Sometimes wage units include more than one firm. In such industries as apparel, lumber, longshoring, trucking, railroads, and steel, employers have banded together in formal associations to establish uniform wage contracts. In other industries firms may not be formally linked, but may have a de facto relationship through pattern bargaining. The Internal Revenue Service is not accustomed to dealing with such matters.

Congressional skepticism delayed action on real wage insurance. Since the plan was designed to influence wages over the twelve-month period beginning October 1, 1978, the delay in enactment tended to reduce the likelihood of enactment. More and more wage setters were forced to make their decisions in the absence of real wage insurance. Thus the incentive effects of the proposal were diminished. Besides, labor support was not enthusiastic. Some unions endorsed the concept, subject to particular adjustments that they wished to see included. The AFL-CIO initially opposed the plan, mainly because it was seen as an appendage of the detested wage guideline. Later the AFL-CIO gave the proposal qualified support, but only if the plan were liberalized to include more workers and combined with an excess profits tax. Business groups did not support the plan. Members of Congress, therefore, felt little urgency about handling the proposal; the main source of support came from the Carter administration itself.

The specific real wage insurance plan presented to the Congress in mid-January by the administration contained three major limits on the potential dollar outlay. First, it limited the maximum rate of inflation that was to be insured to 10 percent over the period October–November 1978 to October–November 1979. Thus a worker with a $10,000 income in 1979 could have received no more than $300 (10 percent minus 7 percent times $10,000), even if inflation exceeded 10 percent. Second, a worker could have received no more than $600 a job. Third, the rebate itself would have been taxable (just as wages paid under a cost-of-living escalator would be). In addition, only wage and salary earners would have been eligible. Self-employed persons and pensioners were to be excluded. The administration estimated that real wage insurance would reduce tax receipts by $2.3 billion a year and raise outlays by $0.2 billion at an assumed 7.5 percent inflation rate. But obviously the cost could have been much higher—or zero—depending on price movements and the number of workers qualified.

A number of compromises were made in drafting the plan. Since COWPS was not prepared to certify the wage increases of every employer in the country, the proposed costing rules for wage increases had to be both understandable to the employer and verifiable to the

Internal Revenue Service. As a result, the rules did not reflect certain exceptions for wage increases permissible under COWPS rules. Furthermore, there were differences between the proposed real wage insurance rules and the guidelines with regard to low-wage workers, fringe benefits, and other costing technicalities. So it was possible for workers to qualify under one program but not under the other. The tension between administrative feasibility for a tax program and the need for flexibility in a guidelines program made these discrepancies inevitable.

Anomalies would have resulted from the treatment of two special groups. Low-wage workers were exempt from the guidelines program but covered by real wage insurance. Increases paid to such workers above 7 percent (like the 9.4 percent increase in the minimum wage on January 1, 1979) might or might not have prevented low-wage workers from being eligible. This depended on such factors as whether they were a significant portion of the firm's work force and what kinds of increases were granted to higher-wage workers. Workers under union contracts signed before the guidelines were announced were to be eligible if their pay increases were 7 percent or less. Thus low-wage workers might have been rewarded for complying with a program from which they are exempt, while workers under pre-guidelines contracts might have been rewarded for complying with a program that did not exist when they negotiated. On the other hand, a decision to exclude these two groups of workers would also have produced results that some would find strange or inequitable.

Despite the anomalies, the plan presented by the administration seemed capable of being administered. But amendments to the plan to deal with the problems of particular groups, to reflect individual circumstance, or to track the COWPS standards more precisely could have easily pushed the plan beyond administrative feasibility. As a result, Congress had to accept the administration's plan more or less as presented or reject it; there was no significant room for compromise. In April the House and Senate Budget committees eliminated real wage insurance from their proposed budget resolutions, an action that made passage of the measure highly unlikely.

Future Use of Direct Intervention

The pressures on government to use direct intervention techniques to deal with inflation are strong. Thus it seems safe to predict that no matter what happens to the particular guidelines program announced in October 1978, there will be other such programs. As for the 1978 program, its fate will be partially determined by price developments in sectors in which direct intervention can have little or no effect. These include prices set in international markets and agricultural prices. The public does not make sectoral distinctions in viewing such programs as successes or failures.

One area of speculation is the possibility that the guidelines program would become a formal, mandatory controls program. Actually, the distinction between a formal controls program and a voluntary program is a matter of degree. Larger corporations appeared to view the program as equivalent to controls, although their cooperation seemed partly predicated on a desire to avoid formal, mandatory limits on prices. They reported to COWPS as requested and followed the detailed rules in the *Federal Register*. The biggest potential for overt noncompliance came from the major collective bargaining settlements due to be reached in 1979.

If the guidelines are to remain practical for an extended period, greater formalization of procedures will be necessary. There will need to be more staff for wage and price monitoring, a formal and acceptable review process for appeals, and a resolution of legal issues, such as the right of the federal government to require its contractors to comply with the standards. Since the program is especially aimed at influencing major collective bargaining settlements, better communication links will need to be established between the administration and the labor movement. The program's administrators will have to prepare themselves to deal more flexibly with sensitive cases than was the original intent when the program was announced. Furthermore, difficult decisions will have to be made about the numerical wage guideline in 1980 and beyond.

Government Regulatory Activities and Inflation*

Traditionally, the federal government's priorities have been set through the budgetary process. For example, after the launching of the first Russian satellite in the late 1950s, public attention was focused on supporting U.S. education and research. This concern

* Robert W. Crandall contributed to this section.

was a major factor in the tenfold increase in federal support to education between 1960 and 1978. But increasingly, important national priorities are being set and policies are being followed in ways that are only marginally reflected in the federal budget. This extrabudget activity is occurring through government regulation. Federal regulations are issued to achieve such goals as improved worker safety or a cleaner environment. These regulations impose costs on private industry rather than on the federal budget, thus making the costs more difficult to detect. To the extent that these added costs are not absorbed by lower profits or wages, they increase the price level.

Types of Regulation

Government regulation is not new. A body of old-style regulatory measures that has existed for many years was often intended to have a direct effect on prices or costs. Farm price supports, as an example, were established to raise agricultural prices in order to benefit farm incomes. Minimum wage laws were enacted to raise the incomes of low-wage workers. Tariffs raise the prices of imported goods, thus providing protection to U.S. import-competing firms.

Some of the newer regulatory agencies like the Occupational Safety and Health Administration (OSHA) and the Environmental Protection Agency (EPA) are not principally interested in price effects.[15] But since the actions of new agencies do affect costs, their decisions affect prices and the efficient use of resources. This fact does not imply that all regulatory actions that have a price-raising effect should be banned; it means simply that the price effect should be considered in determining whether the result is worth the cost.

Two issues arise in connection with old-style regulations designed to influence prices and costs. First, for those policies meant to raise incomes, it can be asked whether alternative income security measures—especially those involving transfer payments—might be both more effective and less inflationary. There has been a long-standing controversy, for instance, over the employment and inflation effects of the minimum wage. Statistical studies suggest that minimum wage floors reduce employment opportunities, so that while those who remain employed (at the same number of hours) receive higher in-

15. The classification of regulatory agencies as old-style or new-style is by no means precise. For instance, federal regulation of food and drugs, which began in 1907, would be a new-style program in this classification, despite its age.

comes, others suffer income losses.[16] According to this argument, the minimum wage is deficient as an income raiser for low-wage workers; at the same time, it tends to raise costs and ultimately prices. It has also been noted that programs that raise farm prices benefit larger and wealthier farmers along with the small low-income farmer who is often viewed as the target.[17]

Even when regulations have adverse or unintended side effects, there is a political obstacle to the adoption of alternatives. It is possible that the income redistributions resulting from price-raising policies would not be acceptable through the standard budgetary process. A natural tendency exists for those who currently benefit from price-raising policies to prefer the more indirect regulatory approach to income support.

Economic conditions and the nature of the regulations can change, producing results contrary to the original intentions. In the late nineteenth century, railroads had a monopoly on long-distance transportation in many parts of the country. Since that time, however, alternative means of transportation—notably trucking—have developed. The regulatory methods of the Interstate Commerce Commission have tended to limit the ability of railroads to initiate price reductions. Moreover, because railroads were regulated, regulation naturally spilled over into interstate trucking, an industry that would otherwise be competitive.[18]

Regulation of airline transportation poses a related dilemma. The Civil Aeronautics Board (CAB) claimed to benefit the consumer by providing incentives for airlines to offer regular and frequent flights, even to areas of comparatively little traffic. This goal was accomplished by keeping prices high and stable, and by permitting airlines to compete in terms of service or by simply requiring minimum levels of service. Inhabitants of a city who themselves rarely fly nonetheless benefit from knowing that a regular flight is available should they suddenly need it. But airlines cannot recapture the costs of providing these benefits except from those who do fly. Hence the CAB

16. Edward M. Gramlich, "Impact of Minimum Wages on Other Wages, Employment, and Family Incomes," *BPEA, 2:1976*, pp. 409–51.

17. Robert W. Crandall, "Federal Government Initiatives to Reduce the Price Level," *BPEA, 2:1978*, pp. 408–14.

18. In 1974 over 65,000 establishments were reported to be in local and long-distance trucking. The average number of employees per establishment was less than sixteen. Only about 37 percent of all truck drivers in 1970 were employed in the "trucking service" industry.

effectively built the service costs into airline price schedules and prevented price competition from eroding those schedules. Although
a service-price trade-off exists, the tilt of public policy toward service
was viewed as excessive by new leadership at the CAB even before
the passage of the Airline Deregulation Act of 1978. In passing that
legislation, Congress effectively decided that the benefits from extra
service did not justify the costs in terms of higher air fares. The CAB
was instructed to be less protective of existing carriers by allowing
more entry and fare competition.

Measuring Costs and Benefits

In recent years economists have pressed the newer regulatory
agencies to use more explicit cost-benefit analyses in making their
decisions. A standard response to arguments relating to costs and
price effects of regulation is that evaluations of the benefits receive a
lesser emphasis. Measures of social output often omit such benefits;
the value of cleaner air is not included in the GNP directly. But there
are also difficulties in assessing costs. Nor is it entirely true that the
benefits from regulation are omitted from all official measurement.
For example, the addition of smog devices to automobiles is im-
plicitly treated as a benefit to the consumer in the consumer price
index, that is, as a quality improvement that offsets the added cost.
The measured rate of automobile price inflation would have been
substantially higher in recent years had not government-mandated
equipment been assumed to provide a benefit to the consumer equal
to the cost of its production. Indeed, the consumer price index has
not been adjusted (upward) for a degrading of quality (from the
consumer viewpoint) inherent in the reduced performance, the requirement to use more expensive unleaded gasoline, and the down-
sizing of larger models. It could be argued that the consumer price
index both overstates the quality and understates the costs of new
cars.

Even the most ardent proponents of regulation are hard put to
come up with specific benefit estimates. Perhaps an estimate can be
made of death and illness rates associated with certain levels of air
pollution and perhaps the costs associated with deaths and illness can
be measured. (Even these suppositions are heavily dependent on
data that often do not exist in reliable form.) But how does one
measure the value of a clean atmosphere to persons who would
neither die nor become ill if pollution controls were relaxed?

From a pure inflation standpoint, the cost side of regulation is especially hard to measure. What matters for overall price effects is the degree to which costs are ultimately reflected in prices. Since some costs could be absorbed by labor or capital, the impact on the consumer price index could be less than the total cost of compliance would initially suggest. If working conditions in an industry are made less hazardous, for example, wages may reflect the greater attractiveness of the job by increasing more slowly than they otherwise would.

Despite these qualifications, estimates of the costs of some of the newer regulatory programs are impressive. For instance, the prospective annual costs of environmental controls for industry required to be in place by 1977 were $25 billion. The cost of OSHA's actual or proposed regulations for nine major health standards have been estimated at more than $4 billion a year. These costs are likely to increase substantially as OSHA moves aggressively to limit possible carcinogenic exposure and as EPA moves toward various statutory deadlines required under the Clean Air Act, the Federal Water Pollution Control Act, and the Toxic Substances Control Act. In 1977 dollars, EPA's regulations are likely to be costing more than $44 billion a year by 1983, excluding emission controls on automobiles.[19] Denison has estimated that in 1974 and 1975 pollution abatement and health and safety expenditures had reduced the measured rate of growth of total factor productivity by 0.3 percentage point a year, a significant reduction in a series that grew at a 2.6 percent rate from 1948 to 1969.[20] Even though these estimates are only approximate, it is evident that substantial resources are being directed by the federal government outside the budgetary mechanism, thereby raising questions of efficient resource utilization as well as of inflationary impact.

The lack of executive review and the difficulties in measuring the results of new-style regulations present a serious problem for government policy. A suggestion has been made that a budget for regulation be created and that each agency be assigned a dollar quota of costs it can impose on the economy. The agency would live within its quota just as conventional agencies live within their budgets.[21] Of course, this proposal assumes that reasonable cost estimates can be

19. Crandall, "Federal Government Initiatives," pp. 420–22.
20. Edward F. Denison, "Effects of Selected Changes in the Institutional and Human Environment Upon Output Per Unit of Input," *Survey of Current Business,* vol. 58 (January 1978), pp. 41–42.
21. Crandall, "Federal Government Initiatives," pp. 429–30.

made. Undoubtedly, were a regulatory budget system established, a bargaining process would develop between the regulatory agencies and whatever group—perhaps the Congress—allocated the dollar volume of costs included in the budget. Ultimately the budget would have to reflect public feelings about regulatory activity, feelings that may be more favorable to it than economists have tended to acknowledge.[22]

Current Anti-Inflation Policies Concerning Regulatory Costs

So far, no attempt has been made to implement a full-fledged regulatory budget. The establishment of such a system would require congressional consent and executive direction. But a more modest program begun in the Ford administration has been expanded by President Carter, most recently as a component of the anti-inflation policies announced last October. The Carter administration formed a regulatory analysis review group to consider economic impact analyses for major new regulations and to make recommendations to the President. An agency must submit these analyses for each regulation with an aggregate impact of $100 million per year. This process has affected some proposed regulations, but the ultimate outcome has yet to be determined.

Deregulation

Deregulation of the airline industry began with a series of administrative reforms at the Civil Aeronautics Board. The new stance taken by the CAB was officially endorsed by Congress in 1978 with passage of the Airline Deregulation Act. From April 1978 to October 1978, airline fares fell at an annual rate of 2.6 percent, whereas from April 1977 to April 1978 they had increased 6.3 percent.[23]

It appears that moves to deregulate ground transportation, chiefly trucking and railroads, may be seriously considered in this Congress. These two sectors pose a more complex problem for the deregulation strategy than airlines do. Trucking and railroads compete for the same customers in many cases, so that a two-industry deregulation

22. A recent survey suggests that a substantial part of the public may be disposed toward the imposition of high costs entailed in pollution control and other environmental programs. See Robert Cameron Mitchell, "The Public Speaks Again: A New Environmental Survey," *Resources* (Resources for the Future, September–November 1978), pp. 1–6.

23. Data refer to the airline fares component of the consumer price index.

approach will be necessary. The trucking industry causes special problems because of the multitude of truck operators and the divergent interest groups within the industry. Regulation of trucking has embedded economic rents in the balance sheets of firms in the industry and in the wage rates they pay. A return to unregulated competition would eliminate these rents. Clouding the prospects for deregulation is opposition from the Teamsters.

Related to deregulation is the ongoing effort to lower tariff and nontariff barriers in world trade. As part of the Tokyo Round of the Multilateral Trade Negotiations, U.S. tariffs on imports are expected to be cut by 30 percent. Such cuts would be phased in over a period of time. The impact of such cuts on aggregate price measures like the consumer price index would be quite small. In any case, the agreement would have to be approved by Congress. And there is always a possibility that pressures for trade protection could build—especially during a period of rising unemployment—thereby obstructing congressional passage. Moreover, pressures for special import-limiting actions could come from certain industries. Under existing authority of the President, import-restricting measures have been undertaken in recent years for shoes, television receivers, and steel. Therefore, the extent of deregulation to be expected in the international trade area is uncertain.

Projected expenditures in fiscal 1980 for farm price support programs are a little more than half of the expected 1979 expenditure levels. This decrease does not signal substantial deregulation in agricultural price support policy. Rather, it reflects an expectation of high farm prices, which reduce the amount of government activity needed to support a particular level of farm income. Farm income is highly volatile, but on a per-farm basis, real income in calendar 1978 rose significantly over the previous year. Compared with the 1973 period, when farm income soared in response to a dramatic rise in world food prices, current farm incomes may seem disappointing to farmers.[24] As in the case of tariffs, government policies affecting farm prices are politically sensitive. A major effort to increase farm income levels could easily overwhelm the effects of deregulation elsewhere.

24. Though it did not reach the peaks of 1973, real farm income was 15 percent higher in the third quarter of 1978 on a seasonally adjusted annual basis than in 1977.

Despite these pitfalls, in several important sectors of the economy a strategy of deregulation can have beneficial effects in an anti-inflation program. And apart from the anti-inflation effects, deregulation can promote increased economic efficiency in the use of resources. However, with increased economic efficiency could come reduced incomes to some participants in target industries. Thus, to ease the transition, it may be necessary to phase in deregulation over an extended period, a strategy that would reduce the anti-inflation impact in any given year. Alternatively, some form of compensation to injured parties may have to be provided.

On April 5, 1979, the President announced a plan for the gradual deregulation of domestic oil prices. Controls on energy prices create a dilemma for the administration. Deregulation will raise prices initially. But controls have produced inefficiencies in usage and production that could lead to cost savings if alleviated. Decreased oil imports would result from higher domestic production and lower consumption, possibly raising the value of the dollar in international markets. This would help moderate the price pressures.

Inflation and Unemployment in the Longer Term

In October 1978 the President approved the Full Employment and Balanced Growth Act, better known as the Humphrey-Hawkins Act. As originally introduced, the act would have mandated achievement of specified employment targets. In its final version the bill simply set forth various objectives and required reports from the President and the Federal Reserve. Indeed, the bill became a hodgepodge of mixed objectives relating to unemployment rates, inflation, the ratio of federal spending to GNP, and "parity" for farm prices.

The targets for unemployment were specified as 4 percent for the overall rate and 3 percent for the rate for workers aged twenty and over. These rates are supposed to be achieved by the end of 1983, and the President is required to set a series of interim goals to accomplish this reduction in unemployment. The 1979 Annual Report of the Council of Economic Advisers (CEA) has dutifully set forth such goals as required.[25] But the targets raise some questions.

First, there is a technical question of the consistency of the unemployment targets. The overall target of 4 percent and the adult

25. *Economic Report of the President, January 1979*, p. 109.

Table 3-5. Unemployment Rates for Selected Groups and Deviation of Real GNP from Trend, 1960–78

Percent

	Unemployment rate					Deviation of
	Workers aged 16 and over	Workers aged 16–19	Workers aged 20 and over			real GNP from trend[a]
Year			Total	Male	Female	
1960	5.5	14.7	4.8	4.7	5.1	−3.8
1961	6.7	16.8	5.9	5.7	6.3	−4.7
1962	5.5	14.7	4.9	4.6	5.4	−2.6
1963	5.7	17.2	4.8	4.5	5.4	−2.2
1964	5.2	16.2	4.3	3.9	5.2	−0.6
1965	4.5	14.8	3.6	3.2	4.5	1.7
1966	3.8	12.8	2.9	2.5	3.8	4.1
1967	3.8	12.8	3.0	2.3	4.2	3.3
1968	3.6	12.7	2.7	2.2	3.8	4.1
1969	3.5	12.2	2.7	2.1	3.7	3.2
1970	4.9	15.2	4.0	3.5	4.8	−0.7
1971	5.9	16.9	4.9	4.4	5.7	−1.2
1972	5.6	16.2	4.5	4.0	5.4	0.9
1973	4.9	14.5	3.8	3.2	4.8	2.8
1974	5.6	16.0	4.5	3.8	5.5	−2.1
1975	8.5	19.9	7.3	6.7	8.0	−6.6
1976	7.7	19.0	6.5	5.9	7.4	−4.6
1977	7.0	17.7	5.9	5.2	7.0	−3.4
1978	6.0	16.3	4.9	4.2	6.0	−3.0[b]

Source: *Economic Report of the President, January 1979*, pp. 184, 216–17.
a. Trend estimated logarithmically over 1947–78.
b. Based on preliminary data.

target of 3 percent are roughly consistent. They imply a rate of unemployment for those sixteen through nineteen years of age of about 13 percent, which rate, historical evidence suggests, would be achieved if the adult rate were to fall to 3 percent.[26] For example, as shown in table 3-5, in recent years the adult rate has differed from the overall rate by about 1 percentage point.

26. Regression analysis suggests that a 1 percent increase in the ratio of real GNP to trend will lower the unemployment rate for adults by about 0.3 percentage point and the teenage unemployment rate by about 0.6 percentage point. Thus the adult unemployment rate would have fallen to about 3 percent in 1978 had the ratio of real GNP to trend been about 6 percent higher (see table 3-5). If the ratio had been 6 percent above its actual value, the teenage rate would have fallen to a little over 12 percent. The combination of the two rates would have produced an overall rate close to the 4 percent target. These estimates were derived from annual regressions—which also included time trends and autoregressive corrections—run over the period 1948–77.

A second, and more fundamental, question is the achievability of a 4 percent overall rate. Table 3-5 shows that the overall unemployment rate dipped below 4 percent during the late 1960s, but has never done so since. A number of factors contributed to the drop in unemployment at that time, including the military draft and the development of a variety of government-supported employment and training programs.[27] Also of importance was the dramatic expansion of the economy into a clear excess-demand boom. As a measure of demand pressure, table 3-5 includes the deviation of real GNP from its trend value as estimated over the period 1947–78. During the late 1960s, the period of the Vietnam War buildup, real output as measured by GNP was 3 to 4 percent above its trend value, indicating an unsustainably high utilization rate of economic resources. The period of the late 1960s was also marked by a substantial acceleration in the rate of inflation. Thus a stimulation of the economy to the labor force utilization rates achieved in the late 1960s would probably lead to acceleration of the current inflation rate.[28] Yet the Humphrey-Hawkins target for the inflation rate is 3 percent by 1983 and zero by 1988.

In recent years it has been argued that the level of demand pressure associated with a given unemployment rate has risen. This change is usually related to demographic changes in the labor force, notably the relative growth in teenage and female participation. As table 3-6 shows, by 1977 the proportion of teenagers (sixteen through nineteen) in the civilian labor force had risen from 8.4 percent to 9.5 percent and the proportion of adult women had risen from 32.9 percent to 36.6 percent. If 1967 is used as a base, these changes alone

27. From 1964 to 1969 the number of people in the armed forces increased by 767,000—substantially drawing from the labor market. Some of these people would otherwise have been employed or not have been in the labor force. Nevertheless, it is likely that the draft did significantly lower the unemployment rate. The Manpower Development and Training Act of 1962 initiated a period of increased federal employment and training efforts. By fiscal year 1969 the Department of Labor reported a total of 889,500 "enrollment opportunities" in training and employment. About 44 percent of these were special summer jobs for youths. One author estimates that the draft and direct government job programs accounted for about three-fourths of the decline in unemployment during 1964–69. See Charles C. Killingsworth, "The Fall and Rise of the Idea of Structural Unemployment," *Proceedings of the Industrial Relations Research Association, 1978* (Madison, Wis., 1979), p. 9.

28. It is impossible to be certain of this statement. During the Korean War utilization rates were also high and yet inflation rates were moderate, partly because of the imposition of wage-price controls.

Table 3-6. Demographic Changes in the Labor Force and Unemployment Rate
in Selected Age and Sex Groups, 1967, 1977, 1985, and 1990

Percent

	Proportion of civilian labor force				Unemployment rate	
Group	1967	1977	1985	1990	1967	1977
Young people aged 16–19	8.4	9.5	7.6	7.0	12.8	17.7
Males aged 20 and over	58.6	53.9	51.9	51.0	2.3	5.2
Females aged 20 and over	32.9	36.6	40.5	42.0	4.2	7.0
Total	100.0	100.0	100.0	100.0	3.8	7.0

Source: Data from Paul O. Flaim and Howard N. Fullerton, Jr., "Labor Force Projections to 1990: Three Possible Paths," *Monthly Labor Review*, vol. 101 (December 1978), p. 29; *Employment and Training Report of the President, 1977* (GPO, 1977), pp. 139, 167; *Monthly Labor Review*, vol. 102 (February 1979), p. 76. Figures are rounded.

would add about 0.3 percentage point to the unemployment rate. For many reasons teenagers and women typically have higher unemployment rates than adult males.[29] Hence, as the proportion of women and teenagers in the labor force rises, the average unemployment rate tends to rise.

Projections of the labor force to 1985 and 1990 suggest that this demographic effect will taper off. The proportion of teenagers in the labor force will drop as a result of the lowering of the birthrate that began in the 1960s. By 1990 this change will just about offset the projected increased participation of adult women in the labor force, a long-term trend.[30] But other factors, such as unemployment compensation and similar social benefits that reduce the economic burden of unemployment, are sometimes cited as contributing to the unemployment rate.[31] Even if these factors are dismissed, a 4 per-

29. Teenagers and women have usually had a looser attachment to the labor force, in part because of school and home responsibilities, respectively. Other factors may include the influences of minimum wage and child labor laws, discrimination, and the availability of other sources of family incomes. As women join the labor force in greater numbers, it is possible that their labor force behavior (as well as employer attitudes) will shift. If so, the use of a base period unemployment rate would overstate the demographic effects. The estimates in the text were made using ten sex-age classifications. For an early paper on this subject, see George L. Perry, "Changing Labor Markets and Inflation," *BPEA, 3:1970*, pp. 411–41.

30. CEA estimates for 1983, however, suggest that most of the demographic effect will still be present in that year. See *Economic Report of the President, January 1979*, p. 119.

31. Other less tangible influences—such as changes in the work ethic—are also sometimes cited.

cent unemployment rate under 1983 conditions would probably be inflationary.

In its 1979 annual report, the CEA expresses as much skepticism about achieving the Humphrey-Hawkins goals as is acceptable in an official report. It notes that the twin goals of 4 percent unemployment and 3 percent inflation by 1983 "are very ambitious" and "would demand not only a performance by the American economy that is unprecedented in peacetime history, but also government programs that can deal effectively with some of our most intransigent problems."[32] Further, the CEA states that "we cannot reach the goals for unemployment and inflation simultaneously by relying solely on monetary and fiscal policies."[33] To supplement these policies, the CEA suggests continued direct intervention in wage and price setting and special targeted programs to deal with high unemployment rates (in particular demographic groups) that seem resistant to substantial lowering through demand policies.

The suggestion of reliance on direct intervention raises two important issues. If the guidelines program were to be continued until 1983, it would necessarily have to operate in a period of economic expansion. According to CEA projections, real GNP would have to expand at an annual rate of about 4.5 percent during 1981–83 to achieve the 4 percent unemployment target. Thus the guidelines program would face the difficulty of rising demand pressures. The initial outline of the guidelines program suggested a temporary effort; extending the program to 1983 would require a more permanent structure and considerable deftness by the administration.

The CEA report suggests that a number of current programs dealing with structural problems could be helpful in lowering the unemployment rate. In particular, the report singles out efforts to aim public-service jobs more effectively at unemployed, and especially long-term unemployed, persons and a special tax credit to employers hiring disadvantaged persons aged eighteen through twenty-four. However, the CEA does not assert that these programs, and others that are currently being planned, will be sufficient to reconcile the Humphrey-Hawkins objectives. The implication is that as-yet-unknown programs might be needed. This is a diplomatic way of warning the public that the CEA does not believe the targets will be met.

32. *Economic Report of the President, January 1979*, p. 110.
33. Ibid., p. 117.

Concluding Observations

Many uncertainties about anti-inflation policies remained in early 1979. Fiscal policy as it appeared in the President's budget was definitely austere. Congress has the last word on the budget, however. Some components of the budget—such as certain cuts in social security benefits—were rejected by Congress almost immediately. Real wage insurance is unlikely to be adopted. Thus the guidelines themselves will be the sole method of direct intervention in wage and price decisions. And the guidelines authorities will be confronted with the task of seeking labor cooperation in the face of considerable price inflation. Indeed, the price fallout resulting from the disruption of Iranian oil exports could easily destroy any possibility of an accommodation with organized labor. Finally, the interpretation of monetary policy is complicated by new institutional structures in financial markets.

The presence of uncertainty in economic decisionmaking is not unusual. But the diversity of viewpoints and forecasts in early 1979 was wider than at any time since 1973, also a year of price pressures. If there is one lesson that can be learned from 1973, it is that inflation forecasts can be badly mistaken, especially if there are strong external sources of price pressures. Under these circumstances, contingency planning can be especially valuable. If prices surge above the levels forecast, or if the economy slows down faster than expected, the President and Congress will be pressured to "do something." Therefore, it is important to consider options in advance of possible events, lest events dictate shortsighted and reactive responses. One possibility, of course, is that there are no feasible, untried options in reserve. But if there are new options, they should be viewed in probabilistic terms; any move has some chance of failure or undesired consequences, even if a successful outcome is expected. Following a given policy always involves some risk, and sometimes the risks outweigh the anticipated benefits.

Both monetary policy and the guidelines program illustrate the dilemma. The Federal Reserve Board could respond to the price surges in early 1979 by a further boost in interest rates. If demand continued to expand rapidly, failure to respond could encourage classical demand-pull inflationary pressures. If, however, monetary policy was already sufficiently tight—but was simply acting with a lag—a further boost in interest rates could precipitate an unwarranted degree of economic slack. Similarly, the guidelines authorities could respond to the price surge by holding tightly to the standards already announced. Such a stance increases the risk of a confrontation with a major union. On the other hand, a loosening of the wage standard increases the risk that what might turn out to be a temporary price surge becomes incorporated in the wage-price spiral.

Since there are risks to any policy, it would be well if these were communicated to the public. Traditionally, statements of economic policy are made with assurance and optimism. Shifts in policy then appear to be repudiations of past assertions, when they actually represent responses to unexpected economic events or outcomes. Given current uncertainties, the temptation to proclaim future victories over inflation must be avoided. It will be a long, hard struggle.

CHAPTER FOUR

The Domestic Budget

HENRY AARON

THE 1980 BUDGET symbolizes the spirit of austerity and the sense of limitations that have come to dominate the political mood of the 1970s. The 1980 budget was formulated under the shadow of seemingly intractable inflation, a drastic slowing in the growth of labor productivity, and overwhelming popular support, as measured by public opinion polls, for a constitutional amendment to require a balanced federal budget. The contrast between these conditions and those of the early and mid-1960s—with steady economic growth, little inflation, and resources sufficient to fight wars against both poverty at home and the Vietnamese abroad—could hardly be sharper.

Against this background President Carter promised to submit a budget with a deficit below $30 billion. To achieve this goal, outlays in 1980 will be held $4.6 billion below those necessary to maintain programs at current services levels and an additional $4 billion to $8 billion below levels required to prevent all existing programs from being reduced by inflation, including those in which adjustments for inflation are discretionary (see chapter 2).

The challenge of preparing a tight budget requires decisions that can be, and invariably are, avoided when resources are plentiful. Not only must the administration resist requests for increases by the nu-

In the preparation of this chapter, Cynthia M. Browning and Amy E. Kessler provided research assistance, and the following people provided useful information: David W. Breneman, Gerald Britten, Robert C. Embry, David F. Garrison, Darwin G. Johnson, Van E. Jolissiant, Marshall Kaplan, Arnold H. Packer, Fred Sanderson, Donna E. Shalala, Mary E. Tuszka, and John D. Young.

99

merous groups clamoring for larger expenditures, it must also choose a strategy for austerity. At least three approaches could have been taken. The administration might have used the necessity for austerity as justification for the elimination of low-priority programs, some of which have been slated for cutback or elimination by other administrations. The same forces that enacted such programs have usually had sufficient strength to resist such proposed cuts. With a few exceptions, the budget does not reflect such a strategy.

As an alternative strategy, the administration might have attempted to impose across-the-board reductions on all programs, with the rationale that all groups within the population should share the sacrifices required by austerity. President Ford moved some way toward adopting this strategy in the 1976 budget when he asked that social security benefits not be increased by the full inflation adjustment then mandated by law. Congress paid scant attention to his request. President Carter asks that increases in federal pay be held to 5.5 percent, well below the increase expected to be justified by inflation under the current pay formula. With this possible exception, President Carter went out of his way to dissociate himself from such a strategy, claiming that the 1980 budget would protect programs that serve needy groups.

The third strategy—the one most apparent in the 1980 budget—involves selective reductions, mostly by relatively small amounts in a large number of programs. Many of the cuts are to be achieved by the simple expedient of spending the same amount of money and allowing inflation to reduce the real level of the program. These cuts lack any overall theme and are bound together only by the belief of the administration that marginal adjustments in priorities are the best way to reduce outlays. The risk of this strategy is that the absence of any overall theme increases the vulnerability of each cut to the special pleadings of the program's supporters.

This chapter is divided into four parts. The first presents a broad overview of changes in the level and composition of domestic expenditures. The second sets forth in some detail issues relating to the administration's decisions in three programmatic areas—health, urban policy, and income assistance. The third surveys three issues of policy that span the budget—financial assistance to states and localities, the varied uses of regulatory policy as alternatives to direct outlays in achieving public objectives, and federal wage policy. The final section reviews the recent history of several dubious federal programs, four of which were highlighted nine years ago in the first issue of *Setting National Priorities.*

Overview

The 1980 budget calls for nondefense outlays of $405.7 billion.[1] Adjusted for inflation, these outlays are unchanged from 1978 and 1979.[2] This three-year pattern raises the question: how can the 1980 budget be austere if the 1979 budget wasn't?

Table 4-1 points the way to the answer. Payments for individuals grew rapidly in real terms between 1970 and 1975 in part because of the rapid increase in social security benefits, spurred by a 20 percent increase in benefits enacted in 1972, and in part because unemployment insurance benefits nearly tripled during the mid-1970s recession. Growth in payments for individuals continued to 1978, but between 1978 and 1979 it virtually stopped. In 1980 real growth will resume, in part because unemployment insurance, which dropped $1.5 billion in constant 1972 dollars between 1978 and 1979, will rise $0.8 billion between 1979 and 1980 (even with the administration's rather optimistic forecast), and in part because social security and federal employee retirement costs are rising rapidly.

As a result of this increase in income security payments between 1979 and 1980, other parts of the budget had to be cut back to hold overall nondefense outlays constant. Measured as a percent of gross

1. Note on budget authority and outlays: most of the tables in this chapter refer to "outlays," the measure of what the government is projected to spend in 1980. The President has made the reduction of the deficit—revenues less outlays—a major budgetary objective. For many programs, outlays provide the best measure of current activity. Payments for individuals, for example, are best measured by outlays, the payments actually made. But outlays often provide a misleading measure of activity of programs in which orders are placed long before products are delivered and paid for or in which projects are undertaken that take years to complete. Grants under the now-defunct urban renewal program sometimes led to outlays a decade or more after the initial agreements. For such programs "budget authority," the dollar amount that program administrators may sign contracts to spend or to lend, provides a better measure of current activity. Consequently, the text refers in some cases to outlays and in others to budget authority. Furthermore, many programs operate through direct loans, interest subsidies, loan guarantees, or administrative requirements that private businesses or individuals or the states undertake certain outlays. In these cases neither outlays nor budget authority may accurately depict the scope of the federal role.

2. In fiscal 1980 dollars, nondefense outlays for 1980 are projected to be $405.7 billion. Estimated nondefense outlays for 1979 and actual outlays for 1978, respectively, are $405.7 billion and $405.9 billion.

Table 4-1. Nondefense Budget Outlays, Selected Fiscal Years, 1970–80

	Outlays in billions of constant 1980 dollars[a]						Outlays as percent of GNP					
Item	1970	1975	1978	1979	1980		1970	1975	1978	1979	1980
Payments for individuals[b]	117.2	204.0	226.7	228.0	237.7		6.2	9.8	9.6	9.3	9.5
All other grants	32.5	49.1	61.7	59.4	54.9		1.6	2.3	2.6	2.4	2.2
Net interest	40.2	39.1	47.7	46.9	46.1		1.5	1.6	1.7	1.9	1.8
All other	59.1	57.7	70.4	71.6	67.0		3.0	2.8	3.0	2.9	2.7
Total	245.2	350.3	405.9	405.7	405.7		12.3	16.5	16.9	16.5	16.2

Source: Office of Management and Budget, "Federal Government Finances," January 1979; and unpublished OMB data.
a. Constant 1980 dollar amounts all equal to constant 1972 dollar amounts reported by OMB multiplied by the ratio of outlays in 1980 dollars to outlays in constant 1972 dollars.
b. Excludes military retired pay. See table 4-3 for total payments for individuals.

Table 4-2. Nondefense Outlays by Broad Functional Categories, Fiscal Years 1978–80[a]
Billions of dollars

Item	Budgeted outlays in current dollars			Budgeted outlays in constant 1980 dollars[b]			Outlays in 1980 for current services[c] (current dollars)
	1978	1979	1980	1978	1979	1980	
Health	49	55	59	59	60	59	61
Income security	156	170	191	181	182	191	191
Energy, natural resources, the environment, and agriculture	25	26	24	28	28	24	25
Commerce and housing credit, transportation, community and regional development	30	30	28	34	32	28	28
Education, training, employment, and social services	30	33	32	34	36	32	33
Other nondefense[d]	57	65	71	65	70	71	72
Total	**346**	**379**	**406**	**405**	**408**	**406**	**411**

Source: *The Budget of the United States Government, Fiscal Year 1980*, pp. 523, 555.
a. Where applicable, veterans' benefits and services are allocated to the appropriate category.
b. Health figures were adjusted by author's estimates of the medical care Consumer Price Index, income security by the CPI projected in the budget, and all other categories by the projections of the GNP deflator contained in the budget.
c. As defined by the Office of Management and Budget; see text note 3.
d. Figure includes undistributed offsetting receipts.

national product, grants to state and local governments for programs other than payments for individuals will decline from 2.6 percent in 1978 to 2.2 percent in 1980, the lowest since 1974. Interest payments in the same period will remain roughly the same percent of gross national product, while all federal programs other than interest, grants, or payments for individuals will decline from 3.0 to 2.7 percent.

Table 4-2 indicates the functions that are curtailed. It separates nondefense outlays into six categories: (1) health; (2) income security; (3) energy, natural resources, the environment, and agriculture; (4) commerce and housing credit, transportation, and community and regional development; (5) education, training, employment, and social services; and (6) all other. The table permits a comparison of trends over time among the functional areas and a comparison between 1980 requested outlays and outlays necessary to maintain current services.[3] It reveals that expenditures on income security have grown sharply in the past two years in real terms, while real expenditures for the other categories, except health, have declined.

Health

The growth of health expenditures largely reflects the fact that the cost of hospital services has been rising 14 percent per year. The 1980 budget calls for a stringent program of hospital cost containment and reductions in expenditures under medicare and medicaid to curb this element of growth in medical costs. Together they would reduce health outlays $2.7 billion. It also calls for a number of small increases.

Income Security

The growth of income security expenditures is traceable to two factors. First, social security benefits—cash payments to the aged, disabled, their dependents, and survivors of deceased workers—rose $10.1 billion between 1978 and 1979 and will grow another $13.5 billion between 1979 and 1980, reaching $115.8 billion. This growth is caused by increases in the number of aged and disabled, by automatic cost-of-living increases in benefits, and by the increased benefits payable to newly eligible beneficiaries by virtue of their wage histories. Second, Congress in 1978 significantly increased veterans' pensions (welfare benefits for veterans), and the administration is seeking to initiate automatic cost-of-living increases in 1980 in veterans' compensation (assistance to veterans with service-connected injuries). Unemployment compensation fell in 1979, with the drop in unemployment, but will rise in 1980 as unemployment drifts upward. Cash welfare outlays (aid to families with dependent children and supplemental security income) will increase slightly in 1980 but will decline in constant dollars. Welfare outlays in 1980 will be 0.5 percent of gross national product, a lower fraction than in any year since 1973.

3. The Office of Management and Budget uses the term "current services" to denote outlays that would occur if programs were continued at their current levels without policy changes. It does not include inflation adjustments unless mandated by law (see chapter 2, note 5). "Current policy," a term used by the Congressional Budget Office, refers to outlays necessary to provide the same level of services as those currently provided. It assumes increases in outlays sufficient to offset inflation whether or not such offsets are required by law.

In an effort to reduce the sharp and automatic increase in income security payments, the budget calls for reductions of $1.2 billion in old age, survivors, and disability insurance and in public assistance.

Energy, Natural Resources, the Environment, and Agriculture

Outlays in these programs will decline by $2.5 billion ($4.3 billion, or 15 percent, in constant dollars) because of a number of factors: a drop of $406 million in spending for the strategic petroleum reserve, attributable in large part to the impossibility of meeting the original schedule for preparing the sites; an increase in receipts of $176 million from sales from the Naval Petroleum Reserve; a reduction in outlays of $298 million on conservation and land management, about 15 percent of current outlays; and reduction of $2.4 billion in price support payments to maintain farmers' incomes.

Commerce and Housing Credit, Transportation, Community and Regional Development

Congress appropriated $6 billion for local public works in 1976 and 1977 in response to the severe recession of the mid-1970s. As projects are completed, expenditures from these appropriations will decline from $2.1 billion in 1979 to $319 million in 1980.

In a major new policy, the administration proposes to curtail freight and passenger railroad service through most of the nation. If approved by Congress, this shift will reduce federal expenditures on railroads by about $600 million in 1980.

The budget calls for a major reduction in the volume of disaster loans and the consolidation of authority to issue such loans in rural areas in a single agency, the Farmers Home Administration.[4] The goal is to limit these subsidized loans when other sources of credit are available. Approval of this recommendation is in doubt.

The budget called for the creation of a national development bank, authorized to lend up to $3.5 billion in 1980. Congress failed to act on a similar proposal contained in the urban policy President Carter put forth last year. Barely six weeks after the budget appeared, the administration announced that it would not ask for the creation of a national development bank but would instead ask Congress to

4. At present the Small Business Administration is authorized to make such loans. Expenditures on such loans by the SBA are projected to decline from $793 million in 1979 to $20 million in 1980.

increase the budget authority of the Economic Development Administration and a number of existing programs.

Education, Training, Employment, and Social Services

Outlays on these functions, which grew significantly in 1978 and 1979, will decline by $446 million in 1980 (nearly 8 percent in real terms). The decline occurs in the Comprehensive Employment and Training Act, a program that was expanded greatly during the mid-seventies recession.

President Carter joins every president since Eisenhower in calling for the curtailment of impact aid, the program of unrestricted grants paid on behalf of children whose parents either work or live on federal property. The 1980 budget would provide such aid only on behalf of children whose parents both live and work on federal property.

The 1980 budget is notable for not seeking any real increase in aid to school districts for the education of handicapped children. In 1975 Congress authorized appropriation of sharply increasing annual sums to support an increasing share of the costs of educating the handicapped, but in 1980 the administration's request for budget authority is virtually unchanged after adjustment for inflation and is just over half of the congressional authorization.

This overview makes clear that the reductions proposed in the 1980 budget are numerous, are not linked by any common theme, and are offset only partially by proposed increases. The next section describes in some detail the changes proposed by the budget in three major areas—health, urban policy, and income security.

Three Major Functions

During the 1960s and early 1970s successive administrations introduced, greatly expanded, and then reformed a broad range of social legislation. An examination of the many and significant reductions proposed for these programs and for some older programs going back to the New Deal gives some flavor of the 1980 budget.

Health*

The 1980 budget sounds three themes in health policy. The dominant theme is the need to contain the costs of medical care. Far lesser

* Louise Russell assisted in the preparation of this section.

Table 4-3. Annual Growth in Hospital Costs and Services, Calendar Years 1970–78
Percent

Year	Total expenditures	Patient days	Expenditure per patient day	Hospital market basket	Net service intensity[a]
1970	17.7	2.6	14.7	7.6	6.7
1971	14.5	1.2	13.2	7.4	5.4
1972	14.1	0.6	13.4	5.9	7.1
1973	11.4	3.2	8.0	6.9	1.0
1974	15.0	3.7	10.8	10.0	0.7
1975	19.4	1.4	17.8	10.8	6.3
1976	16.1	1.7	14.2	8.0	5.7
1977	14.2	0.2	13.9	7.7	5.7
1978	12.8	0.9	11.8	8.3	3.0

Sources: *American Hospital Association, Hospital Statistics*, annual; and Department of Health, Education, and Welfare, Office of Assistant Secretary for Planning and Evaluation.
a. Net service intensity is calculated by extracting the change in price of the hospital market basket from expenditure per patient day.

themes are the need to expand and improve medical services for the poor and the desirability of paying more attention to preventing disease and disability.

COST CONTAINMENT. A feeling verging on panic is spreading that the health budget, public and private, is out of control. Total health outlays for the nation increased 70 percent and federal outlays rose 97 percent between 1973 and 1977. Health absorbed 8.9 percent of gross national product in 1977 and will claim 13 cents out of every nondefense budget dollar in 1980.[5] Americans work an average of more than one month a year to pay for their health care.

Table 4-3 shows the rate of growth in hospital costs and services from 1970 through 1978. Part of this growth can be attributed to the increase in the number of days patients spent in hospitals. Most is explained by the general increase in prices. But about one-third of the growth in costs is caused by such factors as improvements in hospital equipment, the use of more sophisticated and costly procedures, and growth in the relative pay of hospital employees. Without some intervention, health expenditures will continue to rise faster than other federal outlays and faster than gross national product.

Two years ago, Louise Russell examined the reasons for the in-

5. While U.S. health expenditures are large, they are not dramatically out of line with those of other major industrial countries. Germany spends 9.3 percent of its gross national product on health, Sweden spends 9.2 percent, and the Netherlands, 8.7 percent; each spends proportionately as much as or more than the United States. France (8.1 percent), Australia (8.0 percent), and Canada (7.1 percent) spend somewhat less.

crease in total health costs in *Setting National Priorities: The 1978 Budget*.[6] As incomes rise, people demand more health care. Sophisticated health technologies are increasingly expensive. The population is aging. But the structural feature that makes the increase in cost possible is the dominant system of financing health care—third party reimbursement by private insurers and by state and federal governments. This system permits health-care decisionmakers—patients, doctors, and hospital administrators—to insulate most of their health-care decisions, fully or partially, from their financial consequences. This system has succeeded in reducing the number of Americans who lack essential health care, but it has increased the number who receive services that produce small benefits or none at all at very high cost. Newspapers, professional journals, and government reports almost daily transmit new information suggesting that many medical procedures produce negligible benefit and that some inflict harm, that there is a surplus of hospital beds and costly medical equipment, that physicians' incomes are rising far faster than those of other professionals, and even that the much talked-about doctor shortage now threatens to become a doctor glut.

As one of its first actions, the new Carter administration announced in February 1977 its proposal to limit the rate of increase in hospital costs. Under this proposal, total hospital revenues were to be limited to an annual increase of 9 percent. But other provisions allowed the pass-through of the cost of increases in wages of nonsupervisory employees, automatic adjustments for rapid growth in case loads, and special adjustments on a case-by-case basis; they raised the effective limit to about 12 percent, 6 percentage points above the base rate of inflation and 3 percentage points below the projected rate of growth of hospital expenditures. In addition, the administration proposed to limit new investment in hospital construction to $2.5 billion per year; actual investment was $3.5 billion in 1976.

This proposal would have reduced federal outlays $1.6 billion in 1979 and $3.5 billion in 1981 below levels projected for those years and would have reduced the increase in total medical expenditures by $4.9 billion in 1979 and $10.9 billion in 1981. About 17 percent of the savings would have accrued to state and local governments, and about half to insurers, individuals, and other private payers.

6. Louise Russell, "Medical Care Costs," in Joseph A. Pechman, ed., *Setting National Priorities: The 1978 Budget* (Brookings Institution, 1977).

Despite initially favorable reactions to the proposal and the fact that the President consistently listed hospital cost containment as one of his major initiatives, it never reached the floor of either house of Congress.

In its struggle against the administration's cost containment proposal, the American Hospital Association supported the idea of voluntary cost limitations. Congressman Daniel Rostenkowski, then chairman of the health subcommittee of the House Committee on Ways and Means, embraced this approach. So did Senator Gaylord Nelson, who proposed as a compromise that mandatory benefits be imposed only if the voluntary approach was not successful.

The cost containment proposal in the 1980 budget builds on the idea of voluntary cost limitations. If total hospital revenues rise by more than 9.7 percent during 1979, mandatory limitations on the growth of hospital revenues per admission will become effective on January 1, 1980. The administration predicts that the voluntary effort will fail to meet the 9.7 target by a wide margin. Under the mandatory limitations, each hospital would be permitted to increase revenues per admission by the percentage change in the prices each pays, plus a bonus if it has lower routine costs than the median hospital in its class and less a penalty if its routine costs are higher than the median. The mandatory controls would apply to fewer than half of all hospitals, which account for just over half of hospital outlays.[7]

Between issuance of the budget and release of detailed specifications of the plan six weeks later, the administration reduced significantly its estimates of savings from cost containment legislation:

| | Savings in billions of dollars | |
	Fiscal 1980	1980–84
Budget estimate		
Federal	1.7	25.8
Total	4.4	63.1
Revised estimate		
Federal	1.4	21.8
Total	3.7	53.4

7. The mandatory controls would not apply to any hospital whose costs rise 9.7 percent or less and which (a) is located in a state in which total hospital costs rise 9.7 percent or less or in which an approved mandatory cost-control program is in effect, or (b) qualifies as small and nonmetropolitan or new, or (c) primarily serves federally qualified health maintenance organizations.

The Congressional Budget Office puts federal savings in 1980 from the administration proposal even lower, at $1 billion.

The hospital cost containment proposal raises three basic questions. First, will the savings come from more efficient provision of existing services and curtailment of services with no tangible benefit; from curtailment of services generating benefits that, in some sense, are worth less than their cost; or from reduction in services generally regarded as necessary and appropriate? The desirability of cost containment clearly hinges on which of these sources of potential savings is dominant. The administration has argued that large savings can be achieved from the first two sources, especially from the curtailment of pure waste.

Second, is the regulatory approach a promising way to hold down hospital costs? In view of the worldwide rise in hospital and medical costs and the widespread view that third party reimbursement bears responsibility for a large part of this rise in the United States, will purely administrative efforts to hold down costs succeed in blunting the inflationary incentives of current methods of financing health care? Critics argue that regulations will fail because hospital administrators will find ways to avoid the limits and because regulations will induce distortions in the provision of care—for example, by promoting the use of labor whose wages are not included under the limit to provide services that equipment could provide more cheaply or effectively.

Third, has the administration set an achievable goal? Between the issuance of the budget and the issuance of detailed specifications, it reduced its estimate of savings significantly. But even this estimate involves plans about as ambitious as those Congress rejected last year. After all adjustments, controlled hospitals, in the aggregate, would receive smaller increases than would be implied by increases in the prices of things they buy.

The hospital cost containment proposal embodies a decision by the administration that some effort to hold down hospital costs is necessary and feasible and that such a limit is superior, at least in the short run, to other control measures currently available. Senator Herman Talmadge, chairman of the health subcommittee of the Committee on Finance, has favored limits on the rate of increase in the price of routine hospital services. The administration has incorporated elements of the Talmadge approach, but it has refused to rely exclusively on it because it would save little either for the federal government or private payers, and because the principle on which it is based is flawed: hospitals could easily compensate for any decrease in revenues from routine services by raising the price of other services and by inducing doctors to prescribe more of them.

The administration prefers not to use the regulatory powers it possesses under section 223 of the Social Security Act to set limits on reimbursement under medicare and medicaid. But it has begun the process of issuing such regulations so that this power can be used if hospital cost containment fails. By using such powers, the administration unquestionably could reduce the rate of increase of federal expenditures under medicare and medicaid, but nothing would prevent hospitals from segregating medicaid or medicare patients or from setting up separate and higher price schedules for other patients. The net result would be to shift hospital cost inflation from the federal budget to private payers and to re-create the system of second class care for the poor and the aged that medicaid and medicare were designed to end. The failure of Congress to enact any form of hospital cost containment would force the administration to proceed with these regulations in light of its budgetary goals and constraints.

Not only is this year's hospital cost containment plan strict, but it is made in combination with other proposals to limit reimbursement under medicare and medicaid. The combination will eat heavily into hospital revenues.

	Savings, fiscal 1980 (billions of dollars)
Containing hospital costs	1.4
Limiting fraud, abuse, and error	0.7
Reduction of reimbursement for malpractice insurance	0.3
Collection of lower medicare premiums for the working aged	0.2
Other	0.1
Total	2.7

More than half of the estimated $1.3 billion in additional savings is to result from efforts to limit fraud, error, and abuse. Of the $6.3 billion to $7.4 billion leakage due to waste, fraud, error, and abuse in the Department of Health, Education, and Welfare reported last year by the HEW inspector general, $4.5 billion was attributed to health programs, principally medicaid and medicare. A reduction of $674 million from decreased fraud, abuse, and error seems a laudable goal. However, most of the leakage estimated by the inspector general was due to "waste" caused by the basic structure of the program—third party reimbursement—the open-ended commitment to pay a pro rata share of the cost of all buildings and equipment and to pay for all tests and procedures. There is little evidence to support the savings estimated from this source in addition to those from cost containment.

The other proposed sources of savings would shift federal costs to other payers. Because medicare and medicaid patients file malpractice suits less frequently than do other patients, limiting federal reimbursement to actual awards for federal patients will require hospitals to shift charges to other patients. Charging employers premiums for medicare for employees over the age of sixty-five recognizes the fact that some employers terminate insurance coverage for aged employees and that private insurance pays only for eligible services not covered under medicare, but this step will shift insurance costs to private employers.

Underlying each of these proposals for reducing costs are base estimates of program outlays that may be unrealistically low. These base estimates assume increases in hospital services per patient day much below those experienced in recent years.[8] Because of these and other differences with the administration, the Congressional Budget Office estimates that base outlays under medicare and medicaid will exceed the administration's estimates by about $900 million.

OTHER HEALTH SYSTEM REFORMS. In addition to its attempts to stuff the genie of rising hospital outlays into a cost containment bottle, the administration is also proposing to extend or to initiate policies that will deal with some of the root causes of rising medical expenditures.

Perhaps the most important over the long run is the system of grants to encourage the establishment of health maintenance organizations and other systems of prepaid health delivery. There is some evidence that costs of medical care are lower under prepaid health plans than under conventional fee-for-service medical practice. Under prepaid plans, the patient pays annually a sum stipulated in ad-

---

8. The increase between 1966 and 1977 averaged 6.5 percent. The percentage increases estimated or forecast for 1978, 1979, and 1980 are, respectively, 3.0, 2.8, and 4.0.

vance for a specified range of services. There is considerable variation in cost among prepaid plans. Costs of health care under some types of prepaid health plans are 10 to 40 percent below those of care provided on a fee-for-service basis, principally because of much lower rates of hospitalization, while costs under other types of prepaid plans seem to be as high as under fee-for-service.[9] The administration requests authority to spend $74 million in 1980, almost doubling 1979 authority to make grants for feasibility studies for new prepaid health plans, to plan their establishment, to assist their early development, and to aid their expansion.

After many years of federal assistance to increase the construction of hospital beds and the training of physicians, a consensus is emerging among health analysts that the United States now has an excess of hospital beds and soon will have an excess of doctors. The 1980 budget contains initiatives to reduce both the number of hospital beds and the number of medical students. The budget requests $30 million to assist communities with an excess of hospital beds in closing some or all of them or in converting them to some other use, such as nursing home care. This request is the vestige of a much larger departmental request, scaled down because of budgetary stringency despite estimates that each dollar spent will result in savings of $2.60 per year, according to HEW estimates. The budget also calls for termination of payments now made to medical schools to support medical education and proposes instead to provide $28 million to medical schools to encourage young doctors to specialize in primary care rather than in specialties where the surplus of physicians is concentrated. Because all of the doctors who will begin to practice before 1985 have already entered medical school, the number of physicians per 100,000 population will rise from 178 in 1976 to 221 in 1985— a historic high—even if Congress approves the administration's recommendations. The policy Congress makes this year concerning medical education will not have appreciable effect until 1990 and later, because of the length of medical training.

EXTENSION OF BENEFITS. In early 1977 President Carter proposed to revamp the trouble-plagued program of early and periodic screening, diagnosis, and treatment of children, which is administered

9. Harold S. Luft, "How Do the Health Maintenance Organizations Receive Their Savings," *New England Journal of Medicine,* vol. 298, no. 24 (June 15, 1978), pp. 1336–43.

under medicaid. He proposed to require the coverage of children up to the age of six, to assure the provision of treatment as well as screening and diagnosis (a step many cost-sensitive states have neglected to take), and to increase the proportion of the costs of the program borne by the federal government. The congressional committees, to which the proposal was referred, seemed to like the idea so well that they added benefits far beyond those proposed by the President. But neither house of Congress enacted it before adjournment. The 1980 budget calls once again for enactment of this proposal at a cost of $220 million in 1980 and considerably more in future years as the program is fully implemented and participation increases.

Several direct service programs receive recommended increases in the 1980 budget sufficient to offset the effects of inflation, and some of them enough to increase services. These programs include community health centers and community mental health programs. The budget also calls for reorientation of mental health services away from separate mental health clinics and toward regular health-care settings where mental health service would be one in a range of available services. This move would implement one of the recommendations of the President's Commission on Mental Health.

The growing national health service scholarships and national health service corps also receive additional impetus in the 1980 budget. Medical students receive full scholarships for each year they are in school on the condition that they agree to serve an equal period in a health-shortage area or other designated health facility. These programs not only can influence the specialties that new doctors enter but can help increase the number of doctors practicing in areas designated as medically underserved, such as underpopulated rural areas and poor districts in urban communities. Little evidence is available about how many corps physicians remain in the areas where they first practice, about how other doctors in the area view the program, and about how patients view the services of corps physicians.

PREVENTION OF DISEASE.* Over the last several years, the increasing emphasis of health care policy has been on prevention of illness. The shift resulted from widespread recognition that changes in personal habits, such as cigarette smoking, and improvements of the environment, such as reduced air pollution and occupational hazards, could do more to reduce sickness and premature death than

* Lester Lave assisted in the preparation of this section.

could additional physician visits and hospital care. Five years ago, HEW's annual *Forward Plan for Health* emphasized a planned approach to health care, and prevention in particular. A National Conference on Preventive Medicine, hosted by the National Institutes of Health in 1975, and subsequent issues of the *Forward Plan for Health* restated this theme. Joseph A. Califano, Jr., secretary of HEW, made prevention a major theme of health policy, proposing a number of initiatives embodied in the 1980 budget.

The HEW argument is that prevention works and is cost-effective. But, although budget authority for prevention programs increases 12 percent in 1980, it represents only 2.3 percent of health budget authority. Despite the rhetoric, then, the budget seems to reflect an insight derived from prior studies: that prevention can improve health but is unlikely, in the near term, to lower expenditures on health care. Thus, prevention is an additional expense to HEW, not a way of saving funds *currently* committed to health care. The need for fiscal restraint means that no matter how effective prevention programs may be in improving health, they can enter the budget only slowly. Rapid increases in medicare and medicaid costs leave little room for new health initiatives. To increase expenditures further by initiating prevention programs contradicts the need to keep down health expenditures.

Preventive personal medical care is but one of the ways of accomplishing prevention. Of greater quantitative import are the environmental and occupational health and safety programs. Outlays for these programs have risen rapidly, particularly those of the Environmental Protection Administration (EPA). It is a significant comment on priorities that in the last two budget cycles, EPA has come out the major winner in zero-base budget analyses across agencies.[10] Increases have been concentrated in regulatory programs aimed at preventing illness, such as regulating toxic substances, air pollution, and solid waste. These increases are particularly startling when contrasted with old-line EPA programs such as water quality, where expenditures have fallen (from $307.6 million to $284.8 million), and outlays are far below authorizations.

SUMMARY. The administration developed its 1980 health budget under the shadow of medical cost inflation, which has driven up the

10. The budget increases, for other than construction grants, were 23.5 percent for fiscal 1979 and 5.8 percent for fiscal 1980.

costs of medicare and medicaid and exacerbated overall inflation. Thus, the dominant theme is cost reduction. The striking thing, however, is that nearly all of the proposed reductions are in payments to providers, principally hospitals, and little is from reduction in services to patients, especially the needy. But many hospitals and other providers are in fact likely to cut services if cost limitations are imposed. The 1980 budget also calls for some added benefits in medicare and medicaid and in such direct service programs as community health centers, community mental health centers, the national health service corps, and preventive medical programs.

The chief question about the 1980 budget is whether the cost limitations and other cutbacks will be enacted and whether the quite optimistic base forecasts about medicaid and medicare cost trends will be realized. If Congress does not accept the full program of cost limitations as promptly as the administration has assumed or if the underlying increase in medicaid and medicare costs is closer to historical trends than the administration forecasts, health outlays could exceed budget estimates by as much as $2 billion to $3 billion.

Urban Policy and Housing*

Because more than two-thirds of all Americans live in metropolitan areas and 66 percent live in cities of more than 50,000, most domestic programs have some effect on urban areas and the people who live in them. All of the activities of the Department of Housing and Urban Development (HUD) have such effects. But so also do such programs as HEW's aid for elementary and secondary education and loans of the Small Business Administration.

The 1980 budget sets the stage for future cutbacks in expenditures by HUD for urban areas and housing. But present HUD outlays, even more than those of the Department of Defense, depend on policies of previous years and only to a limited degree on current decisions. Thus, HUD outlays will rise 19 percent in 1980, although its budget authority is cut by 7 percent.

Not only does the 1980 budget extend the 1979 reduction of HUD's budget authority, it also signals some changes in policy. Under Presidents Nixon and Ford, HUD moved both to phase down urban-aid programs that gave federal officials discretion to allocate funds among competing applicants and to replace them with programs of

* Anthony Downs assisted in the preparation of this section.

aid distributed automatically according to preestablished formulas. While the 1980 budget retains the centerpiece of this approach, the Community Development Block Grant, President Carter is attempting to assure that these funds reach low-income people and neighborhoods. He is supporting the continuation and extension of other urban development programs under which funds are distributed on a project basis to applicants best able to meet specific objectives set by HUD.

Last year's *Setting National Priorities* described trends in the flow of resources to urban areas under a range of programs far broader than those of the Department of Housing and Urban Development, including education, social services, highway construction, training and public service employment, income assistance, and revenue sharing.[11] The 1980 budget calls for an increase of 2 percent in expenditures and 5.6 percent in budget authority for these programs. Adjusted by the administration's optimistic inflation forecast, outlays will decline in real terms by 5 percent and budget authority by 1 percent. These numbers include the $3.5 billion in requested budget authority and $195 million in anticipated outlays for a national development bank. President Carter first called for the creation of such a bank last year, but Congress refused to act. The 1980 budget calls for it again, but a month after the budget was released, the administration abandoned the idea of creating such a bank and stated that it would ask for increases in the authorizations for a number of existing programs instead. If Congress does not grant these increases, outlays and budget authority for urban-related programs would decline 5 percent in real terms.

PRESIDENT CARTER'S URBAN POLICY. President Carter sent his much-heralded urban policy to Congress in March 1978, two months after he submitted his 1979 budget. The urban policy incorporated a number of proposals for the reauthorization of existing legislation. In this category were the Labor Department's proposal to reform the comprehensive employment and training program and HEW's proposal to concentrate $400 million on aid to school districts with disproportionate numbers of educationally disadvantaged students. Other elements of the urban policy were additions to existing programs: additions to housing rehabilitation loans, increases in social service grants to the states under title XX of the Social Security Act,

11. Anthony Downs, "Urban Policy," in Pechman, ed., *Setting Natonal Priorities: The 1979 Budget.*

liberalization of the investment tax credit, and increases in tax credits to private employers who hire low-income youths. Congress passed each of these proposals either in the form requested by the administration or in modified form.

President Carter also called for a number of major new initiatives, none of which survives. The largest was a national development bank, which would have provided credit to economically distressed urban and rural areas to assist their economic growth directly and to promote their growth indirectly by encouraging the inflow of private credit. The President proposed a $1 billion program of labor-intensive public works to employ the long-term unemployed, the young, and minorities. He called for $1 billion in fiscal assistance to economically troubled local governments and for the extension of the temporary program of countercyclical revenue sharing, authorized by Congress in 1977. The request for the national development bank was withdrawn, and neither of the others appears in the 1980 budget.

HOUSING. The most important housing initiative of 1978 was taken not by the administration or by Congress but by the Federal Home Loan Bank Board. Authorizing thrift institutions to sell six-month money-market certificates at interest rates just above those currently offered on Treasury bills, FHLBB enabled one of the principal sources of mortgage funds to continue to obtain the resources to make home loans in the face of tight monetary policies which in the past have drastically curtailed new construction. For that reason, housing construction remained robust throughout 1978 and forecasts of new construction in 1979 range from 1.6 million to 1.8 million units. If the forecasts are accurate, 1979 will turn out to be an average year for housing starts under money-market conditions previously associated with sharp reductions in housing construction.

The 1980 budget calls for the initiation of construction or the purchase of fewer units of subsidized housing than the 1979 budget—300,000 units, down from 360,000 units.[12] Because of its failure to meet its goals in 1979, however, HUD projects that it will actually complete more units in 1980 than in 1979—274,500 units, up from 248,650. The reduction in newly authorized units will affect completions in the future.

12. In addition, 25,000 units will be reserved for homeownership assistance under section 235 of the National Housing Act. These reservations are proceeding under court order obtained in response to President Nixon's attempt to impound funds in this program.

The largest federal housing program—the section 8 program—is proving to be vastly more expensive than anyone anticipated. It provides subsidies equal to the difference between the fair-market rent of a housing unit and 15 to 25 percent of the income of its low-income occupants. The units may be newly constructed, substantially rehabilitated, or purchased from the existing housing stock. The annual cost for subsidies on regular rental units bought from the existing stock is $2,670 per unit; the cost on new units is currently running about $4,200 per unit.

These costs highlight the hard choice among three conflicting objectives that policymakers face: to provide relatively high-quality units to low-income families, to focus aid on the neediest families, and to support the construction of as many units as possible with a given authorization. These objectives cannot all be achieved simultaneously. Building and housing codes require the provision of high-quality units. Because subsidies on existing housing are less costly than those on new housing, the Office of Management and Budget has urged HUD to shift the emphasis of the section 8 program from new to existing housing.[13]

The 1980 budget moves in the other direction, decreasing the proportion of units that are to be purchased from existing housing stock. The HUD leadership has resisted OMB's suggestion because it believes that increasing reliance on existing housing would make the section 8 program practically indistinguishable from income assistance and vulnerable to the suggestion that housing assistance be merged administratively with income support, because it believes that new construction is necessary to assure an adequate supply of the kinds of housing low-income families require, and because of the need for political support for the program by builders and construction unions.

COMMUNITY DEVELOPMENT GRANTS. The federal government directly assists local development under three major programs: community development block grants, urban development action grants, and loans for housing rehabilitation under section 312 of the Housing Act of 1964. Outlays for these programs will rise significantly because of past increases in budget authority. Outlays persist but are

13. This cost differential previously led HUD to initiate major social experiments to test the feasibility of a national housing allowance—a system of grants much like those provided under section 8 for existing units. These experiments, which cost approximately $163 million, are now nearing completion.

declining under the urban renewal and model cities programs, terminated by the Housing and Community Development Act of 1974.

The community development block grant was the result of President Nixon's successful effort to replace numerous categorical programs of aid to localities with one program of relatively unrestricted financial assistance. Authority for this grant has not kept pace with inflation, rising $150 million in each of the last three years, and reaching $3.9 billion in 1980. The formula was revised in 1977 and now directs relatively more of the funds to older cities than stipulated in the original formula. HUD has attempted through regulations to increase the share of grant funds used for the benefit of low- and moderate-income residents.

The Housing and Community Development Act of 1977 authorized $400 million per year for urban development action grants. Congress appropriated that amount in 1978 and 1979, and President Carter again seeks the full appropriation in 1980. The administration also announced that it would seek $275 million more for such grants when it withdrew its request for a national development bank. In one respect, this program is reminiscent of categorical grant programs: cities and urban counties must apply for grants, and only physically or economically distressed communities are eligible. Because HUD receives more requests for grants than available funds will support, it must select recipients on the basis of the quality of the proposals and the degree of distress. Urban development action grants must be spent within four years (in contrast to urban renewal under which projects sometimes stretched to a decade or more), they focus on construction (like urban renewal, but unlike model cities), and they require the commitment of private investment funds (unlike urban renewal, model cities, or the community development block grant). Indeed the emphasis on leveraging private investment funds is a leitmotiv of the program.

At present, only cities that qualify as distressed are eligible for funds. Congress will consider this year whether to qualify distressed neighborhoods in cities currently ineligible for grants. The criteria now used by HUD for determining eligibility (including age of housing) have the effect of concentrating funds on large cities and urban communities, mostly in the northeast and central parts of the country. Representatives and senators from the South and West, anxious to obtain funds for communities in their districts or states, may seek to change the eligibility rules. The importance of this issue is increased by the fact that HUD uses eligibility for urban development action grants as a criterion for allocating funds for subsidizing home mortgages administered by the Government National Mortgage Association (under the so-called targeted tandem plan).

EMPLOYMENT PROGRAMS. President Carter is proposing to reduce public service employment programs significantly for 1980. Perhaps the most striking aspect of the President's budget for employment programs is his continuing support for these programs at levels unprecedented before his administration, despite the severe pressure he feels to cut expenditures.

In 1978 Congress reauthorized the major employment and training programs (other than the youth employment programs on which it acted in 1977). It retained the basic structure of the programs, under which the federal government provides funds to local sponsors, usually municipal governments or nonprofit agencies, who bear the responsibility for creating job opportunities and making them available to the workers who meet federally established eligibility rules. It consolidated adult employment programs into two titles, one dealing with structural unemployment, one with cyclical unemployment. Under the structural title (title II-D) workers must come from families with incomes below 70 percent of the lower family budget standard of the Bureau of Labor Statistics ($10,481 in 1977 for a family of four) and they must have been unemployed at least fifteen weeks. The prime sponsor cannot supplement from other sources the wage payable from federal funds. Under the countercyclical title (title VI), workers must come from families with incomes below 100 percent of the BLS lower family budget standard and they must have been unemployed at least ten weeks. Furthermore, the prime sponsor may supplement wages at a total cost of up to 10 percent of the federal funds.

Congress anticipated that the number of jobs provided under title II-D would remain relatively constant, while it authorized the number of jobs provided under title VI to fluctuate with the unemployment rate. For 1979 Congress has authorized 267,000 jobs under title II-D and 358,000 under title VI. President Carter proposes to scale down the number of countercyclical jobs under title VI to 200,000 by the end of 1980 and to hold that number constant. He also proposes to retain the 267,000 jobs for the structurally unemployed under title

II-D in 1980. The reduction in actual public service employment may be smaller than these numbers suggest, as the number of workers in public service jobs in 1979 is well below legally authorized levels.

The administration appears to have abandoned its former position that the number of jobs provided under title VI should fluctuate automatically with the unemployment rate and is reported to plan to channel any additional expenditures necessitated by increases in unemployment to title II-D. The real consequences of this decision will be to ensure that additional assistance provided during periods of high unemployment goes to persons whose incomes are somewhat lower and whose period of unemployment is somewhat longer than would be the case if such assistance were provided under title VI. Furthermore, during periods of high unemployment, title VI directs a larger proportion of jobs than does title II-D to industrial cities most afflicted with cyclical unemployment.

The budget seeks the same outlays in 1980 as in 1979 for programs under the Youth Employment and Demonstration Projects Act. This request corresponds to a program reduction because of the rise in the minimum wage from $2.65 an hour to $2.80 an hour, but the number of young people served may not decline because funds will be shifted from relatively high-cost job creation to relatively low-cost training. The budget calls for a reduction in job slots under the summer youth employment program from 1 million in 1979 to 750,000 in 1980.

The cutback in total support for public service employment will cause some problems of adjustment for a number of cities that have come to depend heavily on federal funds to pay for municipal employment. The importance of public service employment in nine major cities is illustrated by the following tabulations:

	Public service employment as percent of city employment
Boston	11
Cleveland	14
Detroit	14
Kansas City	16
Philadelphia	13
Phoenix	16
Rochester	11
San Francisco	12
St. Louis	13

The cutback is justified by the completion of recovery from the 1974–75 recession and is timed to help slow down the economy in order to fight inflation; but the timing comports oddly with the administration's projection that unemployment will rise in 1980. The budget is silent on whether the administration is prepared to recommend increases in funds for jobs programs beyond those in the 1980 budget should unemployment reach the higher totals projected by most private forecasters.

While public employment programs will shrink in 1980, measures to encourage the hiring of disadvantaged workers directly by private employers will increase. The Revenue Act of 1978 created a targeted-jobs tax credit under which employers may receive tax credits of up to $3,000 in the first year and $1,500 in the second year after hiring a worker who would have had difficulty finding employment. These workers include recipients of vocational rehabilitation; the economically disadvantaged young, Vietnam veterans, and ex-convicts; recipients of aid under supplemental security income (welfare for the aged, blind, and disabled) or general assistance (state welfare programs); and youths participating in work-study programs. Total credits are projected to reach $480 million in 1980, up from $140 million in 1979.

Income Assistance

The 1980 budget proposes piecemeal changes in both welfare and social security. The proposed changes in welfare replace President Carter's earlier sweeping plan to revamp welfare, his program for better jobs and income. The proposed changes in social security mark the opening of what promises to be a lengthy, and is certain to be a momentous, debate about the future of social security. While these debates were getting under way, Congress last year enacted a major increase in veterans' pensions for nonservice-connected disability, and the President seeks increases this year in service-connected disability pensions. The 1980 budget amounts to a proposal to shift income assistance to poor and disabled veterans from the aged and other poor. This section describes those proposals.

BACKGROUND. Of the $249 billion in payments for individuals, 66 percent will flow through a number of entitlement programs—old age, survivors, and disability insurance (OASDI), railroad retirement, civil service retirement and disability pensions, military retire-

Table 4-4. Income Assistance Payments for Individuals, Selected Fiscal Years, 1970–80
Billions of dollars

Type of program	1970	1975	1978	1979	1980
Major entitlement programs[a]	43.6	100.4	134.6	146.8	165.6
Major means-tested programs[b]	7.0	17.2	21.2	22.3	24.1
Other[c]	12.1	31.3	48.7	54.4	59.5
Total	62.6	148.9	204.5	223.5	249.2

Source: Office of Management and Budget, "Payments for Individuals—Introductory Notes," January 1979.

a. Major entitlement programs include old age, survivors, and disability insurance, railroad retirement, civil service retirement and disability insurance, military retirement, unemployment insurance, and veterans' compensation for service-connected injuries.

b. Major means-tested programs include aid to families with dependent children, supplemental security income for the aged, blind, and disabled, veterans' pensions for nonservice-connected disabilities, and food stamps.

c. Other payments for individuals include medicare and medicaid, housing payments, other veterans' benefits and services, and other public assistance and related activities.

ment, unemployment insurance, and veterans' compensation for service-connected injuries—under which benefits are paid without a means test. These programs are not only large but rapidly growing—up $65.2 billion in the last five years (see table 4-4).

Payments made under means-tested programs—aid to families with dependent children, supplemental security income for the aged, blind, and disabled, food stamps, and veterans' disability pensions— are much smaller than those made under the entitlement programs and have been growing more slowly in recent years. The last of these four programs is, in effect, a special welfare program for veterans, because disability is presumed if a veteran is poor and sixty-five years old; 51 percent of recipients are over the age of sixty-five. In addition, the federal government provides income-tested assistance through housing assistance and medicaid.

SOCIAL SECURITY. More than 36 million people will receive $115 billion in retirement, survivors, and disability benefits under the social security system in 1980. Measured in these quantitative terms or by its popularity, social security is one of the most successful pieces of social legislation in American history. Nevertheless, the system is undergoing scrutiny by at least four governmental study commissions which are raising basic questions about the character and role of the system. These questions concern the following issues: whether the treatment of secondary earners, which began at a time when few women worked and few marriages ended in divorce, should be amended for a society in which most women work and 35 percent

Table 4-5. Proposed Reductions in Social Security Benefits, Fiscal Years 1980 and 1984
Millions of dollars

	Reductions	
Item	1980	1984
Disability insurance	35	582
Retirement and survivors insurance	465	3,118
Elimination of student benefits	155	1,800
Elimination of lump-sum death benefit	221	378
Elimination of minimum benefit	53	187
Curtailment of widows' benefit when youngest child reaches 16	23	518
Other changes	13	235
Total reductions	**500**	**3,700**

Source: Department of Health, Education, and Welfare estimates.

of new marriages are projected to end in divorce; whether the present exclusive reliance on payroll taxes to pay for benefits should be continued; whether social security coverage should be extended to the 2.5 million exempt federal employees and perhaps to the 2 million exempt employees of state and local governments and the private sector; whether the retirement age under social security should be raised, lowered, or left the same; and numerous other questions. This list makes clear that, despite its popularity and in part because of its size, the social security system is undergoing probing and complete reexamination.

Against this background, the administration has proposed a number of reductions in benefits that would reduce outlays in 1980 by $500 million and in 1984 by $3.7 billion (see table 4-5). The reason for the growth in savings is that none of the proposed changes would apply to current beneficiaries; only those coming on the rolls in the future would be affected.

Disability insurance. Because the number of people claiming disability insurance benefits has increased sharply in the last decade and because of past declines in the rate of recovery, the administration proposed a number of changes that would reduce certain benefits and increase work incentives. To prevent payment of benefits that exceed predisability earnings, the budget calls for a cap on benefits at 80 percent of earnings and other modifications that reduce the risk of lengthy interruption of benefits to people who attempt to work. These changes leave unanswered two more basic questions. How should disability be defined? And to what extent should the income needs of the disabled be met through benefits based on prior earnings and to what extent through benefits based on current income needs?

Retirement and survivors insurance. The 1980 budget addresses none of the basic structural questions about social security. It proposes a number of marginal changes, which the administration defends as desirable and which would reduce costs somewhat in 1980 and more significantly in the future.

1. Social security benefits are now payable to children over the age of eighteen only if they are in school. On the ground that by 1980 student aid will have increased almost 60 percent since 1977, from $3.3 billion to $4.7 billion, the administration proposes to phase out these student benefits.

2. The $255 lump-sum death benefit would be terminated and replaced by a similar benefit under the income-tested supplemental security income program.

3. At present beneficiaries are entitled to a minimum benefit of $122 per month. Workers with long work histories at low wages receive a special minimum benefit of $11.50 a month for every year of covered employment beyond ten and up to thirty. The administration proposes to repeal the $122 minimum but not the special minimum. This repeal would affect only future retirees without long attachment to social security and who, because of excessive income, would be ineligible for benefits under the supplemental security income program.

4. Spouses with young children may receive benefits until their youngest child reaches eighteen years. The administration proposes to deny these benefits (but would retain them for the children) after the youngest child reaches sixteen years, because most parents in fact work. Last year the administration's welfare reform proposal would have subjected parents to a work requirement when their youngest child reached fourteen years.

These cost-saving proposals have generated considerable controversy, although similar proposals have been ignored in the past. Last year, for example, President Carter suggested four changes that would have saved $644 million in 1979, but he could not find a congressional sponsor for any of them. In 1976 Congress refused to accept President Ford's proposal to cut social security outlays by $826 million.

The proposals contained in the 1980 budget are more controversial than those advanced in the past because they come at a time when the fundamentals of the system are undergoing a thorough reexamination and when rising payroll taxes have made the cost of the system increasingly apparent. Although the administration claims that its proposals are modest and leave the basic structure of social security intact, long-time supporters of social security see them as the first round in a lengthy contest over whether the basic structure of the social security system should be modified. The administration holds that its proposals will protect the basic structure by pruning costly and low-priority elements of the program.

Enactment of limits on disability insurance benefits, possibly even stricter ones than the administration proposed, seems likely because key congressional committees have been considering similar limits for some time. But action on the changes in retirement and survivors insurance seems unlikely this year as Congressman Al Ullman, chairman of the Committee on Ways and Means, has declared that he will not hold hearings on them until fall, thereby effectively killing them for fiscal year 1980.

WELFARE. Soon after he took office, President Carter announced that comprehensive reform of the welfare system was one of his foremost legislative objectives. Late in 1977 he sent his plan to Congress.[14] Despite favorable consideration by the special subcommittee to which the plan was referred, neither the House nor the Senate completed action on it. Most observers came to feel that Congress was in no mood to enact a reform as sweeping or as costly as the one President Carter submitted, one that would have cost $17.4 billion, according to the Congressional Budget Office.

The 1980 budget reaffirms the President's commitment to welfare reform, but along lines far more modest than those he pursued last year. The budget commits no funds for welfare reform in 1980 but indicates that the President is prepared to spend up to $5.5 billion in 1982 on a plan that would (1) establish a federal minimum for aid to families with dependent children (AFDC) for one-parent families, (2) mandate coverage under AFDC of two-parent families in the twenty-four states that do not now cover them and under less restrictive conditions than prevail in the other twenty-six states, (3)

14. For a description of the plan, see John L. Palmer, "Employment and Income Security," in Pechman, ed., *Setting National Priorities: The 1979 Budget*, pp. 66–74.

create public service job slots and impose work requirements on the principal earner in two-parent families, and (4) liberalize the earned-income tax credit. In combination, these changes would provide fiscal relief to all states.

This proposal is less costly than the President's 1977 proposal, but it moves some distance toward all but one of the objectives he set then. The exception is program consolidation and simplification, for which this proposal would do almost nothing.

The prospects for enactment seem poor in a year dominated by program reductions and proposals to limit federal and state spending. Its major asset is that it resembles incremental welfare reform plans supported last year by Congressman Ullman, by Senators Howard Baker, Henry Bellmon, John Danforth, and Abraham Ribicoff, and by the New Coalition, an umbrella group for organizations representing governors, mayors, county officials, and state legislators. Its best political chance seems to lie in an agreement on a compromise plan among the administration, congressional leaders, and such outside organizations as the New Coalition.

Whether the President's plan succeeds or fails, welfare as a major issue is likely to vanish from the political scene. Success would mark the achievement of most but not all of the goals the President set for welfare reform in 1977. Failure of the new proposals, after the failure of President Nixon's family assistance plan, the unwillingness of President Ford even to raise the issue, and the lack of success of President Carter's first and sweeping reform proposal, would unmistakably convey the unwillingness of the Congress to alter the welfare system significantly.

The 1980 budget proposes three marginal changes in welfare, two of which would save money right away. The first would simplify the computation of work-related expenses now reimbursed in amounts that vary widely from state to state and from one case worker to another. The second would count stepparents' income that is now disregarded in computing the monthly payment for an eligible parent and child. These two changes would save $170 million in 1980. The third change would tie welfare benefits to actual income of recipients in the previous month, rather than to the income welfare recipients predict they will have in the next month, but this change will not be implemented until 1982, to permit the completion of research on how best to administer the new procedures.

VETERANS' PENSIONS. While Congress was balking on welfare reform, it was greatly increasing welfare for poor veterans. The Veterans Administration provides general income support to veterans and their dependents and survivors under two programs. Veterans' compensation pays benefits ranging from $44 to $1,408 a month, excluding dependents, to veterans with service-connected disabilities. Total payments will reach $7.3 billion in 1980, including proposed cost-of-living adjustments. This program is analogous to disability insurance under the social security system. Veterans' pensions provide benefits to all poor veterans sixty-five years of age or older and to nonaged veterans with disabilities not related to military duty. This program is analogous to supplemental security income— welfare for the aged and disabled. Veterans with as few as ninety days of active duty, including one day during a war, are eligible for benefits.

In 1978 Congress increased welfare-like disability pensions for single and married veterans to $296 per month and $388 per month, respectively. These amounts exceed federal payments under SSI ($190 and $285 per month for single persons and couples, respectively), and they exceed the payments proposed by President Carter under the program for better jobs and income for aged and disabled individuals and couples ($208 and $313, respectively). By requiring that some previously excluded income be counted in computing benefits, and on the assumption that Congress would have increased benefits to offset inflation, the cost of this liberalization was held to $535 million for 1980.

These pensions exceed roughly half of newly awarded social security benefits. Administration estimates of the savings from curtailing certain social security benefits do not take into account partially offsetting increases under veterans' pensions.

SUMMARY. Despite the President's strong desire to hold down expenditures in 1980, the budget calls for significant increases in income assistance because of existing law and increases in the beneficiary population. The reductions below this legislated trend sought by the administration are sizable as measured against most other programs but are small compared to total income assistance or to its growth from 1979 to 1980. Resolution of the major issues—whether to restructure social security and whether to reform welfare—will not occur in time to affect the 1980 budget.

Crosscutting Issues

This section examines three budget issues that cut across particular functions of government. The first is concerned with federal aid to state and local governments: how much of a cutback in federal spending should be achieved through a reduction in these programs and in which ones? This question is sharpened by the facts that state and local outlays have grown far more rapidly in recent years than federal outlays and that state and local governments collectively had a surplus of $28 billion in 1978, when the federal deficit was $49 billion. The second involves the interrelationship between outlays and regulations as methods of achieving policy objectives. In a number of cases, regulatory policy directly affects current outlays or projections of future outlays. Moreover, regulations enable federal agencies to pursue objectives whose costs are borne by subsidiary governments or private businesses or individuals. The third issue is federal employment policy—the cutback in federal employment, the cap on federal pay increases, and the reform of the federal pay structure now under study.

Financial Aid to States and Localities

The 1980 budget calls for $82.9 billion in federal aid to state and local governments. This amount is 20.9 percent of projected federal domestic outlays, 23.6 percent of projected state and local expenditures, and 3.3 percent of projected gross national product. All these percentages are lower than the corresponding values for 1978 and 1979 but are high by historical standards. For 1981 and 1982 the budget projects further declines in grants to states and to localities as a fraction of federal outlays and as a proportion of gross national product. Because these ratios are lower than in the immediate past, they suggest that state and local governments will face dual pressures to cut expenditures—from the reduction in federal grants and from their own taxpayers' calls for fiscal restraint.

The cuts are not evenly divided, however, and grants for some purposes are bucking the downward trend (see table 4-6). The largest reductions are in three programs introduced or expanded to fight the recession of the mid-1970s—countercyclical revenue shar-

Table 4-6. Federal Grants to States and Localities, Fiscal Years 1978, 1979, and 1980
Billions of dollars

Type of federal aid	Grants in current dollars			Grants in constant 1980 dollars[a]		
	1978	1979	1980	1978	1979	1980
Countercyclical aid[b]	9	5	3	11	6	3
Major block grants[c]	19	19	19	22	20	19
Medicaid, public assistance, and subsidized housing	19	21	22	22	22	22
Other	31	37	39	36	40	39
Total	78	82	83	90	88	83

Source: *Special Analyses, Budget of the United States Government, Fiscal Year 1979*, table H-11.
a. Constant dollars are calculated from the GNP deflator (1980 = 100).
b. Includes countercyclical revenue sharing, temporary employment assistance, and local public works.
c. Includes general revenue sharing, other general purpose fiscal assistance, community development block grants, aid to school districts for elementary and secondary education and impact aid, social services grants to the states under title XX of the Social Security Act, and criminal justice assistance.

ing, public service employment, and local public works. Outlays under these programs will drop from $9 billion in 1978 to $5 billion in 1979 and to $3 billion in 1980. Two of these programs—countercyclical revenue sharing and temporary employment assistance—have been particularly valuable to states and localities because they carry few effective restrictions on their use. Countercyclical revenue sharing funds carry few restrictions at all. While temporary employment assistance funds carry many terms and conditions, some localities have succeeded in using those funds, plus funds available under other titles of the Comprehensive Employment and Training Act, to support regular municipal payrolls.

Budget authority for the five major federal block grants—funds that are available for a wide range of purposes with relatively few restrictions—are increasing by less than inflation. These five are general revenue sharing and other general purpose fiscal assistance; the community development block grant; aid to school districts for elementary and secondary education, and impact aid; social service grants to the states under title XX of the Social Security Act; and criminal justice assistance. Budget authority for these programs will decrease by $146 million, a decline of 7.2 percent in real terms. Outlays will rise by 2.3 percent because of growth in past appropriations, although still by too little to keep up with inflation.

The federal government uses states and local governments as its administrative agents for a number of programs. The three largest are medicaid, public assistance, and subsidized housing. Federal grants could increase or decrease either because of a change in the proportion of total costs borne by the federal government or because of a change in total program costs. In the former case an increase in federal outlays helps the finances of states and localities. In the latter case, an increase in federal outlays signals increased burdens on state and local finances. The federal government is not seeking major changes in its matching rates (except for a small increase in medicaid). Federal outlays for these programs will decline slightly in real terms in 1980, signaling a slight improvement in state and local finances on this account.

The largest single federal grant to states and localities occurs under the medicaid program. The size of this grant will jump $600 million in 1980 if cost containment is enacted and $800 million if it is not. This increase is a measure of the stress on both federal and state budgets caused by the growth of medical costs. It is the federal share (ranging from 50 percent in fourteen states to 78 percent in Mississippi) of the increased cost of providing the seven mandatory services of the medicaid program and such additional optional services as states elect to include.

Despite popular misconceptions, cash welfare expenditures have risen negligibly in recent years and have declined significantly after adjustment for inflation. Outlays for AFDC in 1980 are projected to be 10 percent lower in real terms than those of 1976; outlays for SSI are projected to be 5 percent lower. The decline in federal public assistance grants is good news to state and local treasuries because it reflects smaller overall outlays. In some measure, this decline dramatizes the beneficial effects of declining unemployment in reducing the welfare rolls and in slowing the growth of disability. It also reflects the decisions of state and local governments not to increase welfare benefits as fast as prices have risen.

State and local housing agencies are the conduit for about half of federal housing assistance. The increase in these payments reflects the growth of the subsidized housing stock and the increasing costs of maintenance of the portion of that stock owned by local housing authorities.

The remaining federal grants consist of a bewildering variety of programs, including such diverse and unrelated measures as distributions from the federal highway trust fund ($6.8 billion in 1980), the unrestricted grant to the District of Columbia ($327 million in 1980), residual payments under the now-defunct urban renewal program ($280 million in 1980), watershed planning and control ($77 million in 1980), and 128 other categories (some of them combinations of two or more grants). Most of them have fairly specific purposes, although some effectively replace local funds that would otherwise be used for that purpose and confer considerable fiscal relief. These grants are projected to rise by $1.2 billion between 1979 and 1980; after adjustment for inflation, they decline 4 percent.

In general, the budget calls for large real reductions in programs originally justified as antirecession instruments. Despite such design, some cities used these funds to support ongoing activities. Relatively unrestricted aid, through block grants or general revenue sharing, decline modestly in real items. The category "other grants," which includes most narrowly categorized grants, declines somewhat more.

The reductions in federal aid to state and local governments reflect no overall theme or principle other than the judgment that the recovery from the 1974–75 recession is completed. The cutbacks reflect program-by-program decisions on which objectives deserve continued federal efforts. Supporters of the programs that were cut, both within Congress and among recipients, are unlikely to share the particular priorities of the President and his budget advisers. The budget contains no guiding principle on which to defend each proposed cut against the isolated evaluation by the committee that created the program.

Regulatory Policy

If the budget is the principal policymaking instrument in the United States, regulations are a close second. Through regulations the federal government attempts to prevent abuses of monopoly power, promotes civil rights, tries to curb instability in competitive markets, regulates consumer goods, raw materials, and chemicals to protect health and safety, and pursues numerous other objectives. These regulations proscribe certain kinds of behavior and require others. They impose sizable costs on producers and consumers. In fact, most objectives of public expenditures could be sought through regulations or tax incentives, although at some loss of efficiency in many cases. A major purpose behind the congressional requirement that the budget contain a listing of tax expenditures is the recognition that informed policymaking requires decisionmakers to consider whether tax incentives or direct expenditures better promote public objectives.[15] In 1978 President Carter announced that all federal agencies would be required to publish semiannual agendas of forthcoming regulations. Several agencies are rewriting regulations in an attempt to simplify their language.

This section contains three illustrations from among the large number of ways regulations are used and can be used to influence public policy. First, the 1980 budget announces major proposals for modifying regulation of the railroads. This proposal is spurred by recognition that existing service is unacceptably poor and by projections that enormous subsidies will be required to continue providing service under current policies. This example illustrates the fact that regulatory policy can have a major impact on public expenditures by affecting the operating costs of a quasi-public enterprise, the railroads.

The second illustration of regulatory policy concerns environmental safety and health. In this area, the Congress has recently accorded federal regulatory agencies sweeping power to require private industry to make large new expenditures. It also offers tax credits to encourage businesses and individuals to make investments or alter their consumption to reduce air and water pollution. In principle, objectives of these regulatory powers could have been achieved by direct public expenditures instead.[16]

Third, through a variety of policies, including not only direct payments and loans but also regulation of imports, the Department of Agriculture increases the income of farmers and food prices for consumers. In this case, achievement of higher incomes for farmers through regulation tends to lower public expenditures in the short run.

TRANSPORTATION.* Railroads are among the most highly regulated of American industries. Until recently, all railroads were in private hands. With bankruptcy a reality or an imminent threat for many of the largest companies, the federal government stepped in

15. See appendix B for a listing of tax expenditures.
16. The relation between regulation and inflation is discussed in chapter 3.
* Kenneth Small assisted in the preparation of this section.

during the mid-1970s and now has a major interest in Conrail, the successor to several financially troubled eastern and midwestern railroads. For that reason, the profits and losses of the system and funds for necessary capital improvements can directly affect the budget. Regulatory policy now affects not only the profit-and-loss statements of the majority of railroads that remain in private hands but also the budget of the federal government.

Twin shadows hang over policy toward railroads. The first is cast by technological changes that make the airplane and the automobile more attractive than railroads to most travelers and that make the truck more attractive than railroads for shipping many kinds of goods. The second is cast by shifts of population and industry from the East and Midwest to the South and West. Thousands of miles of track in the East and Midwest now run to abandoned factories and shrinking towns.

The 1980 budget calls for a one-fourth reduction in federal expenditures on the railroads. A planned reduction in federal purchases of the securities of Conrail, the organization that assumed responsibility for the freight traffic of the bankrupt railroads of the Northeast, accounts for more than half of the drop. The rest of the 1980 cutback occurs as a result of the reduction in national passenger service by Amtrak, the federal passenger system, and a slowdown in scheduled improvements in Amtrak's Boston–Washington line.

Conrail. In 1978 Conrail issued a five-year business plan that forecast profitability in current operations by 1980. The reduction in federal outlays on Conrail from $799 million in 1979 to $440 million in 1980 seems designed to hold Conrail to its plan. Success in meeting that plan depends on such fortuitous events as decent weather (unlike the severe winters of 1976–77 and 1977–78 and the Johnstown flood), no coal strike (such as the one in 1978), an increase in productivity from changes in work rules, and abandonment of a few high-cost routes. Although the Conrail plan assumes no relaxation of ICC regulation, it does point out that such relaxation would increase revenues.

Conrail could face substantial obligations for payments to workers for layoffs and early retirement required under title V of the Regional Rail Reorganization Act of 1973. In addition, the Railroad Retirement Trust Fund is in actuarial deficit. The administration proposes to close this deficit by cutting benefits and by increasing the payroll tax on all railroads by 2 percentage points, a potential expense not included in Conrail's business plan. The government can enable Conrail to meet these costs—an estimated $140 million—by extending the labor protection fund provided by the Regional Rail Reorganization Act of 1973 and by allowing rate increases. The 1980 budget does not, however, indicate any source for covering these costs.

Amtrak. As mandated by the Amtrak Improvement Act of 1978, the Department of Transportation recently submitted proposals to curtail passenger service. The proposal would reduce route miles by 43 percent and train miles by 34 percent. But the number of passengers served would fall by only 9 percent. The result would be a 19 percent decline in the estimated subsidy, from $779 million in 1979 to $634 million in 1980. Despite these cutbacks, the subsidies necessary to sustain even reduced passenger service are projected to resume their climb, rising to more than $1 billion by 1984. (As a historical note, the Rail Passenger Service Act of 1970 authorized $40 million to tide Amtrak over until it became profitable.)

The proposed reductions can hardly be criticized as excessive (though rail buffs and affected localities do). Three routes would continue to connect the Mississippi River with the West Coast. The proposal would cause only a temporary halt to the ever-larger subsidies necessary to sustain rail passenger service.

Will Congress go along? Past experience leads to pessimism, but under the Amtrak Improvement Act of 1978, the recommended cuts go into effect unless Congress vetoes them. Congress can let the Department of Transportation proposals stand through inaction.

Northeast Corridor improvement. The 1980 budget delays from 1981 until 1983 the faster passenger service between Boston and Washington specified in the Railroad Revitalization and Regulatory Reform Act of 1976. The secretary of transportation has announced an intention to request such a postponement from Congress. This delay permits a reduction in outlays of $102 million between 1979 and 1980. While this delay is asserted to be necessary to avoid disruptions to current service, it is no doubt motivated also by the desire to spread expenditures and thereby reduce 1980 outlays.

Other railroads. Most of the railroad system is privately owned. It consists of some highly profitable lines, mostly in the South and

West, and some lines that are in bankruptcy, mostly in the central states. According to a report issued in October 1978 by the secretary of transportation, the private sector faces a "capital shortfall" over the decade 1976–85 of $13 billion to $16 billion in funds needed to meet deferred maintenance and capital improvements. Rather than commit the federal government to so large a subsidy, the budget proposes to improve the financial health of the industry by permitting and encouraging selective mergers, abandonments, joint track-use agreements, increased rate flexibility, and the elimination of subsidies to competing modes of transport. Communities that would lose service, shippers that would have to pay higher rates, and competing modes that would face new taxes are all likely to fight this plan. Against this background, the administration's proposal for only $1.2 billion for financial assistance during the hoped-for transition to profitability seems optimistic, though perhaps it is an effective device for dramatizing the added costs that congressional rejection of its regulatory changes would entail.

There is a certain irony in the administration's proposals. Many of the gains from the regulatory restructuring would come from mergers, consolidated service agreements, and the freedom to charge higher rates for shipment of commodities, such as grain and coal, that are costly to ship by other modes. It would appear that the financial health of railroads is to be restored in part by encouraging a modest exercise of the very monopoly power that regulation for decades attempted to suppress.

HEALTH, SAFETY, AND THE ENVIRONMENT.* While the administration is working to reduce transportation regulation, it is expanding regulation of health, safety, and the environment. Altogether, the agencies set up to administer these regulations had budgets of $5.8 billion and 18,400 employees in fiscal 1978 at the beginning of this administration, and budget requests for $5.5 billion and 19,100 employees in the 1980 budget. But their employment and expenditures are merely a fraction of the costs of their regulatory actions.[17]

There are two major difficulties associated with the operation of these agencies: setting working goals and designing operating pro-

* Lester Lave assisted in the preparation of this section.
17. This fact does not necessarily imply that these costs exceed the many social and economic benefits they confer.

cedures. Indeed, these two are so intertwined that it is often difficult to decide where one begins and the other leaves off.

Goals and procedures. When it created agencies to regulate health, work safety, and the environment, Congress laid down goals many of which were so vague and others of which were so ambitious that they offer no practical guidance as to where the agencies should begin or what intermediate goals are desirable; in some cases, timetables were completely unrealistic, for example, those concerning reductions in automobile emissions and improvements in air and water quality.

Within such broad guidelines as the elimination of all discharge of pollutants into the navigable waters by 1985, agency administrators must emphasize some areas, neglect others, and violate the timetables of the legislation. But in doing so, the agencies expose themselves to continuous litigation. Some groups sue, asking the courts to force the agency to meet the timetable and the other provisions of the act.[18] Other groups sue, arguing that the regulations themselves are arbitrary and unscientific; or arguing that the agency violated due process, either by failing to solicit comments on the scientific evidence and the proposed regulations or by failing to allow sufficient time for comment.

From the time an agency decides that an action is necessary until something is done, a minimum of several years usually elapses. Background information must be gathered and analyzed in order to come up with a proposed standard. This standard must then be published, comments solicited, and a hearing held. If the prehearing data collection and analysis, the comments, and the hearing record provide a reasonable basis for the standard, it can be issued, after requisite delays for implementation. Then the regulations themselves become targets of suits and criticism. Legal battles delay the implementation of virtually every regulation and may invalidate them. If mis-

18. For example, the Environmental Protection Agency's initial attempts to abate pollution from automobiles (by implementing the emission standards in the 1970 Clean Air Act Amendments) were insufficient to meet the congressional timetable for the improvement of urban air quality. A southern California citizens' group sued the EPA to force promulgation of traffic controls to speed abatement. EPA administrator William Ruckelshaus was forced to order 85 percent gasoline rationing to keep traffic out of central Los Angeles; to no one's surprise, the regulation was never implemented.

takes are made at any stage, the process may have to be stopped and started anew at some future date.

Litigation is a terrible way of setting agency priorities. By its nature, a legal action considers only one issue at a time; the issue is one selected for action by a special interest group and the one that survives the early legal skirmishing. Thus, the timing of the issues surfacing in the courts seems capricious. Furthermore, the issues involve complicated technical and economic problems that the courts are ill equipped to resolve.

A final difficulty is that there is generally a period of some years after a regulation is issued and before its implied costs become evident. Industries often protest that new regulations will be costly, but their testimony is tainted by special interest and it may be years before costs begin to show up in higher prices, shortages, or unemployment.

Regulatory budgets and regulatory costs. Regulatory agencies have systematically sought to shift the burden of record-keeping, analysis, and enforcement to others. They do so because Congress systematically fails to appropriate the funds and staff necessary to carry out the tasks it sets. The powers given the EPA under the Clean Air Act and the Toxic Substances Control Act illustrate two very different legislative approaches.

The Clean Air Act gives EPA sweeping powers, but EPA must bear much of the cost of exercising these powers through its own budget. The act makes the EPA responsible for reviewing research on the effects of various pollutants, sponsoring new research, and setting standards. Congress instructed the EPA to supervise state enforcement and, if states fail to carry out its orders, to take over enforcement. But as a practical matter, the EPA lacks sufficient budget or staff to take over state functions. Furthermore, its own research has been criticized for poor quality and for not providing information that would help improve current regulations.

The Toxic Substances Control Act of 1976 shifts much of the cost of research to the private sector, following the model of the Food and Drug Administration. Under this act, the EPA is not responsible for undertaking research necessary to show the harmlessness of a new chemical; instead the company that wishes to introduce a new chemical into the environment must establish its safety according to criteria and standards established by the EPA. By shifting these costs to the producer, Congress has relieved the EPA of financial responsibility for the costs of its own compliance standards. The Occupational Safety and Health Administration has similar powers and the exercise of those powers raises similar problems.[19] Thus the EPA, OSHA, and the FDA are able to carry out their missions with much smaller staffs and lower budgets than would be necessary if they themselves had to do the research that they can compel private firms to perform.

The real issue should not be the size of the budget and the staff of the government agency but its powers over total expenditures. Shifting financial responsibility to the private sector can increase the cost of regulation even though the agencies themselves do not grow. Therefore, the Congress and the President should reconsider ceilings on agency budgets and cuts in federal employment, many of which represent false savings.

Has health, safety, and environment regulation worked well? After almost a decade, there can be little doubt that this new form of regulation has led to cleaner air and water, safer automobiles, greater safety in the workplace, and less occupational disease. It has worked; but one would have had a hard time showing that it has worked well. Few would hold that the agencies have acted in the most important areas or that they have acted with all deliberate speed. There has been no coordination of regulations among the various agencies or even within an agency. For example, the value of a worker's life implicit in OSHA's benzene standard is ten to twenty times higher than it is in its coke oven standard.

The procedural problems described above have led to numerous attempts to slow health, safety, and environmental regulation. The Congress has systematically constrained agency budgets and staffing and the administration has lengthened the time required to

19. OSHA has required that an employee exposed to hazardous substances (defined by OSHA regulation) must be monitored by the employer. Thus, the employer must test periodic samples to estimate the dose the employee is exposed to, give the employee a physical examination focused on the occupational disease, and maintain records on the exposure and health of the employee. Were the expense associated with these requirements borne by OSHA, its appropriation would have to be many times greater than it is now; but it is doubtful that OSHA would require such elaborate record-keeping if it were paying. Thus, shifting the burden to the private sector not only relieves the agency of the expenditures but produces more stringent requirements than would result if the costs were borne collectively.

issue a new regulation by building in such delays as a regulatory calendar and reviews by the Regulatory Analysis Review Group and the Regulatory Council. The private sector has increased delays by ubiquitous legal challenges. Indeed, the failure to define workable goals and the ever-growing complexity of regulatory procedures ensures that few regulations will be issued.

FOOD.* There is a trade-off between the level of agricultural prices and the budget costs of agricultural price support programs in times of abundant supplies. By taking steps to restrict production and thereby to raise market prices, the U.S. Department of Agriculture can reduce the income payments it is obliged to make to farmers for most basic commodities—wheat, rice, feed grains, and cotton. Other price-supported commodities such as sugar and milk are supported through market intervention, without direct payment to producers.

The President can also affect domestic food prices through his authority to modify quotas on the importation of certain commodities. So far he seems to be leaning toward a restrictive import policy that keeps prices of affected commodities and incomes of affected producers high.

Last year, Martin Abel estimated the cost of commodity programs in fiscal year 1979 to be $5.3 billion, about $1.0 billion higher than estimated by the Department of Agriculture.[20] The 1980 budget estimate for fiscal year 1979 is $5.0 billion.

The 1980 budget projects that commodity programs will cost $2.6 billion in fiscal year 1980, down sharply from 1979. This forecast implies a combination of demand and production that will keep prices of major commodities well above support levels and will result in target price payments lower than those of the previous two years. The support price is the amount the federal government stands ready to lend to farmers on a short-term basis against the security of their crops. The federal government makes additional payments equal to the difference between the support price (or the actual market price, whichever is higher) and the target price. The Department of Agriculture took a number of steps in fiscal year 1979 to increase prices of agricultural products. It reduced 1978 wheat, feed grain, and cot-

* Martin Abel assisted in the preparation of this section.
20. "Farm Commodity Programs," in Pechman, ed., *Setting National Priorities: The 1979 Budget*, table 7-9.

ton crops by encouraging farmers to withhold acreage from production. It allowed large amounts of wheat and feed grain to enter the long-term reserve, insulating these supplies from the market.

These actions kept market prices above support levels, even during the harvest period, and in the case of corn, the price was kept up despite a record crop.

	Wheat (dollars a bushel)	Corn (dollars a bushel)	Cotton (cents a pound)
Loan rate	2.35	2.00	48.0
Target price	3.40	2.10	52.0
Market price range, June 1978 to January 1979	2.78–3.05	1.92–2.28	54.3–61.1

Programs to withhold land from production for the 1979 wheat and feed grain crops, announced by the Department of Agriculture, will, with normal production, continue to keep farm prices well above support levels. No land diversion program was announced for cotton. Continued constraints on production of grains in 1979 together with demand prospects imply relatively high prices and are consistent with the reduced budget costs of commodity programs projected for fiscal year 1980.

Certain other policies do not significantly affect the budget but do influence commodity and food prices. Some are governed by existing legislation and some are governed by administrative action.

Dairy. According to the Food and Agriculture Act of 1977, dairy products and prices must be supported at 80 percent of parity. Dairy price supports were increased in October 1978 and again in April 1979. With the recent increase, dairy prices are now close to support levels, and moderate budget outlays are expected through the end of the marketing year in October. The President has authority to increase import quotas and to augment the flow of lower-cost imports. The issue of dairy imports was addressed in the recently completed Tokyo round of trade negotiations, but the proposed changes will not operate to increase U.S. imports of dairy products in the future.

Meat. President Carter expanded the meat import quota in June 1978 and announced a higher level for 1979. This increase helped prevent greater inflation in beef prices than actually occurred. Cattlemen oppose any further liberalization of meat imports. Had the President authorized higher quotas, some additional imports might have resulted, mitigating somewhat the 25 percent increase in meat prices anticipated during 1979.

Sugar. Federal policy now keeps domestic sugar prices at nearly twice the world level. The current domestic price of raw sugar is about 15 or 16 cents a pound though the world price is 9.5 cents a pound. The price is maintained through a system of fees and charges on imports. The President announced that the raw-sugar price will be at least 15.8 cents in 1979; as much as 0.5 cent may be added as a deficiency payment to farmers, depending on the results of a study of the costs of production. An escalator clause will increase sugar prices automatically in response to increases in the cost of production, which are related to the general rate of inflation. As a result, raw-sugar prices, already far above world prices, will rise another 5.3 to 8.6 percent.

Despite the administration's concern about inflation, it appears to be operating its agricultural programs in ways that reduce budget costs rather than farm prices. This policy is especially evident for grains, the basic feedstuff for livestock production. Similarly, in the case of sugar the balance seems tipped in favor of supporting farm prices and incomes rather than holding down consumers' food costs.

The Federal Civilian Workforce*

The budget proposes a reduction in federal employment and federal pay increases. These proposals follow the Civil Service Reform Act of 1978, which revised procedures for rewarding managerial personnel and for evaluating employee performance. These policy changes have moved employee compensation, ordinarily a recondite topic, onto center stage.

Personnel costs of federal civilian employees amount to about $50 billion in the 1980 budget. Military personnel add another $29 billion. Thus, about one-seventh of the federal budget is devoted to current personnel costs.[21] Although this share is much lower than that

---

* Robert W. Hartman assisted in the preparation of this section.

21. These estimates include direct compensation (regular pay plus overtime) and personnel benefits (the cost of health and life insurance and current retirement benefits). Funds appropriated for future retirement benefits are intragovernmental transfers and not current spending. All estimates in this section exclude the U.S. Postal Service.

Table 4-7. Federal, State, and Local Government Employment,
Selected Years, 1962–80[a]

Year	Federal employees (millions)			State and local employees (millions)	Federal nondefense employees per 1,000 population
	Total	Defense and atomic energy	Nondefense		
1962	1.8	1.0	0.8	6.4	4.3
1965	1.9	1.0	0.9	7.5	4.6
1970	2.0	1.0	1.0	9.6	4.9
1975	2.1	1.0	1.1	11.6	5.2
1980	2.1	1.0	1.1	n.a.	4.9

Sources: *Employment and Training Report of the President, 1978*, p. 333; *Special Analyses, Budget of the United States Government, Fiscal Year 1980*, pp. 249, 252, 258; and author's estimates.
n.a. Not available.
a. Excludes military personnel and employees of government enterprises such as the postal service and local water departments.

of state and local governments, control over employees' pay can clearly play a major role in restraining federal spending.

In the 1980 budget the administration is proposing to limit the annual increase in the civilian employee payroll to 6.1 percent, a significant reduction from previous years. This curb on payroll costs results from curtailment of both employment and annual pay increases.

EMPLOYMENT LEVELS. Over the last ten years civilian employment in federal nondefense agencies has grown about as fast as the nation's population. Table 4-7 shows 4.9 federal nondefense employees for each 1,000 citizens in both 1970 and 1980. Growth in public employment over the past two decades has been concentrated in the state and local government sector, which now employs about 15 percent of the nonagricultural labor force.

In 1978 Congress voted to require that civilian employment in the executive branch at the end of 1979, 1980, and 1981 not exceed the level at the end of 1977. At the President's discretion this ceiling can be increased, but by no more than the percentage growth of the U.S. population after 1978.[22] The 1980 budget keeps federal employment 12,000 under the 1979 ceiling and 41,000 under the 1980 ceiling; by September 1980 total employment will be about the same as it was three years earlier.

22. The resulting ceilings are 2,207,121 at the end of 1979 and 2,226,121 at the end of 1980.

PAY INCREASES. For the past ten years, pay of federal civilian employees is supposed to have been governed by the principle of "comparability."[23] Under this principle, the government each year surveys private-sector salaries in jobs comparable in responsibility, skills, and scope of supervisory authority to jobs in the first fifteen grades of the federal general schedule.[24] The average salary in each grade is then raised to the average salary found in the survey for matching jobs.[25]

Only one comparability pay raise has been granted in the past five years—in 1976. In 1974, 1975, and 1977, comparability pay increases were averaged, and the pay in all grades was raised by 5.5, 5, and 7 percent, respectively. In 1978, the comparability exercise showed that pay increases averaging about 8.5 percent, ranging from 6 to 19 percent, would be required for parity with the private sector, but as part of his anti-inflation program, President Carter asked for, and Congress accepted, an across-the-board 5.5 percent increase in the general schedule.

The 1980 budget once again proposes a 5.5 percent increase in the federal employees' pay schedule. According to the administration's estimates, the comparability procedure would lead to an average increase in federal employees' pay of 10.25 percent to keep up with rises in private pay and to make up ground lost in 1978. The 5.5 percent increase (including similar restraints on military and other pay systems) saves about $3 billion in 1980 outlays.

The administration also proposes to hold federal pay increases in 1980, 1981, and 1982 below those required by the comparability standard. The equity of this proposal, which implies at least temporary abandonment of the pay comparability standard, is addressed below.

23. The description that follows applies to the 1.4 million general schedule (white collar) workers. Pay for blue-collar workers is governed by similar procedures based on local wage surveys. Military personnel and other pay systems (for example, foreign service) are tied to the general schedule.

24. Salaries are surveyed in March; pay increases go into effect the following October. The general schedule is divided into eighteen grades, from GS-1 (a messenger, for example) to GS-18 (a director of a major bureau, for example). Within each grade several pay steps provide more-or-less automatic pay increases after certain periods of service.

25. The averages are smoothed by constructing a pay-line curve for the bottom fifteen grades. These curves are then extrapolated to determine pay for grades 16–18.

Table 4-8. Growth in Payroll Costs, General Schedule Federal Employees,
March 1977 to March 1978

Total payroll cost and components of increase	Amount (millions of dollars)	Percent increase
Aggregate annualized salary, March 31, 1977	22,567.5	...
Changes, March 31, 1977, to March 31, 1978		
Increase in employment	93.7[a]	0.4
Statutory pay increase	1,582.4[b]	7.0
Increase in average grade	236.7[c]	1.0
Other	63.8[d]	0.3
Aggregate annualized salary, March 31, 1978	24,544.1	8.8

Sources: U.S. Civil Service Commission, *Pay Structure of the Federal Civil Service, 1977* (Government Printing Office, 1977), table 4 and p. 44; and ibid., *1978* (GPO, 1978), table 4 and p. 7.

a. Assumes that all additional employees earn the mean salary of March 1977.

b. Computed by applying the 7.05 percent pay raise granted on October 1977 to March 1977 salaries for all grades except those that were frozen at a $47,500 salary throughout the period.

c. Estimated from the change in employment by grade from March 1977 to March 1978 weighted by the mean salary by grade in March 1977 net of increase from employment growth.

d. Computed as a residual; includes increases from different distribution of steps within grades and from the interaction of the factors listed.

OTHER SOURCES OF PAYROLL COST INCREASE. While changes in employment and pay schedules account for most of the change in federal payroll costs, other less visible characteristics also play a role.

The most important of these is grade creep—the tendency for the proportion of employees at higher grades to increase over time. An illustration of the costs of grade creep can be derived from a comparison of the general schedule work force between March 1977 and March 1978 (see table 4-8). If all employees on the rolls at the beginning and at the end of the period worked full time, general schedule salaries would rise by 8.8 percent. One percentage point of this increase (over 11 percent) is attributable to the increase in the average grade. This increased average grade in 1977–78 was the largest such increase since 1970,[26] and had it occurred in all federal pay systems (not just the general schedule) it would have increased the federal payrolls more than $600 million.

In principle, step creep arising from more-or-less automatic longevity increases also can push up federal payroll costs. These increases average about 3 percent of salary after a waiting period of one to three years. If all the employees on the general schedule payroll in March 1977 had remained until March 1978, over 60 percent

26. See U.S. Civil Service Commission, *Pay Structure of the Federal Civil Service, March 1978* (GPO, 1978), p. 6.

of them would have received a 3 percent increase, thus driving up payroll costs by nearly 2 percent. Historically, step creep has averaged about 0.5 percent a year. However, in 1977–78, hiring new workers (at low average steps) to replace experienced workers (with high average steps) who quit canceled any step creep.

Payroll costs also are affected by changes in allowances for such employee expenses as travel (part of the salaries-and-expenses budget of an agency), by changes in the proportion of full-time and part-time workers, and by the length of time job slots are left vacant.

THE FAIRNESS OF ABANDONING COMPARABILITY. The administration justified the 1978 federal pay restraint as a necessary one-time demonstration that federal workers would set an example of noninflationary wage behavior for the private sector. The fact, however, that continued restraint below comparability is called for in the following four years suggests that noninflationary behavior is not the only issue. The public thinks federal employees are overpaid—though employees think they are scapegoats. Some perspective on the issue is needed.

First, the administration is indeed proposing more stringent pay restraint for federal workers than its wage guidelines allow in the private sector. Based on private-sector standards, federal employees would be entitled to maximum pay increases of about 6.5 percent, rather than the 5.5 percent proposed. This 6.5 percent pay schedule boost is equivalent to the 7 percent wage guideline after adjusting for expected step creep and for fringe benefit changes as they are treated for private-sector firms under the regulations implementing the guidelines.

Second, it is hard to prove or to refute the assertion that "federal pay is too high." Since July 1969, when comparability was first supposed to have been achieved, consumer prices have risen an average of 6.7 percent a year and private nonagriculture pay has increased an average of 7.3 percent a year. Federal employee groups point out that general schedule pay increases have averaged only 6 percent a year, implying that federal workers are suffering real and relative income losses (see table 4-9). But federal employees hired in 1969 and never promoted would still have received automatic step increases; as a result of which their pay would have risen an annual average 8.1 percent, about 1.4 percentage points a year more than inflation. Federal employees who received promotions to higher

Table 4-9. Changes in Federal and Private Sector Pay and in Consumer Prices,
July 1969 through October 1978
Percent

Component of change	Cumulative increase	Average increase per year
Pay increase for a given general schedule position	71.8	6.0
Step 1 to step 7 pay increase for a person in a given general schedule position	106.1	8.1
Increase in consumer price index	83.0	6.7
Increase in average hourly earnings, private nonagricultural industries	92.6ᵃ	7.3

Sources: *Pay Structure of the Federal Civil Service, March 1978*, pp. 46, 48; and *Economic Report of the President, January 1979*, pp. 224, 239.
a. Adjusted for overtime and interindustry employment shifts.

grades would have done even better, while employees who were at the upper steps of their grade in 1969 (and never promoted) would have done worse.[27] Comparisons indicate that on the average, private sector pay since 1969 has risen about 1 percentage point more a year than the federal general schedule (table 4-9). Unfortunately, this increase includes any upgrading of jobs in the private sector (akin to grade creep in the federal sector) and thus cannot be used as a basis for comparison with a fixed job in the federal general schedule.

Thus it is fair to say that the real income of most federal employees has increased over the past decade, but such increases are probably not out of line with long-run productivity growth in the economy and with what happened in the private sector.

On the other hand comparisons are sometimes made between average federal employee pay and average private sector pay. Average federal pay ($19,000 in 1979) is much higher than that of the average job in the private sector. But much of this difference reflects the fact that there are proportionately more managerial and professional jobs and fewer unskilled jobs in the federal sector than in the private sector. One study shows that differences in qualifications and socioeconomic characteristics between federal employees and private

27. Federal employees at the top of the Civil Service grades fared worst; their annual pay (and that of most executive level federal employees, judges, and congressmen) rose about 34 percent from 1969 to 1978, or 3 percent a year.

employees account for 50 to 60 percent of the difference between federal and private sector salaries.[28] Remaining differences, which are disproportionately large for women and nonwhites, may reflect affirmative action programs or overpayment for clerical jobs.

In any event, the only procedure available to make job-to-job comparisons between federal and private jobs is the comparability procedure outlined previously; while that procedure indicates underpayment of federal workers in 1978, there is widespread suspicion that the procedure may be flawed in several respects—for example, the pay survey does not cover small firms and state and local governments.

Finally, any full assessment of the equitability and long-run consequences of restraints on salaries must also consider what is happening to nonsalary benefits and, most important, to federal pensions. Most federal civilian jobs are not covered by social security.[29] Instead they are covered by staff pension programs. While these programs differ in detail, they are all more generous than the combination of social security and most private pension plans. Federal retirement plans permit employees to retire earlier with full benefits than do most private pensions or social security, and federal pensions are fully indexed (like social security but unlike private pensions). Federal employees, however, do contribute more than social security participants, and their benefits are more heavily taxed than the benefits of private sector workers. The long-run costs to the federal government as an employer are at least 6 percentage points of payroll greater than the pension costs to private sector employers.[30]

It has been argued on the basis of this greater richness of the federal employees' benefit package that their salaries should be held below comparability with private sector pay. In that way, total compensation comparability—equal pay plus fringes—could be achieved.

28. Sharon P. Smith, *Equal Pay in the Public Sector: Fact or Fantasy* (Princeton University, Department of Economics, 1977), p. 63.
29. Many federal employees secure social security coverage by private-sector work before, during, or after their stint with the federal government and collect two pensions in retirement.
30. This estimate refers to the largest federal plan, civil service retirement. It is based on a special study commissioned by the Congressional Budget Office. See *Options for Federal Civil Service Retirement: An Analysis of Costs and Benefit Provisions* (GPO, 1978), especially pp. 28–30.

The administration's budget projections of salary increase are certainly compatible with trading low pay for high fringe benefits.[31] However, it seems premature to hold down salaries in anticipation of a continued generous federal pension plan. The administration is now studying proposals that would put federal civilian employees under social security. Such participation would necessitate the creation of a supplementary federal employees' pension plan; the debate over such a plan cannot escape the issues of the desirability of full indexing, early retirement, and the receipts of double pensions until the system is fully reformed. Only after decisions are made on these issues can salary levels (and employee contribution levels) be meaningfully addressed.

The reader will have to supply his own conclusion for this discussion. What can be said firmly is that the answer to the question of whether federal salaries are too high is far from obvious, and confident declarations on either side of the issue should be avoided.

Continuing Problems in Older Programs

Nine years ago, the first volume of *Setting National Priorities* ended its analysis of a budget that promised "new directions" and "a significantly different set of priorities" with a critical review of four entrenched programs so flawed that they could not conceivably accomplish their publicly declared purposes. The authors of that book remarked that "only as the public widely understands the characteristics of such programs will any President be able to secure the support he needs to achieve reforms."[32]

In a commentary on a budget that President Carter has described as "lean and austere," and that promises to eliminate programs that are unworkable, it is appropriate to revisit the flawed programs of almost a decade ago in order to see how much progress has been made in reforming them; it is important also to consider tax provisions that suffer from flaws as serious as those of the four programs reviewed then.

31. More than one observer has noted that the gap between comparability pay and the administration's 5.5 percent pay raise proposal is in the same ball park as the benefit plan excess.

32. Charles L. Schultze, with Edward K. Hamilton and Allen Schick, *Setting National Priorities: The 1971 Budget* (Brookings Institution, 1970), p. 161.

An Update

The four programs criticized nine years ago accounted for outlays in 1970 of $6.6 billion to $6.8 billion: water resources projects, impact aid, farm price supports, and maritime subsidies. All four of those programs remain in existence. All have been modified by legislation, and the relative importance of some of their objectives has shifted. In 1980 they will account for nearly $6 billion in outlays, a significant real decline. This section reviews the evolution of these programs and briefly sketches some continuing problems.

WATER RESOURCES PROJECTS.* The major criticisms of water resources projects nine years ago were that they were approved even when they yielded low rates of return, that evaluation methods used tended to overstate the rates of return, that irrigation projects served to subsidize high-income farmers, and that flood control projects encouraged the uneconomic location of businesses and residences in floodplains. Furthermore, Congress required the use of budgeting procedures for water resources projects that it prohibited for other programs and that systematically concealed from the public the full project costs.

In the last decade this picture has changed in a number of important respects, but it is qualitatively similar. Services from water resources projects continue to be free or underpriced. For example, at the San Luis irrigation canal and distribution project in the Central Valley of California, the users of irrigation water will repay only an estimated 20 percent of project costs. Beneficiaries of flood control dams pay nothing for the higher capital values produced by them. Benefit-cost analysis has been improved but continues to be criticized for double counting of benefits, for ignoring adverse effects, and for counting as benefits such services as water recreation even if an area is oversupplied with them. In addition, those who oppose water resources projects on environmental grounds have not hesitated to attack them on economic grounds.

One of President Carter's earliest acts was to call for the cessation of planning on nineteen water projects. The political uproar caused by that announcement forced him to back down, but he ended the Ninety-fifth Congress by vetoing the public works appropriation bill.

* Clifford S. Russell assisted in the preparation of this section.

The continuing resolution under which the Corps of Engineers is now operating kills, at least for this year, the seventeen worst projects from the President's point of view.

One of the recent targets of environmentalists, the Tennessee-Tombigbee Waterway, was cited in *Setting National Priorities: The 1971 Budget* to illustrate the "camel's-nose" budget techniques used for water resource projects—only $1 million of the $320 million cost was contained in the 1971 budget. President Carter in the 1980 budget proposes to end this deceptive procedure. He asks Congress to authorize the full cost ($578 million) of the twenty-six new projects he is requesting.[33] The budget also calls attention to the fact that $2.1 billion requested to continue ongoing projects is merely an installment payment; another $19 billion is needed to complete them.

FARM PRICE SUPPORTS. Nine years ago farm price supports went overwhelmingly to farmers with higher than average income, an anomalous feature in a program justified in large part as a device for maintaining agricultural incomes and helping the small farmer to stay in business. Last year, *Setting National Priorities: The 1979 Budget* described the major reform of legislation to support farm incomes enacted in 1977. As that chapter made clear, the new legislation continues to make large and highly variable payments to farmers to insulate them from fluctuations in the prices of agricultural commodities. In addition, it increases farm incomes by keeping prices of certain grains and fibers and other commodities from declining. This approach to maintaining farm incomes not only is inflationary, but also gives most to large producers, those with net farm income of $40,000 a year or more. Recent analysis shows that a strategy of maintaining farm incomes by maintaining prices directs three-fifths of all assistance to farms with sales of more than $100,000 a year, a group with an average farm value of over $500,000 and an average income (including capital gains) of more than $150,000 per year.[34]

The fact that Congress consistently elects to give most assistance to farmers through price enhancement rather than direct

33. The Tennessee-Tombigbee Waterway has still not been started, but it is included in the Corp's 1980 agenda. Its scope has been enlarged and its cost has grown to $1.7 billion. It is now under attack in the courts.

34. Robert W. Crandall, "Federal Government Initiatives to Reduce the Price Level," *Brookings Papers on Economic Activity*, 2:1978, pp. 407–17, reports that average income, including capital gains, for farms with sales of $100,000 a year or more was $197,270 in 1973 and $164,742 in 1976.

payments, with some limit on aid to the largest farms, suggests that Congress seeks to accomplish objectives other than protecting incomes of small farmers. One purpose is to reduce price fluctuations; but the policies it has adopted to accomplish this purpose augment the incomes of all farmers without regard for the size of the farm or the income of the farmer—and do so more generously for large farmers than for small farmers.

The result, not surprisingly, has been a large increase in the price of agricultural land.[35] With a perverse logic the rules for determining target price levels depend in part on estimated costs of production which, in turn, are based in part on the price of agricultural land.

IMPACT AID. Every President since Eisenhower has asked Congress to reduce impact aid—the program of financial aid to school districts on behalf of students whose parents either work or reside on nontaxable federal property. President Carter is continuing this bipartisan and, so far, futile tradition by calling for a reduction in budget authority for the program to $528 million, $317 million below the level necessary to maintain current services. Real expenditures under this program have declined over the last decade, although Congress has broadened the categories of students counted in the formula used for computing aid. Most observers of the program agree that the federal government should provide some help to school districts on behalf of students whose parents both work and reside on federal property. The disagreement has concerned whether districts require aid for students whose parents reside on federal property or work on federal property, but not both. Under present law, for example, a student whose parents live on taxable property inside the school district but work on federal property outside the school district triggers aid to his school district, although he imposes no greater burden than does another student whose parents work for a private employer outside the district.

The key to the popularity of the program today, as it was in 1971, is that the aid under this program goes to school districts represented by all 100 senators and by 415 of the 435 members of the House of Representatives. In 1971, impact aid was often unrelated to the presence in the district of nontaxable federal property (as in the example

35. Crandall reports that the price of farmland approximately doubled in Iowa, Kansas, and Wisconsin between 1972 and 1976 despite declines in the prices of farm products, presumably in anticipation of direct federal aid or of higher prices induced in part by federal policies (ibid.).

above), most of the districts that received funds were negligibly affected by the federal presence, the impact aid formula distorted efforts by states to equalize educational opportunities, and the formula for distributing aid was so constructed that, without any real change in circumstances, districts could acquire or lose eligibility for significant amounts of aid.

At least one of these criticisms remains valid today. Of the 4,192 districts expected to receive some aid in 1979, 2,560 had fewer than 10 percent federally connected children. These districts received about 20 percent of impact aid payments.[36] Only 614 districts were heavily impacted (25 percent or more federally connected children). These districts received less than one-half of federal impact aid payments. On the other hand, Congress in 1974 reduced the degree to which impact aid interferes with state equalization programs.

The prospects for any reduction in impact aid significantly below the current services level of $845 million are uncertain. In 1978 President Carter submitted a proposal to reduce the impact aid program gradually while maintaining aid to school districts with large numbers of federally connected students. Congress paid little attention to these proposals and only after intense lobbying by the administration did the conference committee on the bill to reauthorize the Elementary and Secondary Education Act delete a House-passed proposal that would have required greatly expanded appropriations.

MARITIME SUBSIDIES. The federal government continues to subsidize the American shipbuilding industry and the merchant marine. The cost of these subsidies was $650 million to $750 million in 1971. In 1980 the budget calls for subsidies of $218 million for new construction, $308 million in operating subsidies, and $169 million for Public Health Service hospitals, built and maintained in large part to serve merchant seamen. These figures do not include the estimated $150 million in added costs borne by the U.S. government because of the requirement that government cargoes travel in ships flying the American flag. These subsidies achieve to only a very limited extent their stated purpose of sustaining American shipbuilding capacity and maintaining a fleet of ships available to the Department of Defense in time of war. The U.S. shipbuilding industry produces far more ships a year than the two for which subsidies were given in 1978 or

36. Department of Health, Education, and Welfare, *Impact Aid Two Years Later*, Technical Analysis Report Paper 15 (DHEW, 1978), p. 65.

the thirteen anticipated in 1979. There has been no military emergency recently like that during the Vietnam War; for that reason it is not possible to fault U.S.-flag operators now, as it was a decade ago, for their reluctance to make their subsidized ships available for military cargoes.

The basic structure of these subsidies has remained essentially unchanged for ten years. The same questions raised a decade ago about these programs remain. Is it worth an average of $189 million a year to support the construction of a handful of ships that sustain a very small proportion of shipbuilding capacity? Is it worth $300 million a year in subsidies to U.S.-flag operators (the difference between their operating costs and the costs of foreign vessels), when hundreds of foreign-flag ships are contractually obligated to serve the United States and thousands more ships belong to NATO allies?

Tax Incentives

Congress frequently uses the tax code to achieve its objectives. By providing tax incentives of various kinds—credits, deductions, exemptions—unrelated to conventional definitions of income, Congress can induce individuals and businesses to make expenditures for purposes that otherwise might necessitate public spending or regulation. Since 1976 the budget has contained a special analysis which lists such special tax provisions under "tax expenditures." This term is heuristically useful because it indicates that the objectives of public expenditures can also be accomplished with tax provisions, but it obscures the fact that there is no direct comparability between ordinary government outlays, which measure something the government does, and tax expenditures, which measure something the government does not do (namely, collect certain revenues).

Terminology aside, the compilation of tax expenditures highlights the importance of examining whether direct expenditures or tax provisions are superior devices for achieving public objectives. The 1980 budget lists ninety-two such tax provisions.[37] Because of interactions among the various provisions, the simultaneous repeal of all those tax provisions would increase federal revenues more than the sum of the revenue changes from repealing each one alone.

Many of the provisions are controversial because observers disagree about whether they are efficient devices for achieving their

37. See appendix B.

stated objectives. For example, some supporters of the exclusion from taxation of 60 percent of long-term capital gains hold that this provision is an effective spur to saving and capital formation; opponents hold that these objectives can be achieved more efficiently in other ways and that the capital gains exclusion disproportionately benefits the well-to-do. The repeal of this exclusion would increase federal revenues in 1980 by $10.8 billion.

In a number of cases, however, tax provisions are demonstrably inequitable or inefficient devices for achieving their stated objectives. Such provisions remain in the code because they accomplish unstated objectives or for a variety of other reasons. Their effects may be poorly understood. The value of the tax provision may have become incorporated in the prices of assets that have changed hands, so that the repeal of the tax provision would inflict capital losses on current holders. More generally, the repeal of any tax provision will increase the tax liability of some taxpayers, even if Congress returns the full additional revenue from the repeal through lower tax rates; in accord with the principle that government actions should directly and palpably injure no one,[38] such changes in the tax code are avoided.

Among the tax provisions that are hard to justify on any grounds are the following:

DOMESTIC INTERNATIONAL SALES CORPORATIONS (DISCS). Under this provision of the internal revenue code, exporters may set up separate corporations to act as agents to handle exports of commodities and to receive profits from such sales. A portion of such profits are exempt from taxation until they are returned to the parent corporation. This provision will reduce federal revenues by an estimated $1.3 billion in 1980. Its purpose is to encourage exports. A Treasury Department report indicated that, under the best of circumstances, it is a highly inefficient device for achieving this objective.[39] Under the system of floating exchange rates, which went into effect two years after Congress authorized DISCs, however, much of the benefit of any increase in exports accrues to DISCs at the expense of other exporters or investors, for whom DISCs make the exchange rate less favorable.

President Carter proposed the gradual termination of DISCs as

38. See Charles L. Schultze, *The Public Use of Private Interest* (Brookings Institution, 1977), p. 23.
39. *The President's 1978 Tax Program: Detailed Description and Supporting Analysis of the Proposals, January 30, 1978*, pp. 275–76.

part of the tax reform bill he submitted to Congress in 1977, but Congress took no action on this proposal.

SOCIAL SECURITY BENEFITS. Under a ruling of the Treasury Department in 1941, social security benefits are not subject to taxation. This ruling applies a different rule to social security than is applied to private pensions. Taxpayers do not have to pay taxes on that part of private pensions that represents repayment of contributions they made out of income already subject to tax. They must pay tax on the portion of private pensions that their employer paid or that represents the interest earnings on contributions by themselves or their employers. The logic of this rule is that taxpayers should have to pay taxes once, but not twice, on private pension income.

Equal taxes on employees and employers support the social security system.[40] However, workers typically receive far more in benefits than the combined taxes on themselves and their employers; the difference is the implicit interest earned on these contributions. Under the principle that applies to private pensions, social security recipients would pay taxes on all of their benefits except the portion that represents the repayment of their own payroll taxes. For an average retiree, 85 percent or more of benefits should be taxable. The inclusion of all social security benefits in adjusted gross income would increase federal revenues by $6.4 billion in 1980.

Not only is this exclusion contrary to the policy applied to other forms of pension income, but it also violates common notions of equity. For a taxpayer in the 14 percent bracket, a $100 tax-exempt benefit is worth as much as a $116 taxable benefit. But for an aged couple in the 54 percent bracket (which requires income of $67,000), a $100 tax exempt benefit is worth $217. The exclusion of social security from taxation is worth nothing until the combination of social security and other income exceeds $4,300 for single persons and $7,400 for couples, the income levels at which aged individuals and couples become subject to taxation in 1980. If they have deductions—such as for medical expenses or property taxes—the taxable income level is correspondingly higher. The exclusion of social security is most valuable for taxpayers with substantial amounts of income from sources other than social security. Furthermore, because the social security earnings test denies benefits to persons

40. The self-employed pay tax at a rate higher than the employee rate but lower than the combined employee-employer rate.

under the age of seventy-two years (seventy years, beginning in 1982) with sizable earnings, such outside income typically must come from investments of considerably greater total value.

MUNICIPAL BOND INTEREST. Interest paid on state and local bonds is tax exempt. As a result the federal government will collect $7.7 billion less in 1980 than it would if interest on currently outstanding bonds were taxable. Tax exemption enables states and localities to sell bonds with lower yields than would be demanded if the interest were taxable. The difference between the yields of taxable and nontaxable bonds varies over time. In early 1979 the yield on municipal bonds was about two-thirds that on taxable bonds of equivalent quality. That means equivalent tax-exempt and taxable bonds yield the same after-tax return to an investor in the 33 percent tax bracket. For taxpayers in higher tax brackets, exempt bonds yield more after tax than do equivalent taxable bonds, because tax savings from the exemption rise with the tax bracket.

A Treasury Department study indicates that the federal government could offer a credit to states and localities that issue taxable bonds sufficient to make them cheaper than tax-exempt bonds, tax the interest on such bonds, and come out ahead—the added tax revenue would exceed the cost of the credit. Some municipalities fear that provision of such a credit and issuance of such bonds would undermine their legal claim that the interest on municipal bonds is constitutionally immune from taxation, but these legal fears are not well-founded. In 1978, President Carter recommended the adoption of a taxable-bond option along with a federal credit of 35 percent of the interest paid in 1979 and 1980 and 40 percent thereafter. The failure of Congress to offer states and municipalities an option to issue taxable bonds with an interest subsidy is hard to understand.

Summary

The most important question to raise about the 1980 domestic budget is whether the rhetoric of restraint and the promised savings are a one-time exercise or constitute a sustainable commitment to curtail the role of the federal government. In some respects, the 1980 budget does look like a one-time effort because much of the spending slowdown is from reductions that cannot be repeated; the most notable are the program cuts tied to completion of the recovery from the 1974–75 recession.

In most respects the 1980 budget hints at but does not engage in a basic debate about the domestic role of the federal government. The proposals to curtail certain social security benefits suggest the need for such a debate and for a discussion of the proper role and the appropriate cost of social insurance. The administration's proposal to control hospital costs should be interpreted in the same light. Similarly, the change in regulatory policy with respect to railroads represents an important and controversial shift in long-standing policy. Furthermore, the projections of expenditures for 1981 and 1982 promise further reductions in the proportion of gross national product absorbed by the federal government, although the growth of real nondefense expenditures is projected to resume.

Nor is the budget devoid of calls for increased expenditures in selected areas. Perhaps the most notable are the renewed, although reduced, commitments to welfare reform and to a national health plan.

The vision projected by the 1980 budget is one of a federal sector that expands to deal with growing social problems and military challenges, but one that grows less rapidly than the rest of the economy because of curtailments in the resources devoted to a number of existing programs. Inflation assists in this curtailment by permitting the budget to reduce program commitments through the simple expedient of asking for the same amount of money Congress appropriated last year. This tactic avoids futile and divisive debates about the desirability of the programs while it slowly reduces them.

The budget projections show that federal spending can be held in check if major new initiatives in the nondefense area are avoided. The test of the congressional mood to cut spending will come when it addresses the dozens of specific proposed reductions of programs dear to powerful interest groups.

CHAPTER FIVE

The Defense Budget

THOMAS A. DINE, JOHN C. BAKER, ROBERT P. BERMAN,
G. PHILIP HUGHES, *and* WILLIAM P. MAKO

THE DEFENSE BUDGET proposed by the President for 1980 continues a pattern of real spending increases that began in fiscal year 1976. Budget authority of $135.5 billion is proposed for the Department of Defense and $3 billion for the Department of Energy. Outlays of $122.7 billion are estimated for 1980 for the Department of Defense, with an additional $3 billion for defense-related activities in the Department of Energy. The commitment the President made at the May 1977 meeting of NATO to increase defense spending by 3 percent is interpreted to apply to the total outlays of the Defense Department. Under official assumptions, which include favorable congressional action on supplemental requests for the 1979 budget, the outlay total of $122.7 billion would represent an increase of 3.1 percent above the 1979 total in constant 1980 dollars. Moreover, budget authority is projected to increase by 1.7 percent in constant 1980 dollars. The accumulation of budget authority increases since 1976 and in the next few years implies a real increase of about 3 percent in Defense Department outlays for each year through 1984 (table 5-1).

These continuing increases in defense outlays reflect a major shift in national priorities. Given the limit on the federal budget inspired by strong voter sentiment, increases in defense spending come at the

John Steinbruner, James Shufelt, and Peter Fitzwilliam contributed to this chapter. Penelope S. Harpold provided research assistance.

Table 5-1. Budget Authority and Outlays of the Department of Defense, Constant and Current Dollars, Fiscal Years 1976–84
Dollar amounts in billions

	Budget authority		Outlays	
Fiscal year	Amount	Percent change from previous year	Amount	Percent change from previous year
	Constant 1980 dollars			
1976	124.7	4.2	114.6	−3.2
1977	130.9	4.9	116.5	1.7
1978	131.8	0.7	117.4	0.8
1979	133.2	1.1	119.1	1.4
1980	135.5	1.7	122.7	3.0
1981	138.4	2.1	126.4	3.0
1982	141.5	2.2	130.5	3.2
1983	145.9	3.1	134.4	2.9
1984	150.5	3.2	138.4	2.9
	Current dollars			
1976	95.8	11.2	87.9	3.5
1977	108.2	12.9	95.6	8.8
1978	116.5	7.7	103.0	7.7
1979	125.7	7.9	111.9	8.6
1980	135.5	7.8	122.7	9.7
1981	145.7	7.5	133.7	8.9
1982	155.7	6.9	144.9	8.4
1983	166.8	7.1	155.5	7.3
1984	177.7	6.5	165.7	6.6

Sources: *Department of Defense Annual Report, Fiscal Year 1980* (1979); and data provided by the Office of the Assistant Secretary of Defense (Comptroller), March 1979.

cost of other programs (see chapter 4). This unusually sharp turn in political commitment has been stimulated by widely shared perceptions of potentially dangerous increases in Soviet military capability and a drift in world political affairs that is unfavorable for the United States. The Ford administration emphasized these considerations when it turned the defense budget around in fiscal 1976. Improvements in the technical capability of Soviet strategic missiles and the extraordinary turbulence in the Middle East have intensified the concern of Congress and the administration about the U.S. defense capability.

Although defense budget increases provide a means of stating a serious national commitment, by themselves they do not necessarily produce increases in real military capability. The effectiveness of defense spending depends on how resources are allocated in the defense budget, and at the moment that is a more important question than marginal percentage increases or decreases. The most significant problem in contemporary U.S. defense policy, moreover, does not involve budget choices in the first instance but rather clarification of the basic military purposes of U.S. forces. To produce the kind of military capability that can respond to challenges around the world requires clarity of purpose and appropriate allocation of defense resources.

At this point in their development, the basic military purposes of U.S. forces are in serious dispute. In part this is true because defense programs are becoming more complicated and are changing in character. The primary potential enemy—the Soviet Union—is stronger, and the occasions for potential conflict are more diverse. Well-established U.S. military programs, which are the result of three decades of investment, inevitably generate demands for additions to military capabilities along favored, familiar lines. The range of choice for further investment provided within these traditional programs does not necessarily correspond to the most urgent national security needs.

The 1980 budget on the surface does not represent a sharp departure from previous defense budgets. As can be seen from table 5-2, its pattern of allocation across basic military purposes shows orderly continuity with the past, and the five-year defense plan projects an orderly progression to 1984. In the struggle over the military budget, however, serious questions have prompted new lines of thought that might well lead to basic changes beginning soon enough to alter the course of the current five-year plan. It is too early in this process of transition, if that is what it is, to define desirable reallocations of the defense effort in detail, but it is not too early to expose the issues that need to be resolved.

These issues are encountered in four areas of military activity: the strategic deterrent, theater nuclear weapons in Europe, ground force and tactical air force operations on the European central front, and general purpose naval deployments.

Table 5-2. Distribution of Total Obligational Authority by Category, Constant and Current Dollars, Fiscal Years 1976, 1980, and 1984

Billions

Category	1976	1980	1984
	Constant 1980 dollars		
Strategic nuclear forces[a]	24.8	25.8	28.6
General purpose forces[b]	85.9	93.2	103.3
Mobility forces[c]	3.5	4.4	4.9
Retired pay	9.8	11.5	13.9
Support to other nations	0.3	0.6	0.4
Total	124.7	135.5	150.5
	Current dollars		
Strategic nuclear forces[a]	19.0	25.8	33.8
General purpose forces[b]	66.2	93.2	122.0
Mobility forces[c]	3.1	4.4	5.8
Retired pay	7.3	11.5	15.7
Support to other nations	0.3	0.6	0.4
Total	95.9	135.5	177.7

Sources: Authors' estimates derived from data provided by the Office of the Assistant Secretary of Defense (Comptroller), March 1979.

a. The costs of strategic nuclear forces are the sum of the following portions of strategic forces programs: 50 percent of the intelligence and communications program; 10 percent of the National Guard and Reserve program; 40 percent of the research and development program; and a percentage of the three support programs—central supply and maintenance; training, medical, other general personnel activities (excluding retired pay); and administration—which varies each year in direct proportion to the ratio of operating costs between strategic and all other forces.

b. The costs of baseline general purpose forces were taken as Department of Defense total obligational authority less the cost of strategic nuclear forces, strategic mobility forces, support to other nations, and retired pay.

c. The costs of strategic mobility forces are the sum of the airlift and sealift programs, 5 percent of the intelligence and communications program, 5 percent of the National Guard and Reserve program, 1 percent of the research and development program, and a variable percentage of the three support programs.

Strategic Forces

For 1980 the Carter administration proposes $10.8 billion of direct spending for U.S. strategic force programs. This is a $2.2 billion increase over the previous year's appropriation and supplemental request and represents nearly a 17 percent real increase. If most of the major strategic weapon programs now under development are approved for deployment in the next few years, by the mid-1980s funding for these programs will increase dramatically as a series of new weapon systems simultaneously enter into advanced development and production.

This renewed emphasis on strategic forces stems primarily from two factors. First, as in the late 1950s and early 1960s, the United

States is now entering a cycle of across-the-board modernization of its strategic forces. These new, more advanced, and more expensive weapon systems will increasingly replace most of the current intercontinental ballistic missiles (ICBMs), submarine-launched ballistic missiles (SLBMs), and strategic bombers during the 1985–95 period. Spending for the development and production of most of these new systems is already well under way. Second, while the second round of strategic arms limitation talks (SALT II) will be valuable in reducing the uncertainties with which defense planners must cope, it will not eliminate the Soviet Union's capability to threaten the survivability of American strategic forces. Some of this increased spending for U.S. strategic force programs could be moderated—but not eliminated—if the SALT II agreement is signed and ratified by the United States and the USSR.

The 1980 budget request for strategic forces reflects the U.S. commitment to provide for a moderate level of modernization in the near term and to add new forms of strategic capability in the long term. (Table 5-3 gives estimated costs of major strategic programs for the five-year defense plan.) Current deployment programs primarily seek to improve the effectiveness and flexibility of the so-called triad of ICBMs, SLBMs, and strategic bombers that constitute U.S. strategic forces. For instance, guidance improvements have been made to the 550 Minuteman III ICBMs carrying multiple independently targetable reentry vehicles (MIRVs), and the higher-yield MK-12A warheads will be placed on 300 of these missiles in the early 1980s.

The budget request also includes full funding for the construction of the eighth Trident (*Ohio*-class) nuclear-powered ballistic missile submarine (SSBN), which was deferred last year owing to payment problems between the contractor and the navy. The first of these larger and faster SSBNs will become operational in 1981. The Tridents will carry twenty-four launchers each for the Trident I SLBM, which has a range of 4,000 nautical miles. This missile is currently scheduled to be retrofitted on twelve of the older Poseidon SSBNs, the first of which will be deployed in October 1979. The longer range of the Trident I missiles will expand the potential patrol area available to U.S. SSBNs, thereby improving their survivability against enemy antisubmarine forces.

The triad's aircraft and air-launched missile components are also undergoing modernization. Advance funding for the production of

Table 5-3. Cost of Major Strategic Development and Acquisition Programs, Fiscal Years 1980–84[a]

Total obligational authority in millions of constant fiscal 1980 dollars

Strategic force	Program cost					Total, 1980–84
	1980	1981	1982	1983	1984	
Offensive	**4,464**	**4,613**	**5,140**	**6,460**	**8,745**	**29,422**
Improved Minuteman ICBM	135	150	50	15	0	350
MX mobile ICBM[b]	675	1,230	1,500	2,300	2,600	8,305
Trident submarine[c]	1,575	1,315	1,220	1,200	2,360	7,670
Trident I SLBM	861	660	735	800	630	3,686
Trident II SLBM[b]	41	120	540	950	1,340	2,991
B-52 modifications	657	550	500	500	450	2,657
Air-launched cruise missile	475	490	420	365	315	2,065
Cruise missile carrier and missiles[b,d]	40	75	150	300	1,000	1,565
New manned bomber[b,e]	5	23	25	30	50	133
Defensive	**418**	**441**	**344**	**346**	**348**	**1,897**
Antiballistic missile research	228	230	232	234	236	1,160
Space defense	81	101	n.a.	n.a.	n.a.	n.a.
Civil defense[f]	109	110	112	112	112	555

Command and control	306	279	250	280	235	1,350
Advanced airborne command post	193	190	150	130	120	783
Extremely low frequency submarine communications program[b,g]	14	15	40	90	55	214
Navy submarine communication aircraft	99	74	60	60	60	353
Total	5,188	5,333	5,734	7,086	9,328	32,669

Source: Figures for 1980 are based on information in *Department of Defense Annual Report, Fiscal Year 1980*; Department of Defense, *Program Acquisition Costs by Weapon System* (1979); and data from a statement by Vice Admiral Charles H. Griffiths before the Senate Committee on Armed Services, February 1, 1979. Figures for 1981–84 are authors' estimates.

n.a. Not available.

a. The weapon systems in this table include most of the largest and most important U.S. strategic force programs. In the 1980 budget these programs will amount to over two-thirds of the total Department of Defense request for funds for research, development, and procurement in the strategic forces category.

b. No decision has been made to procure these weapon systems at this time. Figures in this table are based on publicly available estimates of the numbers and costs of these systems. The initial operational capability for these programs is assumed to be as follows: an MX missile in a mobile basing system, 1986; Trident II SLBM, 1989; wide-body cruise missile carrier aircraft with improved air-launched cruise missiles, 1987; and a new manned bomber, 1992.

c. The current five-year naval shipbuilding program includes six Trident submarines. Calculations in this table include the costs of Trident I missiles for these submarines and for certain Poseidon submarines.

d. Assumes a program of 100 wide-body aircraft and includes the cost of additional numbers of an improved air-launched cruise missile.

e. Assumes a program of 120 new manned penetrating bombers based on a new, advanced strategic bomber.

f. Not to be included in the Defense Department budget after fiscal 1980.

g. Assumes a decision to deploy and be operational by 1984.

the air-launched cruise missile (ALCM), which will be deployed on existing B-52G bombers, is being received. Operational deployment of the first squadron of B-52G aircraft equipped with ALCMs is planned for December 1982.

In accord with the 1972 treaty limiting antiballistic missiles (ABMs), U.S. strategic ABM research programs are maintained at relatively modest levels of funding. The minimal U.S. bomber defenses will be strengthened over the next few years by the addition of six new airborne warning and control system (AWACS) aircraft. In addition, various improvements to the ground-based radar system are under way. For the time being the Carter administration has deferred procuring a new interceptor aircraft for continental air defense, preferring instead to assign some interceptors of the Tactical Air Command to serve in the event of a crisis.

Finally, substantial funds are continuing to be allocated to improvements in the U.S. strategic command and control system as well as in the early warning and space defense systems. Of special importance is the planned acquisition of six E-4B advanced airborne command post aircraft that are intended to provide survivable command centers in the event of nuclear war. Numerous programs seek to improve the capability for warning of enemy missile and bomber attacks and for assessing them. The United States is also working on ways to make its satellites less vulnerable to enemy attacks and to destroy enemy satellites in the event of war.

In the short run, current strategic force modernization programs will incrementally improve the existing force structure at modest costs. But in the long run the new strategic forces now being considered for deployment in the second half of the 1980s raise fundamental questions about U.S. strategic doctrine, spending, and force-level priorities.

The Purpose and Missions of U.S. Strategic Forces

The purpose of the strategic forces is to provide the United States and its allies with a credible deterrent against both a nuclear attack and political coercion by hostile states. Thus U.S. strategic forces have been assigned three military missions: assured destruction, escalation control, and damage limitation.

The *assured destruction* mission continues to be the foundation of U.S. strategic deterrence. It requires the United States to maintain sufficient forces to be capable of countering a nuclear attack with a retaliatory strike that would inflict an unacceptable degree of damage on the Soviet Union's urban-industrial base. Some observers doubt that the United States has the capability to effectively carry out this mission—a doubt prompted by the USSR's civil defense effort. The U.S. capability to perform the mission, however, is accepted by most defense analysts.

Similarly, despite some debate over the scope and definition of *escalation control,* most analysts agree that some degree of flexibility and selectivity is desirable in the employment of strategic forces. Improvements in the strategic command and control system and in targeting plans could make the United States capable of responding more effectively to less than all-out nuclear attacks, thus enhancing its ability to terminate such attacks. A new part of this flexibility mission appears to be the explicit requirement to withhold a certain portion of U.S. strategic forces as a strategic reserve.

Controversy over U.S. strategic weapons policy concerns the final mission—*damage limitation.* This mission calls for U.S. offensive and defensive strategic forces to attempt to limit the amount of damage the Soviet Union could impose on the United States and its allies by limiting attacks to the adversary's military forces only. The tension between various U.S. strategic objectives, such as essential equivalence and strategic stability, is manifested to the greatest degree in the debates concerning the role of U.S. forces in damage limitation.

Some analysts, primarily arms control proponents, argue that the United States should only deploy strategic forces that enhance strategic stability between the United States and the Soviet Union. Such forces would seek to maintain their survivability without threatening the survivability of the Soviet Union's deterrent forces, thus promoting greater stability between the two superpowers in times of crisis. Those holding this viewpoint also generally see the requirement for essential equivalence between U.S. and USSR strategic forces as meaning an overall balance of various strategic weapon capabilities.

Another set of analysts, however, are more concerned about relative imbalances between the United States and the USSR. These analysts strictly interpret the requirement for essential equivalence, focusing on specific types of strategic capabilities. Consequently they worry that asymmetries in the ICBM capabilities of the Soviet Union and the United States could have serious consequences. They particularly fear that the USSR may gain certain political and military advantages if it acquires a disarming, countersilo capability in the 1980s that the United States cannot effectively thwart. This viewpoint is less sensitive to arms race stability and is more concerned with matching or exceeding the USSR in all major strategic capabilities so that strategic stability and a credible political deterrent can be achieved.

Consequently the primary strategic force question is whether the United States should offset only the Soviet capability to threaten the U.S. ICBM force or should also acquire a matching capability against USSR hardened targets, including ICBM silos. In short, how much and what kind of hard-target kill capability does the United States want in the future? How should it deal with the potential threat to the survivability of its silo-based ICBM force?

The Carter administration evidently has no firm answers to these questions at this time, but it is aware of the tension caused by a desire for strategic stability on the one hand and pressure to prevent Soviet acquisition of an advantage in strategic capability on the other. In the annual report of the Defense Department the administration has declared a "countervailing strategy" by which the United States should make certain that it has the capability to respond to any attack "in such a way that the enemy could have no expectation of achieving any rational objective, no illusion of making any gain without offsetting losses."[1] Under this strategy the United States will maintain the capability to (1) cover hard targets, such as silos, command bunkers, and nuclear weapon storage sites, with at least one reliable warhead capable of destroying the target; and (2) have the retargeting capability necessary to permit reallocation of these warheads to a smaller number of hard targets or to other types of targets such as Soviet general purpose forces and their support elements.[2] Furthermore, U.S. strategic forces must continue to be capable of attacking urban-industrial targets. Another part of this strategy is the maintenance of a "strategic nuclear reserve," which has not been defined.

In essence, the annual report implies a commitment to a second-strike counterforce capability while taking pains to distinguish this from a disarming first-strike capability against the Soviet strategic forces. A second-strike counterforce capability would give the United States the option to effectively target Soviet strategic and conven-

1. *Department of Defense Annual Report, Fiscal Year 1980*, p. 77.
2. Ibid., p. 78.

tional military forces that would be held in reserve. How the administration intends to acquire this capability and how the countervailing strategy would specifically affect U.S. strategic force decisions are not explained in the report.

New Strategic Force Capabilities

A number of important strategic arms decisions face the Carter administration and Congress in the next two years. Those that will have the most important arms control and fiscal implications concern (1) the MX missile and its mobile basing structure, (2) the Trident II missile and the Trident submarine, and (3) the future bomber force.

MX MISSILE AND MOBILE BASING. Despite the uncertainties involved in a large-scale countersilo attack, the Defense Department has decided that it is necessary to deploy a new ICBM that would be mobile and more survivable. A final decision on the type of missile-basing system may be made by late 1979, and a production decision for the MX missile system could possibly be made in mid-1983.

Two basing arrangements for the MX are currently under consideration: the vertical shelter basing concept and an airmobile ICBM concept. The vertical shelter would rely on the deployment of about 4,500 alternate shelters to exhaust the attacking Soviet warheads; the airmobile would rely on short takeoff and landing aircraft for dispersal until the missiles were air-launched. The air force prefers the lower-cost vertical silo arrangement, which would also make fewer demands on the accuracy of the new ICBM, would require far less support, and would not depend on warning of an attack for its survivability. Others in the Carter administration favor the airmobile system because of its greater compatibility with the SALT verification requirements.

Outside the administration a general debate has arisen concerning the need for and desirability of deploying the MX and its mobile system. Critics have emphasized the destabilizing character of the potent counterforce capability of the MX and the SALT verification problems the basing system would create. Many of these critics desire a shift toward more survivable bomber and SLBM forces.

Proponents of the MX system have emphasized its importance as a solution to the growing vulnerability of the U.S. ICBM force. They also stress the political and military need to prevent the USSR from attaining an unmatched capability in the form of large numbers of highly accurate ICBM warheads.

TRIDENT II MISSILE AND TRIDENT SUBMARINE. Another important future weapon system decision is whether the United States should continue to produce the large and expensive Trident submarine and to develop and deploy the Trident II missile. The substantial cost of each Trident submarine, currently $1.4 billion, has led the Defense Department to consider the cost-effectiveness of an SSBN-X once again.[3] Even if promising, such a lower-cost submarine would not become available until fiscal 1984, by which time 11 Tridents with 264 SLBM launchers are projected to be deployed or under construction. Consequently the United States faces the question of whether to procure a longer-range, large throw-weight Trident II missile for these submarines.

Current defense planning calls for the Trident II to be designed with increased accuracy in order to be effective against all types of USSR targets. A new, longer-range SLBM with sufficient accuracy to destroy hard targets will be expensive, possibly costing about $23 billion in fiscal 1980 dollars. It will also be the first time an SLBM has had such a capability, thereby raising important questions about the nature of the SLBM force and its future implications for strategic stability.

An important issue concerns the projected drop-off in U.S. SLBM launchers in the late 1980s and early 1990s. At this time Poseidon submarines will reach their appointed retirement age, but not enough Trident submarines will be ready to replace them. One solution to this decrease in the number of SLBMs available in the future is to adopt a more flexible retirement policy for the Poseidons. The navy could retain some Poseidons beyond their projected twenty-five-year service life, thereby postponing and mitigating the SLBM drop-off. This policy move could be assisted by the adoption of more flexible deployment practices for the older SSBNs.

THE FUTURE OF THE BOMBER FORCES. A final important question concerns the type of bomber force the United States will maintain through the late 1980s and early 1990s. The present conception of future bomber force requirements is unclear. After canceling the B-1 bomber, the Carter administration initially portrayed the B-52G

3. In the mid-1970s the navy considered and rejected the idea of this smaller SSBN based on the Narwhal submarine design.

Table 5-4. Total Acquisition Costs, Strategic Offensive Forces, Fiscal Years 1980–95
Millions of constant 1980 dollars

	Acquisition costs	
System	Fiscal 1980–95	Total
Land-based missile forces		
Improved Minuteman ICBM	350	980
MX mobile ICBM[a]	20,800	21,500
Sea-based missile forces		
Trident submarine[b]	16,000	21,600
Trident I missile	3,700	8,500
Trident II missile[c]	17,500	17,500
Strategic bomber forces		
Air-launched cruise missile	2,550	3,750
Cruise missile carrier and associated cruise missiles[d]	14,775	14,800
New manned bomber[e]	10,000	10,000
Advanced strategic air-launched missile[f]	2,450	2,600
Total	88,125	101,230

Source: Authors' estimates based on Defense Department statements and congressional testimony.

a. Estimates based on current projections of a force of 200 MX missiles in a multiple shelter basing system.

b. Official U.S. Navy figures for the cost of the Trident submarine program include only the number of Trident submarines and Trident I missiles in the current five-year defense plan. Under the current five-year shipbuilding program, this would be thirteen Trident submarines and associated missiles. Defense Department officials have stated that the United States will eventually procure at least twenty Trident submarines. The figures listed here project the total acquisition cost of a force of twenty Trident submarines and associated Trident I missiles for these submarines as well as the installation of twelve Poseidon submarines with Trident I missiles. A twenty-ship fleet including some lower cost SSBN-X submarines could cost about $18 billion.

c. Figures are estimates of the cost of a sufficient number of Trident II missiles and spares for a force of twenty Trident submarines. They are based on a Trident II missile of modest accuracy using conventional guidance techniques. A missile system with a high accuracy, terminal guidance system could total about $23 billion.

d. Estimates assume a force of 100 wide-body aircraft carrying seventy-five advanced air-launched cruise missiles each. A smaller force of fifty such cruise missile carrier aircraft and associated missiles could cost about $9 billion.

e. Costs are based on a force of 120 advanced strategic bombers. A similar number of less advanced penetrating bombers derived from the FB-111 program is estimated to cost about $6 billion.

f. This missile would begin to replace in 1989 the short-range attack missile currently carried by U.S. strategic bombers. A variant of it would be used as a bomber defense missile against Soviet air defense forces.

bombers as serving exclusively as cruise missile carriers. Now these bombers are characterized as both standoff cruise missile launch platforms and penetrating bombers that will carry gravity bombs or short-range attack missiles in their bomb bays. This has resulted in stretching out the procurement of the number of ALCMs required for the B-52 bombers. Moreover, the deployment of a wide-body cruise missile carrier force would be an expensive proposition (see table 5-4), although it could become operational in the late 1980s because of the availability of wide-body aircraft and the previous production of air-launched cruise missiles.

There is the further issue of whether (and when) the United States should procure a new manned penetrating bomber to replace the B-52s as USSR air defenses are upgraded. Administration officials currently project a requirement for this new bomber in the early 1990s; the air force, however, is openly pushing for its procurement by the late 1980s. Proponents of a new manned penetrating bomber contend that a mixed force of standoff and penetrating bombers would prevent the USSR from maximizing its air defense resources to counter any single type of attacking bomber force.

U.S. Strategic Planning for the Long Term

U.S. strategic force policy has proceeded on an expedient, piecemeal basis. A number of increasingly important factors give rise to the need for a longer-term, more coherent plan in which the purpose and structure of the strategic forces are directly linked. Among these factors are the four discussed below.

STRATEGIC THREAT ASSESSMENT. One important influence on the general direction of U.S. strategic force development has been the way American defense planners view the threat posed by Soviet strategic forces. In the annual defense reports to Congress and in other official statements, the USSR is perceived as being engaged in an effort to develop and deploy various weapon systems aimed at neutralizing the effectiveness of the U.S. strategic forces.

The Soviet strategic threat that currently most concerns many defense planners is the projected deployment of large numbers of highly accurate MIRV warheads on the USSR's new ICBMs. Official U.S. estimates conclude that such a force could theoretically provide the USSR with sufficient capability to destroy most of the American ICBM silos by the early 1980s. This possibility has led many American analysts to worry that in a future crisis the USSR might be tempted to seek some type of political advantage by threatening the U.S. land-based missile force with a limited nuclear strike.

The USSR's countersilo capability is seen as the most serious threat. While Soviet air defenses are projected to improve in the future, U.S. cruise missile technology is expected to stay significantly ahead of Soviet efforts. Finally, official statements often portray Soviet antisubmarine warfare (ASW) forces as oriented toward strategic ASW against U.S. missile submarines, despite the limited effectiveness of Soviet forces at the present time.

The official threat assessment is accepted by most defense analysts, with some variations. Some find the USSR civil defense program worrisome. Others are concerned that regional Soviet systems, such as the Backfire bomber, would be used for intercontinental strikes against the United States.

Despite the general acceptance of the official threat assessment, however, there are some indications that the major threats posed by the Soviet strategic forces may be different from those familiar to most defense analysts. In the past most attention has been paid to the survivability and effectiveness of U.S. strategic weapon systems. Of even more importance may have been Soviet interest in developing a capability to effectively neutralize the U.S. strategic forces by disabling the American command, control, and communications system. Thus before the United States commits itself to major weapon programs in the future it should examine more closely the possibility that vital U.S. command and control systems may be more vulnerable to a Soviet nuclear attack than the strategic weapons these systems direct. In particular, this raises questions about all mobile strategic systems including SSBNs and mobile ICBMs.

The assumption that the USSR is intent on developing a capability for undertaking a limited nuclear strike against the U.S. land-based missile force is questionable. One reason is that Soviet military writing contains little to encourage the belief that the USSR finds Western conceptions of limited strategic strikes either desirable or feasible. Second, unlike U.S. ICBMs, Soviet ICBMs have a predominant and demanding role in the strategic force structure. Because USSR strategic land-based missiles must strike a wide range of targets, not merely U.S. ICBM silos, the design of Soviet ICBMs is distinctive.

Another alternative assessment is that current Soviet ASW forces are given the primary task of protecting their own strategic submarines from superior Western ASW forces. Consequently the real threat to U.S. submarine survivability in the future is likely to come from unconventional means of ASW detection such as satellite-based or airborne sensors. This raises the question of whether an alternative to the large Trident submarine might better serve as a hedge against such ASW developments. Furthermore, the Soviet Union's concept of actively defending its SSBNs by using conventional naval forces might be worth future American consideration as the United States searches for better ways to ensure the long-term survivability of its SSBN force.

STRATEGIC STABILITY CONSIDERATIONS. It is not clear that American defense planners have adequately thought through the effect of their present strategic arms programs on strategic stability. To some degree U.S. conceptions of stability appear to be based on the presumption that Soviet non-ICBM forces are survivable to the same degree as American SSBNs and bombers. Closer examination shows that the Soviet SSBN force has not been as invulnerable to ASW threats as the U.S. SSBN force has been, a weakness that has compelled the Soviet navy to make fundamental changes in its mission structure in order to improve the survivability of its submarine force. Furthermore, Soviet bombers do not play the significant role that U.S. bombers do, nor are they kept on high alert.

Another tendency in the United States has been to ignore the effect that the acquisition of a new SLBM with a hard-target capability could have when added to a similar land-based capability. Given the projected acquisition of a similar hard-target kill capability for both the MX and the Trident II missiles, the USSR could reasonably perceive the combined capability of these two systems as a substantial new threat to its land-based forces.

FUTURE AFFORDABILITY. With a substantial increase in strategic spending, fiscal 1980 marks the beginning of a sustained and heavy investment of new funds for strategic force modernization. The total future cost of these weapon programs for the MX and its mobile basing system, the Trident submarine and Trident I missiles, and the ALCM for the B-52G cruise missile carrier is about $43 billion in constant fiscal 1980 dollars. The three new strategic weapon programs under consideration by the Defense Department—cruise missile carrier aircraft and associated ALCMs, a new manned bomber, and Trident II SLBMs—could cost an additional $42.3 billion (see table 5-4).

In light of the projected operational deployments for both the current and new strategic programs during the late 1980s and early 1990s, these strategic systems will require even higher levels of real growth in the future. The continuing production of many of the currently projected programs such as the MX system and Trident submarines through the last half of the 1980s will coincide with the increasingly expensive advanced development–initial procurement phase of a number of new weapon systems such as the Trident II and the new strategic bomber. The peak in this overlap of expenditures for several current and new strategic weapon programs is likely to occur about 1986 if the United States adheres to its present projected deployment schedules for these systems.

Even if spread over the next fifteen years, these costs would probably be prohibitive, given competing defense and domestic priorities. Yet there is little indication of which way the Defense Department intends to go at this time. Considering the large sums involved, it is unlikely that the United States will be able to procure both the MX and its mobile basing system and the Trident II missile, as well as to continue to fully modernize the strategic bomber force. Consequently it is imperative for the U.S. government to decide which of these weapon systems it can either defer or forgo before committing itself to the advanced development of these new types of strategic forces.

SALT CONSIDERATIONS. Because of projected strategic deployments the United States will be compelled to choose between dismantling some number of MIRV-equipped Minuteman III ICBMs or Poseidon C-3 SLBMs in order to remain under the SALT II ceiling of 1,200 ICBM and SLBM launchers with MIRVs.[4]

The United States currently has a total of 1,046 MIRV-equipped Minuteman III and Poseidon missiles. As new Trident submarines are deployed beginning in 1981, the U.S. launcher level will gradually increase toward the SALT II ceiling of MIRV-carrying missiles. With the sixth new Trident, the United States will reach the ceiling and will presumably choose between dismantling some Minuteman III missiles or retiring some Poseidon submarines. The delivery and deployment dates of the sixth Trident are currently estimated by the navy to be in 1985.

The total number of older MIRV-equipped ICBM or SLBM launchers that will have to be dismantled will depend on two considerations. One of these is whether the SALT II limit of 1,200 MIRV launchers continues in effect beyond 1985. Assuming that it does, the major factors determining the number of older launchers that must be dismantled are the pace at which new Trident submarines become

---

4. Both sides are also allowed to deploy 120 aircraft carrying long-range cruise missiles. Each additional aircraft of this type must be counted as one of the 1,200 MIRV launchers constituting the SALT limit.

operational and the number of aircraft carrying long-range cruise missiles in excess of the 120 aircraft that are allowed under the SALT II treaty. In light of the revised procurement program for the air-launched cruise missile, the United States will probably be able to avoid surpassing the cruise missile carrier limit until 1985. Yet eventually, as additional cruise missile carrier aircraft are converted or procured, this shift in forces will become an important factor in compelling the United States to retire older MIRV-equipped missile launchers.

To date no decision has been made concerning whether MIRV-equipped ICBMs or MIRV-equipped SLBMs will be dismantled. It would seem prudent to make this decision before current programs are allowed to continue much longer. Finally, it is also necessary to have a clear idea of future U.S. strategic force preferences in order to avoid many of the conflicts in the SALT negotiations that arose as new systems, such as the ALCM and MX mobile basing system, came into being.

In summary, to some degree all these factors argue for the development of a more comprehensive, long-term American strategic force framework as well as the avoidance of the piecemeal rush into commitments to add new strategic weapon capabilities before a better understanding of their role and implications has been established. It is also important to this planning framework to have a much clearer understanding of Soviet strategic force developments and the specific threats that these developments pose to the United States.

Theater Nuclear Forces

The Carter administration's 1980 defense budget includes programs to update every element of the U.S. theater nuclear arsenal.[5] Secretary of Defense Harold Brown describes modernization of theater nuclear forces as a "key program objective."[6]

In the budget request are five nuclear weapons programs: one to produce new nuclear warheads for the Lance tactical missile, and

5. Almost all theater nuclear delivery systems are based in or allocated to units with wartime missions in Western Europe.
6. *Department of Defense Annual Report, Fiscal Year 1980*, p. 136.

four engineering programs to develop new 8-inch and 155-millimeter nuclear artillery shells, a more accurate, longer-range, lower-yield Pershing II missile, and a highly accurate, longer-range ground-launched cruise missile (GLCM).[7] More than $1.6 billion is provided for continued procurement of the new, nuclear-capable F-16 fighter, which will replace the F-4 fighter in nuclear and conventional roles. The administration is also considering theater nuclear versions of the air-launched and sea-launched cruise missiles, although the time for developing the latter has been indefinitely extended, and a new mobile medium-range ballistic missile (MRBM) to take the place of missiles with longer-range delivery capabilities. Finally, $48.3 million is requested to study survivability and security improvements for current and future theater nuclear forces.

The total fiscal 1980 cost of all theater nuclear weapons programs is small—about $2 billion—half of which appears in the Department of Energy budget. These programs, however, represent the most thoroughgoing modernization the theater nuclear forces have had in two decades and are significant both for U.S. strategic nuclear programs and for NATO allies. The United States' choice of a theater nuclear modernization program, which was influenced by the threat facing NATO, will affect NATO members' perception of the U.S. commitment to the defense of Western Europe.

Assessment of Missions and Threats

THE STANDARD ASSUMPTION. NATO defense planning is based on the assumption of an attack by large numbers of Warsaw Pact conventional forces on Central Europe. NATO theater nuclear forces, in conjunction with the U.S. strategic deterrent, would be relied upon to deter Soviet use of nuclear weapons during the attack. Later, if NATO conventional forces were unsuccessful in their defense, NATO theater nuclear weapons could be used to destroy the attackers and perhaps force a favorable truce. Recently there has been renewed questioning about the length of time the Soviet Union would require to mobilize for such an attack, the amount of warning and preparation time that NATO defenders might have, and the consequent swiftness with which the Soviet-led forces might achieve

7. The new Lance warheads and nuclear artillery shells do not have increased radiation features—they are not "neutron bombs"—but are designed so that these features could be incorporated later if the President so decided.

victory. If the mobilization and warning time were very short and NATO defenders were caught relatively unprepared, the prospect of a swift victory by the Warsaw Pact countries could force NATO to use nuclear weapons sooner than it might otherwise, especially if quick Soviet seizure or conventional destruction of large portions of the NATO nuclear arsenal seemed likely unless these weapons were used first. It is difficult to believe that NATO theater nuclear delivery systems, many of which are used to deliver conventional munitions also, would survive the chaos of an unsuccessful conventional defense. The heightened possibility of an early NATO nuclear response to a conventional attack with so little warning would surely affect Soviet readiness to launch it.

REASONS FOR QUESTIONING. Soviet military writing has long emphasized the decisive use of nuclear weapons at the very outset of an attack. NATO planners, however, have persisted in the conventional attack planning assumption in part because of the strength of the U.S. strategic deterrent and the increasing capability of Soviet conventional forces. Recent Soviet writing and military exercises acknowledge the possibility of a purely conventional phase of combat, and even of a limited theater nuclear phase.

The modernization and strengthening of Soviet theater nuclear forces, combined with their doctrine of disrupting all types of threatening targets outside their territory in the event of war, cast doubt on the NATO assumption. The Soviet Union has improved the flexibility of its theater nuclear forces, replacing the Frog and Scaleboard tactical missiles with the new SS-21 and SS-22 missiles, both of which have conventional capabilities, something their predecessors lacked. The Soviet Union has also improved the flexibility of its conventional cannon artillery in recent years, giving it for the first time a nuclear delivery capability similar to that of NATO forces. The replacement of SS-4 and SS-5 missiles with SS-20 missiles has both reduced the vulnerability of the Soviet striking force and increased its ability to attack fixed sites such as NATO airfields and nuclear storage sites. This capability was further enhanced by the deployment of nuclear-capable later-model MIG-21, MIG-27, SU-17, and SU-19 fighter-bombers with the Frontal Aviation forces in Central Europe and the deployment of the Backfire bomber with the Long Range Aviation forces in the USSR in the early and mid-1970s. The possibility that the Soviet Union might use nuclear-armed sea-based ballistic and cruise missiles against targets in the European theater also adds to this capability.

This growth in the size and flexibility of the Soviet Union's theater nuclear forces has alarmed U.S. allies in NATO and added impetus to suggestions that the United States undertake offsetting initiatives. At the same time, the ambiguity of Soviet doctrine about whether the attack would be initially conventional or nuclear, combined with force improvements, raises a vital question for NATO. Can the alliance afford to assume that it will be allowed the luxury of choosing the time and place for the first use of nuclear weapons in a war with the Warsaw Pact countries? This question can be answered affirmatively only if the United States adopts a coherent doctrine and structures its theater nuclear modernization plans to intensify deterrence of a Soviet nuclear attack in Europe.

The Necessity for a Coherent Policy

The Carter administration's program for theater nuclear modernization replicates and adds to the current stockpile of tactical nuclear weapons and delivery systems. That stockpile, the accumulation of twenty years, was begun at a time when the United States did not have to worry about deterring a Soviet theater nuclear offensive. No policy has since been developed to indicate how this might be done and to justify additions to the stockpile. It is therefore difficult to see how adding to this much-criticized stockpile without developing a theater nuclear deterrence doctrine will assure the United States of a credible deterrent to a Soviet nuclear attack. It is also unclear what concept or doctrine of theater nuclear deterrence is behind the programs proposed by the administration. Are the forces intended to deter Soviet attack by threatening to destroy attacking Soviet forces, to disrupt military targets in Eastern Europe, or to carry out reprisals on nonmilitary targets in Eastern Europe or in the Soviet Union itself? Are they to be used in large numbers or in selective, individual strikes, in planned attacks or in improvised attacks? And what are the intended effects of this use—prompt military relief, the signaling of serious intentions, coercive bargaining, or punishment?

In his annual statement to Congress for fiscal 1980, Secretary Brown justifies this wide array of programs by pointing out the need for diverse and flexible forces that can be used in different ways for different purposes. There is something to be said for this approach. It could show the Soviet Union that the United States has many options available for responding to various provocations. But uncertainty about how the United States might react increases the risk of any Soviet provocation. Deploying a great variety of weapons can also be very costly. Moreover, unless the variety of weapons and possible responses is backed by well-reasoned contingency plans, it may simply perpetuate U.S. confusion about what to do. Having many types of weapons may merely be a way of avoiding difficult choices among alternative theater nuclear systems and strategies. Thus a variety of flexible weapons does not seem an adequate substitute for an articulated theater nuclear strategy.

Until last year, when President Carter deferred making a decision on producing enhanced-radiation tactical nuclear weapons (neutron bombs), the army contemplated delivering "pulses" of such low-yield weapons in planned "packages" of detonations that would blanket sparsely populated avenues of attack by the Warsaw Pact countries with lethal radiation. U.S. Air Force tactical nuclear bombing doctrine was similarly modified to minimize damage to civilian facilities.

The President's decision, however, denied the army a weapon that was crucial to employment planning. At the same time, serious questions were raised about whether these plans were really workable and about the possbility of Soviet retaliation, which would result in great civilian destruction. Consequently, although the army's nuclear employment concept is still in its field manuals, it has been dropped as a practical matter. No new doctrine has yet been developed to take its place and guide the modernization effort. Instead, the army seems to have reverted to its earlier plan of using nuclear weapons on individual tactical targets of opportunity when it becomes necessary.

Without enhanced-radiation weapons and the employment doctrine that supported them, the United States is back in the position it was in more than five years ago. Then, as now, the Defense Department was proposing to produce new blast-type artillery shells and missile warheads for existing delivery systems—without a credible, articulated theater nuclear doctrine. Then, as now, the justification for these programs was that the shells and warheads they would replace were based on old technology, were very inefficient, were cumbersome to use in the field, and produced inappropriate nuclear yields. The now-defunct Joint Committee on Atomic Energy found these justifications weak in 1973, and they seem weak now. While the technology of existing weapons may be old and reliability may not always be perfect, if the United States is to use blast-type weapons for individual target destruction, as was planned in the 1960s, it is difficult to see why the current stockpile of weapons would be inadequate for this task. If decisions were to be made on strategic grounds alone, it might be better to defer these theater nuclear modernization plans until a clear concept of how and when the weapons are to be used is developed.

Theater nuclear modernization cannot be considered only in the context of "warfighting" options, however, as these forces have political and symbolic importance to NATO allies. This was recently emphasized by concern in NATO about Soviet deployment of the mobile SS-20 medium-range ballistic missile and the desire to offset the weapon with additional long-range capabilities in Europe. Without such capabilities, allies fear that the United States might be unwilling to use its strategic forces in retaliation for a Soviet attack with SS-20s on Western Europe.

The justification for such added systems seems doubtful, however, since they would surely not be used to attack the SS-20 preemptively before it was moved. Moreover, justifying them requires an assumption that the Soviet response to nuclear attack from Western Europe would be different from the response to an attack with U.S. strategic forces. If this distinction is not made by the USSR, the need for additional long-range weapons in Europe is dubious. If the NATO allies have confidence in the United States' willingness to use its strategic forces in their defense, those forces should be more than adequate to counter the threat of an SS-20 strike. If they lack confidence, the longer-range systems based in Europe could not reassure them militarily. They would view the United States as just as reluctant to use these forces against the USSR as to use its own strategic forces, since the Soviet response would be the same in either case.

Although the strategic rationale for more long-range nuclear capability in Europe may be weak, such deployments might nevertheless give NATO visible psychological reassurance of U.S. commitment. If the purpose of these deployments were political and psychological, however, fewer weapons would probably be needed than for demanding military missions. Thus long-range Pershing II, GLCM, and MRBM programs should not all be required to provide this symbolic reassurance.

The administration's program of theater nuclear modernization is directly related to strategic nuclear programs, such as the MK-12A warhead for Minuteman III, the MX missile, the Trident I and II missiles, and the air-launched cruise missile, which will increase the number of U.S. nuclear warheads by an estimated 40 percent through 1985. At the same time, the U.S. supply of available nuclear material to build these weapons is limited.[8]

This supply limitation, if severe enough, could prevent the completion of all these strategic programs unless additional nuclear material was obtained. The problem could be solved by producing more material, but this would be extremely costly and would lead to innumerable environmental complaints. Alternatively, additional material could be obtained by replacing older tactical nuclear weapons, which used material very inefficiently, with new, more efficient weapons. Thus if new material cannot be produced, it may be impossible to achieve all the planned strategic nuclear force improvements without simultaneous theater nuclear modernization. This situation would mean that the pursuit of aggressive strategic nuclear programs might make it necessary to undertake a concurrent theater nuclear modernization program even though its underlying strategy had not been fully thought out. But the situation presents an opportunity as well: if the pace of U.S. strategic force deployments were slowed, theater nuclear modernization might be less urgent and more time would be available to decide what measures, if any, the United States really should take.

Ground and Air Forces

The 1980 budget request reflects the administration's continued interest in improving the ability of the United States to help defend its NATO allies. The President wants $56 billion for the ground and air forces oriented toward Europe. Included is $4.0 billion to continue modernizing the air force inventory of tactical combat aircraft and $2.6 billion to develop and procure fifteen new ground combat systems for the army, which is just beginning a major modernization program. All this comes partly in response to improvements over the past decade in the military capabilities of the Warsaw Pact countries.

8. W. S. Bennett, R. P. Gard, and G. C. Reinhardt, "Tactical Nuclear Weapons: Objectives and Constraints," Informal Report LA-5712-MS (Los Alamos Scientific Laboratory, September 1974), pp. 6–7; "LASL Panel on Tactical Nuclear Warfare, Report of the Third Meeting," Informal Report LA-6059-MS (Los Alamos Scientific Laboratory, September 1975), p. 29.

The Warsaw Pact Threat

Since the late 1960s the Soviet Union has come to accept the possibility of a conventional phase in any European war. Consequently it has sought to increase its military flexibility by augmenting the Warsaw Pact's conventional combat power.

There is general agreement about what this has meant. The Warsaw Pact armies have increased and modernized their inventories of tanks, infantry-fighting vehicles, artillery, and antitank and air defense weapons. Moreover, the Soviet Union has deployed a large number of attack helicopters. In addition, the personnel strength of Eastern European armies has increased slightly, and the Soviet Union appears to have added about 100,000 troops, mostly between 1968 and 1973. Some of the additional personnel seem to have gone to bolster the Warsaw Pact's support establishment. Finally, the Warsaw Pact seems to have further increased its ability to sustain conventional operations by expanding its forward stocks of combat consumables.

The deployment of more and better weapons has given Warsaw Pact ground forces the mobility and firepower needed to generate the shockpower and achieve the rapid advance rates long emphasized by Soviet military doctrine. Moreover, increases in organic firepower and air defense capabilities have freed Soviet ground forces, at least, from dependence on tactical aviation for air defense and close air support. At the same time, the Soviet Union's deployment of new tactical and long-range aircraft has increased its ability to carry more ordnance over longer distances, to fly more at night or in bad weather, and to employ precision-guided munitions for conventional ground attack.[9]

The Soviet Union now expects its tactical and long-range aviation to conduct independent air operations at the start of any conflict. These would involve concentrated strikes against such NATO targets as airfields, nuclear storage sites, command centers, and stockpiles of pre-positioned equipment.

Several things seem certain from all this. First, Soviet (if not Eastern European) ground and air forces have moved to positions

9. The offensive load-carrying capability of Soviet air forces in Europe perhaps doubled between 1965 and 1975. See Robert P. Berman, *Soviet Air Power in Transition* (Brookings Institution, 1978), p. 55.

where they would operate largely independently of one another. Second, the ability of Warsaw Pact ground forces to wage and sustain conventional operations has increased. Third, modernization and force improvement programs have decreased the amount of mobilization and reinforcement the Warsaw Pact would need to attain a given level of conventional combat power. But it is not clear how much improvements in the Pact's conventional capabilities would affect the amount of attack warning, the duration of any conflict, or the Soviet Union's readiness to use nuclear weapons.

Five years ago Soviet ground doctrine for the conventional phase clearly called for carefully prepared, massed breakthroughs along a few axes of attack. This type of campaign would require several weeks of mobilization and reinforcement. But the 1973 Middle East war raised doubts among Soviet planners about the ability of armored forces to break through well-prepared defenses thick with guided antitank missiles. Believing that a hasty attack against an uneven defense would actually involve less risk than a prepared assault against a solid defense, some Soviet theorists have argued for a preemptive campaign—a "daring thrust"—designed to achieve quick and deep advances before NATO could fully prepare its defenses.[10]

A preemptive campaign would be extremely risky for the Soviet Union. Because of the low readiness of Eastern European armies and the time needed to move reinforcements from the western USSR, the initial ground attack would probably involve only those Soviet forces already deployed in Eastern Europe. Moreover, after the attack began NATO almost certainly would try to delay the arrival of Soviet reinforcements and mobilized Eastern European armies. Finally, while training routines might make their ground combat units ready for a standing-start attack, the Soviet Union would still need time to set up the command and support systems needed to control and sustain an offensive.

Other factors might serve to lessen the USSR's risks in launching a preemptive ground offensive. Force improvement and modernization programs during the past decade might have given forward-deployed Soviet armies an ability to go it alone against an ill-prepared NATO defense. The Soviet Union might also be able to hide some preparations for an attack and to finalize its command and support arrangements under the cover of military exercises.

10. See Phillip A. Karber, *The Tactical Revolution in Soviet Military Doctrine* (McLean, Va.: BDM Corp., 1979).

Whereas NATO once expected several weeks' warning of an attack, it now counts on no more than eight to fifteen days. NATO's confidence about having that much warning stems from its ability to monitor military activity in the Warsaw Pact countries. In expecting eight to fifteen days of usable warning, NATO supposes that its surveillance apparatus would largely be able to see through the Soviet Union's efforts to screen its attack preparations. NATO also assumes that its analysts and decisionmakers would be perceptive enough to discern the significance of available attack indicators, despite Soviet attempts at deception, and decisive enough to act on them in a timely manner.

Numerous uncertainties make it impossible to predict how much usable warning NATO would have of a Warsaw Pact attack. But it is reasonable to conclude that NATO would now have less warning than it would have had ten years ago, and that assured warning time may decrease still further.

Despite acceptance of the possibility of a conventional phase, Soviet military writers still show a predisposition toward using nuclear weapons to achieve singularly decisive results throughout the European theater. This stems from their belief that the high stakes would probably provoke nuclear fire by the losing side, their doubts about the possibility of tightly controlling nuclear exchanges, and their appreciation of the military benefits to be gained from a first strike. Moreover, the Soviet Union seems to believe that any use of nuclear weapons would benefit its side because it would force NATO's defenses to disperse, thus giving Warsaw Pact armies greater opportunities for maneuver. In general the Warsaw Pact's investment in protective equipment and its emphasis on training in simulated nuclear environments at least indicate high Soviet readiness to use nuclear weapons.

Increases in the number of Warsaw Pact support personnel and the amount of pre-positioned supplies probably are the result of a Soviet desire for greater military flexibility, through improvements in the Pact's overall conventional capabilities, and a realization that another conventional war would consume an unprecedented amount of matériel. These steps need not suggest Soviet plans for a protracted conventional campaign. Appreciating the West's superiority in manpower and economic capacity as well as the advantages of compressing its period of risk, the Soviet Union has always planned for a quick campaign.

The availability of large nuclear stockpiles, the likelihood of strong pressures and incentives for a cease-fire, and the anticipated high rate of matériel consumption raise strong doubts about any conflict continuing or staying conventional beyond, say, thirty days. Of course, it is conceivable that both sides would hold their nuclear fire and, perhaps conserving their resources, fight conventionally for a longer period.

U.S. Missions, Operational Concepts, and Projected Spending

The Seventh Army's presence on West German soil demonstrates the U.S. commitment to Western Europe's security. The combined power of this force and allied armies serves to deter military threats or conventional aggression by the Warsaw Pact. The basic wartime mission of that portion of the U.S. Army dedicated to Western Europe would be to participate in the forward defense of allied territory.

The army is embarking on the most extensive and costly modernization program in its history; the budget seems likely to peak between fiscal 1982 and 1984. Two things account for this. First, the Vietnam War absorbed most of the funds that would otherwise have gone for the development and procurement of new weapons for Europe. Once U.S. involvement in Vietnam ended, the army began developing a variety of new systems. Second, development problems disrupted what plans the army had made for phasing in new weapons. For instance, high costs forced it to cancel the Cheyenne attack helicopter and the MBT-70 main battle tank and virtually start over again. As a result, many new systems are currently reaching maturity and entering low-level production. Hence, as table 5-5 indicates, development funding for fifteen new systems will drop off rapidly between fiscal years 1979 and 1984. But over that same period the army's plans for buying those systems would require about a fivefold increase in their procurement funding.

Between fiscal years 1979 and 1984 the army plans to triple its investment in major systems for close combat. Funding for the new XM-1 tank, infantry-fighting vehicle (IFV), and cavalry-fighting vehicle (CFV) will account for most of this increase.

The army's desire for these new armored fighting vehicles, which offer greater firepower, mobility, and survivability than their predecessors, reflects two beliefs. First, the army believes that its superior

Table 5-5. Costs of Planned Modernization of Selected Ground Combat Systems, Fiscal Years 1979–84

Millions of fiscal 1980 dollars

	Cost					
Ground combat system	1979	1980	1981	1982	1983	1984
Close combat[a]	**818**	**1,167**	**1,790**	**2,200**	**2,315**	**2,335**
Development	370	314	217	...	...	...
Procurement	448	853	1,573	2,200	2,315	2,335
Fire support[b]	**137**	**176**	**312**	**470**	**475**	**475**
Development	90	83	78	...	...	...
Procurement	47	93	234	470	475	475
Air defense[c]	**749**	**1,013**	**1,349**	**1,350**	**1,255**	**1,255**
Development	371	184	80	20	...	...
Procurement	378	829	1,269	1,330	1,255	1,255
Command, control, communications, and intelligence[d]	**116**	**218**	**244**	**280**	**370**	**335**
Development	116	171	109	45	35	...
Procurement	...	47	135	235	335	335
Total	**1,820**	**2,574**	**3,695**	**4,300**	**4,415**	**4,400**
Total development	947	752	484	65	35	...
Total procurement	873	1,822	3,211	4,235	4,380	4,400

Sources: Figures are authors' estimates drawn from *Department of Defense Annual Report, Fiscal Year 1980*, pp. 144–55; Department of Defense, *Program Acquisition Costs by Weapon System*, p. iv; and *Department of Defense Authorization for Appropriations for Fiscal Year 1979*, Hearings before the Senate Committee on Armed Services, 95 Cong. 2 sess. (GPO, 1978), pt. 2, pp. 168, 900–02. Figures are rounded.
a. Includes the XM-1 tank, infantry-fighting and cavalry-fighting vehicles, advanced attack helicopter, and Hellfire missile.
b. Includes the general support rocket system, Copperhead laser-guided shell, and ground laser designator.
c. Includes the Patriot and Roland missiles, DIVAD gun, and Stinger missile.
d. Includes the TRI-TAC radio, standoff target acquisition system, and remotely piloted vehicles.

firepower and tactical mobility make heavy forces—armored and mechanized infantry—the most appropriate for use in Central Europe.[11] All American infantry units in West Germany have been mechanized since the early 1960s. And heavy divisions are coming to dominate the active army: the portion of heavy divisions in the active army's divisional structure increased from 45 percent in fiscal 1972 to 63 percent in fiscal 1979 and will increase to 70 percent by fiscal 1984. Second, the army believes that the capability to move more quickly and deliver more firepower can obviate the need for more men on the battlefield. In peacetime it has never been politically feasible for the United States to maintain ground forces as large as those of the Soviet Union. Indeed, the continued "heavying-up" of

11. See table 5-7 for a comparison of heavy and light divisions.

the army and the procurement of better armored fighting vehicles can be seen as instances of technological substitution.

Technological substitution shows up more clearly in the army's interest in new systems for command, control, communications, and intelligence (C^3/I). The army's investment in three C^3/I systems will grow significantly between fiscal years 1979 and 1984. These are the standoff target location and tracking system, an airborne radar for detecting enemy ground forces, the TRI-TAC communications system, and a remotely piloted vehicle for reconnaissance.

As electronic systems have improved, the army has seized upon them as a means for managing its relatively scarce combat assets more effectively. The army's interest in a new airborne radar and a new reconnaissance drone reflects the fact that the army now counts heavily on airborne and ground-based sensors to accurately locate the enemy so that American commanders can feel more confident in deploying their outnumbered maneuver battalions. While the growing electronic warfare capabilities of the Warsaw Pact have raised concern about the reliability and security of present radios, the army's interest in new communications systems is heightened by its requirement that division and brigade commanders exercise tighter control over their subordinate units. In general, numerical inferiority has created a need for reliable target location and tracking, data-processing, and communications systems.

Some degree of substitution between ground attack aircraft and ground combat weapons, particularly artillery, is possible. The army now counts heavily on air force ground attack aircraft to destroy a substantial portion of army targets. The army, however, is in the process of building up its fire support capabilities. Over the next five years the army intends to increase the number of howitzers in many of its artillery battalions by 33 percent; and in fiscal 1981 it plans to request funds for the procurement of a general support rocket system, which is capable of rapidly delivering a large volume of fire. But these programs are largely needed to counter the recent modernization and expansion of Warsaw Pact artillery. The Copperhead laser-guided shell, for which funds have been requested for continued procurement, will theoretically give the army's artillery an ability to hit moving tanks, but the Copperhead has several operational limitations. Despite these improvements in fire support, it appears that the army will continue to require tactical air support to implement its plans for forward defense.

The army is in the process of reducing somewhat its dependence on the air force for air defense. It plans to nearly double its annual investment in major air defense systems between fiscal years 1979 and 1984. These include the Patriot, an army-level, radar-guided missile system; the Roland missile and DIVAD gun, which are short-range, radar-guided systems for the division; and the Stinger, a short-range infrared-guided missile for the division.

The 1980 budget also requests funds to increase the speed with which the army could deploy heavy divisions to Europe, to improve the readiness of home-based and forward-deployed forces, and to maintain forces for a protracted conflict.

Army matériel stockpiles in Europe now include the equipment for seven brigades (the equivalent of two and one-third divisions) that are currently based in the United States. Upon mobilization the personnel from these units would fly to Europe and take this pre-positioned overseas matériel configured to unit sets (POMCUS) out of storage. This arrangement reflects the difficulties that the United States would encounter otherwise in moving heavy units to Europe. Whereas the United States might be able to fly the personnel for a heavy division to Europe within twenty-four hours, it could take as long as eleven days to airlift the personnel and equipment of a heavy division.[12] Moving heavy forces by sea would take at least thirty days.

Currently the United States could send about one additional heavy division to West Germany within a week and a half. The apparent decrease in attack warning time has prompted the United States to seek to attain by 1983 the capability to send about five divisions to Europe within the same amount of time. Because of current limits on its ability to airlift outsized cargo, such as tanks and armored personnel carriers, the United States plans to meet its goal by adding another division's worth of POMCUS by the end of fiscal 1980 and two more divisions' worth by the end of fiscal 1982.

Congress has not authorized the purchase of extra equipment for POMCUS. The equipment will therefore have to be drawn from war

12. Robert Lucas Fischer, *Defending the Central Front: The Balance of Forces,* Adelphi Paper 127 (London: International Institute for Strategic Studies, 1976), p. 22.

reserve stocks and the inventories of active and reserve units based in the United States. But the administration did receive $59 million in fiscal 1979 to construct additional POMCUS storage sites and to maintain this extra stored equipment. It is requesting another $33 million in 1980 for the maintenance of the additional POMCUS.

Plans for increasing POMCUS will decrease the amount of equipment that home-based units have to train on and thus seemingly conflict with the administration's desire to increase the readiness of home-based units as part of an overall program to raise the readiness of all army units oriented toward NATO. The interest in increased readiness likewise stems from concern about decreased warning time. Readiness is a vague term, but a unit can reasonably be judged ready when it has enough well-trained people and enough working equipment on hand to perform its mission; for U.S. Army units in Europe, the ability to quickly take up forward defensive positions could serve as an additional criterion of readiness.

The administration is pursuing a modest program to increase the readiness of forward-deployed and early-arriving army units. For instance, it is increasing training and is beginning to man selected units above their authorized levels to ensure the presence of at least 95 percent of their personnel at all times; in West Germany it is now keeping selected combat vehicles loaded with ammunition and is constructing ammunition storage sites in forward areas. The administration is also studying the possibility of spending about $30 million per battalion to reposition selected army units already stationed in West Germany. This is partly prompted by the fear that many of these units may be based too far west of their forward defensive positions. Because Warsaw Pact ground forces are generally stronger in the north, however, the orientation of the relatively strong U.S. ground force toward the south central German border has also caused concern in recent years. Last year, in response, the army moved a brigade to northern Germany. This brigade is part of a U.S. corps that upon mobilization would deploy to northern Germany.

Finally, the administration wants to maintain funding for the Army Reserve and the National Guard, which would provide additional combat and support units after mobilization, at the fiscal 1979 level of about $2.7 billion. Because the army deactivated some support units to provide personnel for the three new divisions and two new brigades it established in the mid-1970s, it counts on the reserves to augment its support establishment in wartime. In addition the army maintains eight divisions and twenty-four brigades in its reserve force structure. With the possible exception of the four reserve brigades attached to active divisions, it is reasonable to expect that these units would take months to achieve combat readiness.

The U.S. Air Force currently bases twenty-six of its fighter–ground attack squadrons in Western Europe. Within ten days it could deploy another forty squadrons. U.S. aircraft in Central Europe could bring their great firepower to bear in a matter of minutes on the central front and within hours on the northern and southern flanks.

Although almost all the air force's tactical combat aircraft could operate worldwide, most of the existing and planned forces are oriented toward Central Europe. In a European war air force missions would be to establish some degree of air superiority and to assist allied and U.S. ground forces. The air superiority mission would involve the continuous defense of friendly airspace and could also involve air combat over enemy territory and strikes against enemy air bases. The present extent of the air force commitment to these extra elements of the air superiority mission is unclear. To assist U.S. and allied ground forces, the air force would fly reconnaissance, airlift, battlefield and deep interdiction, and close air support missions.

While the air force will continue to have some specialized aircraft (A-10s and F-15s), it will retain a large number of multipurpose aircraft (primarily F-4s now and F-16s in the 1980s). The air force wants a lot of aircraft that can be used for air combat or ground attack as the situation requires. This emphasis on flexibility discourages any precise definition of mission priorities.

The air force has made numerous responses to the changing Warsaw Pact threat. In the early 1970s it embarked on programs to procure several new aircraft: the E-3A, F-15, A-10, and F-16. The E-3A airborne warning and control system is designed to detect enemy aircraft and to direct the operations of NATO's fighter and ground attack aircraft. The F-15 is an all-weather fighter for the air superiority mission. The A-10 is basically a daytime aircraft designed solely for close air support. Charges that the air force was ignoring army needs encouraged its procurement. A multipurpose aircraft, the F-16 will replace the F-4. While it has a limited capability for ground attack in adverse weather, the F-16 could not be used for air combat at night or in bad weather.

Table 5-6. Size and Cost of Major Air Force Modernization Programs, Fiscal Years 1979–84

Costs in millions of fiscal 1980 dollars

Program	1979		1980		1981		1982		1983		1984	
	Number	Cost	Number	Cost	Number	Cost	Number	Cost	Number	Cost	Number	Cost
F-16	...	**1,669**	...	**1,699**	...	**1,745**	...	**1,710**	...	**1,710**	...	**1,710**
Development	...	114	...	27	...	39	...	...	...	...	...	...
Procurement	145	1,555	175	1,672	180	1,706	180	1,710	180	1,710	180	1,710
F-15	...	**1,526**	...	**990**	...	**1,011**	...	**505**	...	...	...	...
Development	...	11	...	1	...	9	...	...	...	...	...	...
Procurement	78	1,515	60	989	60	1,002	30	505	...	...	...	...
A-10	...	**888**	...	**904**	...	**559**	...	...	...	...	...	...
Development	...	19	...	18	...	...	...	...	...	...	...	...
Procurement	144	869	144	886	106	559	...	...	...	...	...	...
E-3A	...	**319**	...	**407**	...	**363**	...	**300**	...	...	...	...
Development	...	62	...	74	...	61	...	...	...	...	...	...
Procurement	3	257	3	333	3	302	3	300	...	...	...	...
Total	...	**4,402**	...	**4,000**	...	**3,678**	...	**2,515**	...	**1,710**	...	**1,710**
Total development	...	206	...	120	...	109	...	...	...	...	...	...
Total procurement	370	4,196	382	3,880	349	3,569	213	2,515	180	1,710	180	1,710

Sources: Figures for 1979–81 are from *Department of Defense Annual Report, Fiscal Year 1980*, pp. 186–87; figures for 1982–84 are authors' estimates. Figures are rounded.

As table 5-6 indicates, the air force plans to finish procuring the E-3A, F-15, and A-10 during fiscal years 1981 and 1982, but it will continue buying F-16s through the mid-1980s. While the annual funding for procurement of all these aircraft will decrease by about two-thirds between fiscal 1979 and 1984, the air force's annual budget for the modification of existing aircraft will more than double between fiscal years 1979 and 1981 and may increase further in subsequent years.

In response to the increased threat from Soviet theater aviation and Warsaw Pact air defenses, the air force also wants to improve the survivability of its aircraft on the ground and after takeoff. Thus the 1980 budget request contains funds to continue programs designed to increase the survivability of U.S. air bases. It also requests funds for the development and procurement of new systems designed to deceive or destroy enemy air defenses. Finally, the 1980 budget request almost certainly contains funds for the continuation of army–air force exercises that are partly designed to promote the coordination of the capabilities of the two forces for suppressing enemy air defenses. As the threat from enemy air defenses has grown, the air force has increasingly sought help from the army, which would use electronic warfare equipment as well as some of its artillery and attack helicopters to aid in defense suppression.

Budget Issues and Alternatives

The future level and allocation of army funding for procurement is the foremost issue in the fiscal 1980–84 program for ground and air forces. The army's plans for buying the fifteen new systems shown in table 5-5 would require about a fivefold increase in their procurement funding between fiscal years 1979 and 1984. The Defense Department is planning to increase the army's total procurement budget from $6.6 billion in fiscal 1979 to $8.5 billion in 1981 and $9.5 billion in 1983.[13] But the procurement of the fifteen new systems as planned would absorb a disproportionate share of these increases in total army procurement. Whereas the procurement of these systems consumes 13 percent of the army's total procurement budget for fiscal 1979, it would absorb 38 percent in 1981 and 46 percent in 1983.

13. "New Systems Pose Huge 'Bow Wave' for Army Budget," *Armed Forces Journal International* (June 1978), p. 12. Figures are expressed in fiscal 1980 dollars.

This budget contains hundreds of additional items, however, and if the army plans to maintain fairly constant funding for their procurement, it cannot go ahead with the procurement of the fifteen new systems as planned. Hence it appears that the army will have to cancel some of these systems, stretch out their procurement, or obtain extra funding from somewhere else. Accordingly, the rationales behind these procurement programs—as well as spending for POMCUS, readiness, and hedges against a long war—warrant close examination. Moreover, since the army and the air force perform some identical missions—notably air defense and fire support—the relationship between their performance of these missions deserves an attempt at clearer definition.

FUTURE PROCUREMENT OF ARMORED FIGHTING VEHICLES. Before buying large numbers of XM-1s, IFVs, and CFVs, the administration and Congress would do well to address two questions.

First, how many heavy forces will the army want for use in Central Europe ten or twenty years from now? The army has recently come to recognize that a war there would now involve almost continuous combat in built-up areas. It would also involve a lot of fighting in woodlands. Since afforestation and controlled urbanization is proceeding at a slow but steady pace, the open areas in West Germany most suitable for armored and mechanized operations will continue to shrink in the years ahead.[14]

Light forces (infantry, airborne, or airmobile) are more suitable for defensive combat in close terrain. As table 5-7 indicates, they also have considerable combat power. While light units are more vulnerable to artillery fire, the assignment of extra artillery to suppress that of the enemy would mitigate this problem. By the 1990s it is possible that the United States might want or be prepared to trade in some of its heavy units—equipped with XM-1s, IFVs, and CFVs—for such light units.

Second, with heavy units retaining some role in Central Europe, what will be a suitable mixture of armored fighting vehicles in quality and quantity? The growing lethality of modern weapons and the consequent likelihood of high attrition in any European war warrants further consideration of this question. While the XM-1 appears to be nearly invulnerable to current antitank missiles, how much more

14. Paul Bracken, "Urban Sprawl and NATO Defense," *Survival*, vol. 18 (November–December 1976), pp. 254–60.

Table 5-7. Characteristics of Heavy and Light U.S. Divisions

Characteristic	Heavy divisions		Light divisions		
	Armored	Mecha-nized infantry	Infantry	Airborne	Airmobile
Authorized strength (number)					
Personnel	16,850	17,800	18,146	16,682	18,313
Main battle tanks	342	216	54	0	0
Artillery[a]	66	66	72	54	72
Guided antitank weapons	680	738	813	684	1,242
Ground-launched	344	402	429	300	522
Helicopter-launched	336	336	384	384	720
Defensive combat power					
Notional value[b]	50,000	46,000	44,000	35,000	39,000
Airlift requirements (thousands of tons)					
Outsized cargo[c]	29.0	21.0	14.0	11.0	9.0
Non-outsized cargo	40.5	42.0	37.5	29.0	27.0
Total cargo[d]	69.5	63.0	51.5	40.0	36.0
Addendum: Ratio of defensive combat power to weight[e]	719.4	730.2	854.4	875.0	1,083.3

Sources: Selected Department of the Army "H-series" Tables of Organization and Equipment; International Institute for Strategic Studies, *The Military Balance, 1978–1979* (London: IISS, 1978); methodology extracted from U.S. Army Concepts Analysis Agency, "Weapon Effectiveness Indices/Weighted Unit Values," vol. 1 (Bethesda, Md.: USACAA, April 1974); and the Boeing Aerospace Co., *The 747 Tanker/Transport* (Boeing, April 1973), p. 76.

a. Heavy divisions have 155-mm and 8-inch artillery, infantry and airmobile divisions have 105-mm and 155-mm artillery, and the airborne division has 105-mm artillery.

b. This index sums up the effectiveness of all the weapons in a particular unit. Estimates of the effectiveness of each weapon are based on formulas that take into account its firepower, mobility, and survivability.

c. Consists of cargo that because of its bulk can only be carried on the C-5 aircraft.

d. Included is 60 percent of the initial support increment needed in the first thirty days of deployment. Excluded is the bulk cargo that would be carried by mobilized civilian aircraft.

e. Weighted unit value per 1,000 tons.

protection it will offer against new armor-piercing shells fired from tank guns is not clear. In the 1973 Middle East war, tank guns caused almost all the tank kills. Because tank guns are highly accurate and have many advantages over guided missiles, including a higher rate of fire, it is reasonable to assume that they would pose the greater threat in conventional combat in Europe. If this is true, the United States might still stand to lose a lot of XM-1s. Moreover, losses of any kind of tank would presumably be higher still in nuclear combat.

The XM-1's overall survivability seems to be the chief issue. Unless it offers substantially greater survivability than current tanks, the XM-1's extra firepower and mobility will not be worth their expense.

If indeed the XM-1 does not offer a significant decrease in vulnerability, overall survivability of the U.S. tank force will improve more with increases in number. In this case, instead of spending more than $7 billion on 7,000 XM-1s over the next eight years, the administration and Congress might want to think about limiting the XM-1 purchase and using some of the money to procure additional M-60A3s, to turn additional M-60A1s into M-60A3s, to accelerate development of a new low-cost tank, and to create additional maneuver battalions for deployment in West Germany.[15]

Because of their profile and lighter armor, the survivability of the IFV and CFV is even more questionable. Again, the administration and Congress might want to think about limiting their purchase and pursuing other alternatives. These alternatives might include the development and procurement of another infantry-fighting vehicle, derived from the XM-1, to accompany the XM-1 into battle; the modification of some M-113 armored personnel carriers to give them increased standoff firepower; or the development of a wheeled combat vehicle for use in an urbanized environment such as Central Europe. Wheeled combat vehicles are much cheaper to operate and maintain. The savings in support costs that would probably result from these alternatives could fund other things.

Apart from these larger issues, there are questions about the XM-1, IFV, and CFV themselves. In operational testing the XM-1's engine is experiencing problems. Current plans for refitting the first thousand or so XM-1s with West Germany's 120-millimeter gun will involve additional costs. As for the IFV and CFV, their designs have been severely criticized for poor operational and strategic mobility, low survivability, and other faults. All in all, more thought about the army's direction in armor development might be in order.

STRATEGIC MOBILITY THROUGH POMCUS. Increasing the number of POMCUS to five is generally applauded for being the most cost-effective way of increasing the U.S. ability to rapidly send heavy reinforcements to Europe. These sets of equipment, however, would be stored at a relatively small number of obvious sites, which seem extremely vulnerable to attack by conventional, chemical, or nuclear munitions, or airborne troops. The Defense Department's response that there are many rear area targets around to draw Soviet fire offers

15. As of last year the army considered its M-60A3 superior to the two new Soviet tanks, the T-64 and T-72. *Hearings on Military Posture and H.R. 10929, Department of Defense Authorization for Fiscal Year 1979,* Hearings before the House Committee on Armed Services, 95 Cong. 2 sess. (GPO, 1978), pt. 2, p. 225.

cold comfort, for it is reasonable to assume that a disruption of U.S. reinforcement, through a surprise strike at POMCUS, would come as a severe blow to NATO. Another problem with increasing POMCUS is that some equipment would have to be taken away from units in the United States, thereby decreasing their readiness.

Hence the administration and Congress might want to consider the following Defense Department alternatives: (1) give the strategic mobility forces more money to increase their ability to carry outsize cargo, thereby increasing America's worldwide military flexibility; (2) plan on sending some entire light units at the start of any reinforcement;[16] (3) substantially increase the number of planned storage sites and allocate more money for POMCUS maintenance; or (4) make provision for emergency dispersal of the additional POMCUS.

SPENDING FOR READINESS. While readiness has received greater attention in recent years, several things seem worthy of still further study. How serious is the threat of a standing-start attack by Soviet, and perhaps Eastern European, ground forces? And how much can NATO count on its capacity to detect, appreciate, and act on indications of a Warsaw Pact attack? Finally, what would be the rewards of additional spending on readiness and the costs of increasing the number of POMCUS division sets to five?

Further study might indicate that the army's current level of readiness is sufficient. If so, funds programmed for additional increases in readiness could be diverted to other uses. Alternatively, a need for greater readiness might become apparent. If this were the case, the administration might want to spend more on training, reposition some army units already in West Germany, and perhaps deploy additional ground units to Europe.

WORLDWIDE FLEXIBILITY VERSUS COMMITMENT TO NATO. Programs such as those to "heavy-up" the army and increase the amount of POMCUS in West Germany may very well increase the army's capacity to carry out its NATO mission of forward defense. They may also decrease the army's ability to respond adequately to military challenge elsewhere in the world.

Because of the distances and the terrain involved, the United States

16. As table 5-7 indicates, light units possess considerable combat power and require less airlift capacity. Indeed, it is estimated that the defensive power of these divisions outweighs the offensive power of the notional Soviet heavy divisions. U.S. Army Concepts Analysis Agency, "Weapon Effectiveness Indices/Weighted Unit Values," vol. 1 (Bethesda, Md.: USACAA, April 1974).

will continue to rely on light forces for contingencies outside Central Europe. Counting the marines, the United States currently has nine light divisions in its active forces. One marine division is oriented toward NATO's flanks, and one army infantry division is deployed to defend Korea. It is planned to convert the latter unit into a mechanized infantry division upon its return to the United States.

Of the remaining seven divisions, the army's airborne and airmobile divisions maintain high readiness, as may the two other marine divisions. But two of the three infantry divisions would each require the time-consuming mobilization of one reserve brigade to achieve combat readiness. Perhaps it is more important that equipment may be taken away from these army divisions to increase the amount of equipment pre-positioned in West Germany. Finally, it may be that insufficient attention has been paid to the development of easily transportable equipment that would increase the tactical mobility and organic firepower of the army's light forces.

For contingencies in such regions as the Persian Gulf or the Middle East, the Defense Department now seems to plan on sending a corps-sized force of about three divisions. It currently appears that the United States could quickly deploy at most only four or five light divisions. Depending on the situation, this might or might not be a sufficient force.

Western Europe, whose security is vital to the United States, is at present in a stable relationship with Eastern Europe. Given the tendency toward political turmoil in many other regions, more urgent threats to U.S. security could easily arise in other parts of the world. Thus before the administration spends much more money on ground forces for NATO and converts any more light divisions into heavy ones, it might do well to think more about potential military threats and ground force requirements elsewhere in the world.

HEDGING AGAINST A LONG WAR. The size and organization of the selected reserves deserves further examination. In a European war, the army probably would need some of the extra support capability that selected reserve units could provide. But how much would it need for a conflict that seemed likely to be of short duration? Likewise, given the generally low readiness of these forces, the administration should ask whether it can really afford to maintain the equivalent of sixteen combat divisions in the National Guard and the Army Reserve. While the maintenance of this hedge against a protracted conflict may be a source of comfort, the money might better go toward increasing the army's short-war capabilities. Unfortunately, domestic politics make it difficult to effect substantial or even minor changes in the selected reserves. But at the very least the administration and Congress might more vigorously pursue ways to make these reserve combat units more responsive to the threat of an intense, brief war in Europe.

C^3/I AS A "FORCE MULTIPLIER." The notion that C^3/I systems can serve as a force multiplier deserves careful examination. While it is natural to want a better view of the enemy and better control over one's own forces, is it realistic to suppose that electronic systems will reliably allow the army to get by with fewer maneuver battalions than would otherwise be needed? Atmospheric conditions, terrain, electronic warfare, and nuclear effects can all degrade the performance of electronic systems to varying degrees. Radar for locating and tracking targets, short-range communications equipment, and data-processing equipment are particularly vulnerable to nuclear effects.

There seems to be a consensus that many of the army's current C^3/I systems are unacceptably vulnerable to interference or exploitation by an enemy. Funds are in this year's budget request to continue the development of various systems that promise increased security and reliability. The procurement of these systems promises to significantly increase C^3/I budgets in the 1980s.

In considering future expenditures and C^3/I's potential as a force multiplier, the army may need to think more about the operational limitations of these systems. The army might also consider how different assumptions about the nature of a future European war would affect C^3/I requirements and whether it wants to promote a further centralization of command and control. A future European battlefield might well discourage efforts by division and brigade commanders to fine tune the operations of their subordinate units. If it seemed that future European combat might be more chaotic and fast-moving and more likely to involve nuclear weapons than is currently assumed, the army might want to think about decentralizing command and control, increasing its number of maneuver battalions, and relying still more on the initiative of battalion commanders.

AIR TO GROUND FIRE SUPPORT. The attractions of ground attack aircraft were mentioned earlier. But two things raise questions about the army's reliance on the air force for close air support and battlefield interdiction.

First, the combined threat from the Soviet Union's theater aviation, surface-to-surface missiles, and airborne forces suggests an ability to partly neutralize the U.S. Air Force in Europe or disrupt its operations. In recent years the air force has taken a number of steps to increase the survivability of its air bases, and it has spent much money to defend rear area targets from air attack. The question is whether this is enough to guarantee a reasonable degree of security against a broader threat, which has likewise increased in capability.

Second, quantitative increases and qualitative improvements in the Warsaw Pact's ground-based air defenses raise questions about the ability of U.S. ground attack aircraft to survive and successfully perform their missions. Through the use of jamming equipment, Warsaw Pact ground forces might be able to disrupt the communications required for the air-ground coordination of close air support; through the use of complementary weapons, they might be able to exact unacceptable attrition. Depending on the projected length of the conflict, seemingly low aircraft loss rates (for example, 2 percent per sortie) could quickly curtail operations. Higher loss rates have occurred in recent wars. The United States is, of course, continuing to develop active and passive countermeasures and tactics to increase the survivability of its ground attack aircraft. But the competition between air defenses and combat aircraft is highly dynamic, and it holds great potential for technological surprise. It is impossible to predict with any confidence who would prevail in actual combat. It may be that neither side would gain a decisive edge.

Finally, in questioning the future contribution of offensive air support to the ground battle, it is worth noting the unequal wartime burdens that would be placed on the ground attack elements of the Soviet and U.S. air forces. The Soviet air forces would be out to get a rather modest number of fixed and generally soft targets in NATO's rear area. In contrast, the U.S. Air Force would have to deal with thousands of moving and generally hardened targets. Moreover, the Soviet deployment of a larger number of precision-guided air-to-ground munitions seems likely to further increase the inequity.

All this suggests that a lot of uncertainty surrounds the role of U.S. ground attack aircraft in any European war. But none of it suggests that air power is obsolete. At the very least the ground attack aircraft currently in the U.S. inventory could serve as a highly mobile strategic reserve to be used against ground breakthroughs. Air power could probably do more, but the question is how much more?

It seems reasonable to suggest further examination of the army's reliance on tactical air power. It may also be reasonable to suggest some redistribution of funds between the air force and the army. The magnitude of this redistribution would depend on a better determination of the degree of uncertainty associated with tactical air support. Attack helicopters and ground-based fire support systems, such as tube artillery and general support rockets, may present fewer command and control problems; and they certainly seem to offer greater survivability. Hence the administration might want to think about decreasing procurement and modification funding for the A-10 and perhaps the F-16 and using the money instead to increase the organic firepower of the U.S. Army in Europe.

AIR DEFENSE. Before proceeding as planned with large expenditures on the F-15 and F-16 aircraft and the Patriot and Roland missile systems, the administration and Congress might further consider the integration of these weapons. Although these systems differ in having been designed for either all-weather or clear-daylight use, either area or point defense, and use against targets either within or beyond visual range, they are also redundant to some degree. The expenditure of much more money on air defense would increase operational flexibility. But given the demand for funds, it might be necessary to more closely examine possible trade-offs in the continued procurement of these systems.

General Purpose Naval Forces

Budget authority of $42 billion is proposed for general purpose naval forces in the 1980 budget.[17] Within this total are sharp increases and decreases for new resources. Budget authority of $4.8 billion is provided for the construction and conversion of fourteen general purpose ships—60 percent higher (in constant dollars) than the comparable part of the 1979 budget. For all other naval functions the increases average less than one-half of 1 percent in real terms. Spending for the marine corps (particularly for tactical aviation) and for

17. The Trident submarine program is a strategic system and is discussed in the strategic mission section above.

naval support forces such as oilers, tenders, tugs, and repair ships is decreased.

The emphasis on ship construction and associated investment is projected to continue in the five-year defense plan. Approximately $30 billion of budget authority in constant dollars is included for 61 new ships and 13 conversions, with another $12 billion for the purchase of 525 naval aircraft for use on aircraft carriers. If implemented, this program will absorb 25 percent of the new resources devoted to naval programs over a period of five years.

In fiscal 1980 budget authority for general purpose ship construction is dominated by three large commitments—$1.6 billion for a conventionally powered aircraft carrier of medium size; $1.3 billion for continued construction of patrol frigates; and $825 million for a new destroyer with an advanced fleet air defense system (AEGIS). The carrier and the destroyers, as well as proposed authority of $1.7 billion for F-14 and F/A-18 aircraft, are the principal budget items around which debates about the purposes of naval forces revolve.

The executive and the legislative branches agree that naval forces are an important symbol of America's political presence throughout the world and a flexible means of responding to crises. The currently programmed force of 12 aircraft carriers with their associated aircraft and some 175 supporting ships are frequently justified by these requirements. In support of political commitments to European and Asian allies, the United States has long kept two carriers permanently stationed in the Mediterranean and two more in the western Pacific. To meet overhaul schedules, conduct training, and facilitate personnel management, the navy believes it must have three carriers to support one on station and defines its peacetime need as six carriers in the Atlantic to support the Sixth Fleet in the Mediterranean and six in the Pacific to support the Seventh Fleet in the Asian theater.[18]

Though this determination of peacetime requirements for the navy's capital ships has been questioned, it is apparent that any change in habitual deployment patterns would be strongly resisted by U.S. allies. Also, any contemplated reductions in the established level would probably have to be compensated for by increasing support efficiency enough to enable the navy to maintain a carrier on station

18. Naval missions and their budget implications are reviewed by the Congressional Budget Office in *Navy Budget Issues for Fiscal Year 1980* (Government Printing Office, 1979).

with fewer than two in reserve. In recognition of these difficulties, much of the recent debate has focused not on the number of carrier task forces but rather on the appropriate size, cost, propulsion system, and aircraft complement of new carriers to be added to the force as older ones are retired. This debate hinges on one important fact—that the central problems of current naval force planning concern missions to be performed in a conflict with the Soviet Union. The F-14 fighter and the AEGIS fleet air defense system are specifically designed to counter Soviet force capabilities. Though it has not been authoritatively determined whether these systems would be unnecessary and whether other naval assets could be eliminated or redirected if the Soviet threat did not exist, it is nonetheless apparent that U.S. naval development is driven by the prospect of war with the Soviet Union. Far from apparent, however, is what the general purpose navy, particularly the carrier forces, might appropriately seek to accomplish in such a war. The fact that this issue is unresolved is reflected in the content of the 1980 defense budget and the five-year force plan.

Assessment of the Threat

The first step in defining the Soviet naval threat is readily taken; in the most general sense Soviet naval capability has increased significantly in the past two decades. From 1962 to 1976, 331 ships classified as major combatants were delivered to the Soviet fleets. Over this period, the rate at which major ships were added declined as the total tonnage of new additions increased (table 5-8), a crude indication of the increasing emphasis on technical sophistication.

Table 5-9 shows the change from 1968 to 1978 in the composition of major combatants in the Soviet fleet, mainly a shift toward nuclear power in the Soviet navy—which is also a rough measure of sophistication—and reflects some of its priorities. In particular, the large increase in strategic missile submarines—up to the limit allowed in the SALT I agreement—has given the Soviet navy a capability for global projection of strategic power comparable to that of the United States. This particular element of the Soviet navy seems to fulfill the requirements of the Soviet armed forces, particularly the navy.

The Soviet navy has clearly been given the general military mission and the forces to protect the waters adjacent to the Soviet Union from the incursions of hostile powers. Large numbers of coastal patrol

Table 5-8. Major Combat Ships Added to the Soviet Navy, 1962–76

Type of ship[a]	1962–66			1967–71			1972–76		
	Number of ships	Tonnage	As percent of total tonnage	Number of ships	Tonnage	As percent of total tonnage	Number of ships	Tonnage	As percent of total tonnage
Aircraft carriers	0	...	...	0	...	...	1	3,700	7
Helicopter cruisers	0	...	...	2	34,000	7	0	...	...
Guided missile cruisers	6	46,500	12	7	52,500	11	10	86,000	15
Guided missile destroyers	17	72,500	19	18	76,700	15	16	64,900	11
Frigates	40	46,000	12	24	27,600	6	0	...	...
Cruise missile submarines	40	142,500	37	13	58,500	12	10	45,000	8
Attack submarines	32	69,000	18	20	70,000	14	17	56,500	10
Ballistic missile submarines	2	10,000	2	22	176,000	35	34	276,000	49
Total	137	386,500	100	106	495,300	100	88	565,400	100
Addendum: Ballistic missile submarine production as percent of total		2.6			35.5			48.8	

Sources: Ship deliveries are primarily based on those constructed by Michael McGwire, "Comparative Warship Building Programs," in McGwire, ed., *Soviet Naval Developments: Capability and Context* (Praeger, 1973), pp. 144–50; Michael McGwire, Ken Booth, and John McDonnell, eds., *Soviet Naval Policy: Objectives and Constraints* (Praeger, 1975), pp. 424–25; and Michael McGwire, "Soviet Naval Programmes," in Paul J. Murphy, ed., *Naval Power in Soviet Policy* (Government Printing Office, 1978), pp. 77–107. Also consulted were Siegfried Breyer and Norman Polmar, *Guide to the Soviet Navy*, 2d ed. (U.S. Naval Institute, 1977); and John E. Moore, ed., *Jane's Fighting Ships* (Franklin Watts, 1978), pp. 483–519.

a. Types of ships are U.S. designations.

Table 5-9. Changes in Major Soviet Types of Naval Vessels, 1968–78

Type of ship	1968	1978	Percentage change
Surface ships	**121**	**135**	**12**
Antisubmarine cruisers	1	2	100
Rocket cruisers	8	8	0
Cruisers[a]	16	13	−19
Large antisubmarine ships	10	63	530
Destroyers	86	50	−42
Submarines	**341**	**333**	**−2**
Multipurpose			
Attack, nuclear	14	40	185
Attack, conventional	243	134	−45
Cruise missile, nuclear	25	45	80
Cruise missile, conventional	24	24	0
Strategic missile[b]			
Nuclear	13	70	438
Conventional	22	20	−9

Sources: Numbers of ships, International Institute for Strategic Studies, *The Military Balance, 1967–1968*, and *1978–1979* (London: IISS, 1967, 1978); categorization of ship types according to Soviet classification systems, MccGwire, "Soviet Naval Programmes," pp. 89–90; and Admiral S. G. Gorshkov, commander-in-chief of the Soviet navy, in "The Navy," *Translations on U.S.S.R. Military Affairs* (Joint Publications Research Service, November 22, 1978), pp. 30–34.

a. U.S. Navy officials have reported that the USSR no longer designates *Kiev*-class carriers as antisubmarine warfare (ASW) cruisers but instead calls them simply "cruisers." Consequently, the two *Kiev*-class carriers in operation by 1978 are included in the "cruiser" category. Had they retained their former designation, the ASW cruiser category would have increased by 300 percent and the cruiser category would have been further reduced by 31 percent.

b. Soviet naval literature also refers to nuclear strategic missile submarines as submarine missile carriers and missile-armed submarines and to conventional strategic missile submarines as submarine cruisers.

craft, antiship missiles, and land-based aircraft (including a substantial portion of the Backfire bomber inventory) have been deployed to support the Soviet fleets in the Barents Sea, the Baltic Sea, and the waters between Vladivostok and Petropavlovsk. These have become areas of impressive Soviet naval strength. A somewhat less impressive but nonetheless substantial and clearly conceived Soviet naval presence has also been established in the Mediterranean. The Soviet Mediterranean squadron would be a respectable opponent for the U.S. Sixth Fleet.

These general characterizations of Soviet naval forces are widely accepted. However, there is serious disagreement among analysts about the capabilities and intentions of Soviet fleets in the open oceans.

Official estimates by the U.S. Navy, undoubtedly influenced by its most memorable combat experience, project a range of Soviet naval missions similar to those carried out by enemy forces during World War II. Thus it is estimated that in a war the Soviet navy would attack U.S. fleets in the open oceans, would interdict shipping between the United States and its European and Asian allies, and would support amphibious landings by Soviet troops on the flanks of NATO. Also, while acknowledging currently poor Soviet antisubmarine capability in the open ocean, analysts of the Soviet threat are particularly sensitive to any challenge to U.S. ballistic missile submarines, and most credit the Soviet Union with systematic efforts to develop such a challenge.

Disagreement with standard conceptions of the Soviet threat come from analysts who do not believe that the Soviet navy has actually acquired the capability necessary to conduct open ocean operations against U.S. naval resistance.[19] Their assessment is that Soviet surface fleets could not successfully emerge from their areas of strength under full war conditions to attack the navies of the United States and its allies. In fact, they estimate these fleets to be so inadequate for such a mission that they doubt whether the Soviet Union would attempt it. U.S. carrier task forces in the Atlantic and the Pacific might be attacked with remotely based Soviet missiles, but analysts also doubt that Soviet missile systems have the capability to fix on and track targets accurately. Soviet submarines might operate in the open oceans alone or in small squadrons with considerable risk, but not in combined fleet operations.

Such doubts lead dissenting analysts to limit the purposes of the general Soviet navy to two. The first is to support land combat operations in the European and Asian theaters adjacent to the Soviet Union by direct attack on the forward operations of U.S. fleets. The second is to protect Soviet strategic missile submarines operating in areas of primary Soviet strength from U.S. antisubmarine warfare. Both of these missions are in keeping with the general policy of

19. See V. D. Sokolovsky, *Soviet Military Strategy*, 3d ed., ed. and trans. by Harriet Fast Scott (Crane, Russak, 1975), p. 254; S. G. Gorshkov, "The Sea Power of the State," a translation of the book reprinted in *Survival*, vol. 17 (January–February 1977), p. 28; Bradford Dismukes, "The Soviet Naval General Purpose Forces: Roles and Missions in Wartime," in Michael MccGwire, Ken Booth, and John McDonnell, eds., *Soviet Naval Policy* (Praeger, 1975), p. 582; Commander Richard T. Ackley, USN (Ret.), "The Wartime Role of Soviet SSBNs," *United States Naval Institute Proceedings*, vol. 104 (June 1978), pp. 34–42. The term "SSBN support" has also been used by U.S. Navy officials to describe Soviet antisubmarine operations. See the testimony of Admiral James L. Holloway, Chief of Naval Operations, in *Hearings on Military Posture and H.R. 10929*, pt. 1, p. 690.

strongly defending ocean areas near the Soviet Union. If the second conception is valid, it may explain why, despite having such poor antisubmarine warfare capability in the open oceans, the Soviet Union has invested so heavily in large surface combatants for anti-submarine warfare (see table 5-9).

Esoteric as such arguments may seem, they have potentially strong implications for U.S. defense programs. If the dissenting opinion should ever prove to be correct, it would affect the direction of U.S. naval force developments.

U.S. Naval Combat Missions

As with the problem of assessing the threat, there is a range of opinion about the appropriate combat missions for which U.S. naval forces ought to be designed. Dissension on this point undermines the coherence of naval posture and effectiveness in allocating naval re-sources. Though many specific variations of opinion can be found, there are a few general themes.

In its recent comprehensive planning exercise, "Sea Plan 2000," the navy advanced the concept of a two-front war against the Soviet Union that would require carrier task forces to attack land targets both on the Kola Peninsula and in Soviet Asia.[20] Forward attack of this sort against the core strength of Soviet naval deployment and a clear Soviet commitment to defend these areas would be an extremely demanding task. It would endanger a significant portion of the U.S. Navy, and it is unlikely that current forces or those programmed in the five-year defense plan would be sufficient.[21] Such a mission would probably demand additional aircraft carriers, more AEGIS destroy-ers, and an increased number of the more expensive F-14 fighters. The cost of such increments would probably run close to $10 billion.

Both the cost and the basic wisdom of this mission are sharply questioned outside the navy. Attacks on the Soviet Union of this sort would clearly be strategic if only because Soviet ballistic missile sub-marines seem to be the principal targets. Circumstances that moti-vated such attacks would also motivate strategic operations, which would be aimed at many of the same targets.

20. U.S. Department of the Navy, "Sea Plan 2000, Unclassified Executive Sum-mary" (1978).
21. The Congressional Budget Office, in *Navy Budget Issues,* chapters 3 and 4, assesses the prospects and requirements for performing this invasion and finds the current plan inadequate for the purpose.

The secretary of defense in his 1980 annual report presented a less demanding concept of the missions of the surface navy in a war with the Soviet Union.[22] In explaining the proposals for carrier task forces and other elements of the surface fleet, he emphasized defensive missions against Soviet attacks in the open ocean—protecting allied shipping from air and submarine attack and defending against any operations in the Atlantic or the Pacific of the Soviet surface fleets. For these purposes the current shipbuilding program seems adequate to most authorities. Though a war in which nuclear weapons remained in reserve on both sides is highly unlikely, in such a war the United States could expect to use carrier task forces, land-based aircraft, and attack submarines for supporting combat operations in many areas of the globe.

Few doubt that the protection of the Atlantic and the Pacific is intrinsically desirable if war should occur, but doubts about the more defensive mission concepts do arise when assessing the threat. If the Soviet navy is not being designed for major conventional naval combat in the Atlantic and the Pacific, desirable trade-offs can be made to direct U.S. naval development toward less demanding contingencies elsewhere in the world. These include the construction of cheaper, smaller, less capable ships in greater numbers and an emphasis on more modest aircraft, which could be purchased and maintained in greater numbers under existing and prospective budget levels.

In short, attaining the goal of clear-sighted, efficient naval planning for these and other issues will require a more stable, more explicit, more authoritative policy than now exists relating the character of the Soviet naval threat to the missions of U.S. forces.

Conclusion

The increase in defense spending in the President's 1980 budget is intended to serve notice that the United States is not lowering its military guard. But national security cannot be purchased merely by spending more money. At any level of spending, defense resources must be effectively directed to actual military needs. There is currently wide disagreement about the definition of these needs. In the principal areas of military activity, the relationship between basic

22. *Department of Defense Annual Report, Fiscal Year 1980*, pp. 183–84.

objectives, major missions, and actual force deployments has not been made clear. Those who seek to form an opinion about the defense budget and those who must act on it are entitled to ask whether its allocation of resources is fully consistent with national security requirements. Resolution of such doubts through sharp and constructive debate is necessary to achieve greater clarity of purpose in defense policy and will help the United States play a more effective role in world affairs.

APPENDIX A

Proposals to Limit Federal Spending and Balance the Budget

BRUCE K. MACLAURY

A GALLUP POLL in July 1978 found that 81 percent of the respondents favored a constitutional amendment requiring Congress to balance the federal budget every year. At the end of March 1979, twenty-nine of the necessary thirty-four states had approved some form of resolution asking Congress to call a constitutional convention for the purpose of proposing such an amendment. And the Ninety-sixth Congress itself started off with a flurry of bills and resolutions in a hasty effort to get at the head of the stampede.

Demands for balanced budgets, reduced taxes, and limited federal expenditures are nothing new in this country. But they have taken on a new political dimension with the passage last year of California's Proposition 13, which drastically cut property taxes in that state. For years, bills to require balanced federal budgets have been introduced in Congress as a matter of ritual, but never before have they received a serious hearing.

The public's frustration with government has many probable causes—the past decade's unexpectedly large increases in income transfer programs, continuing reports of inefficiency and waste, rising social security taxes, and the expanding web of regulations and red

The author thanks Robert W. Hartman for helpful comments and Amy E. Kessler for research assistance.

tape. But no single factor, it seems, has had a more corrosive effect on public attitudes, particularly attitudes toward government, than the persistence, and recent acceleration, of inflation. Few people blame government alone for the nation's inflation problems—rising energy and food prices did play a role. But most people do assign government an important responsibility in the inflation process—and with reason.

The administration and the Congress have contributed to inflation in a number of separate actions that individually seemed negligible for inflation arithmetic, but that cumulatively added to the momentum of rising wages and prices—hikes in payroll taxes and minimum wage rates, acreage allotments and higher crop support prices, import limitations and steel trigger prices, inadequate consideration of costs in regulatory decisions, and so forth.[1] Given the underemployed state of the economy, the cost-raising effects of actions such as these may well have contributed more to inflation in the last few years than the level of federal spending or the budget deficits have.

But those who blame government for inflation usually have in mind "excessive" government expenditures or budget deficits as the major culprits. For this reason, they propose a variety of limitations on spending and on deficits.

A good case can in fact be made for further strengthening controls over the federal budget. The risk, however, is that some of the proposed cures are far worse than the present disease. In evaluating this risk, it is important to distinguish between limitations imposed by constitutional amendments and those effected through changes in federal law.

Rationale for Budgetary Limitations

A fundamental issue in the current debate is whether deficits in the federal budget in and of themselves contribute to inflation. No one would argue that such deficits never add to inflationary pressures —they did add to them during the Vietnam War and in 1972–73. On those occasions, the excess of federal expenditures over receipts was superimposed on an economy whose resources were already fully

1. See chapters 3 and 4 and Robert W. Crandall, "Federal Government Initiatives to Reduce the Price Level," in Arthur M. Okun and George L. Perry, eds., *Curing Chronic Inflation* (Brookings Institution, 1978), pp. 165–216.

employed. Under such circumstances, additional demand, whether from government or from the private sector, results not in additional output but in inflation.

Under different circumstances, however, when resources—human and capital—are underemployed, an increase in total demand can increase output and employment without necessarily creating pressures that generate inflation. Then the use of the federal budget to counter slack in other sectors has obvious advantages and, conceptually at least, few costs. Moreover, fiscal stimulus can be achieved through tax cuts as well as by expenditure increases (though not necessarily with the same incidence, timing, and multipliers), so that during recessions countercyclical policies need not result in swollen outlays even when they do result in deficits.

But even though there is no necessary link between federal deficits and inflation or between countercyclical fiscal policy and an expanding government role, the record is pretty clear:

1. Federal deficits *have* contributed to excess demand pressures and inflation in critical times in the past.

2. The difference between an economy that is "underemployed" and one that is "fully employed" is difficult to gauge, partly because it is defined by a range rather than by a point. Moreover, the range itself is changing with changes in the competitive structure of industries, the work force, income maintenance programs, patterns of employment, and the availability of efficient plant capacity.

3. The processes by which fiscal policy is consciously adapted to changing economic conditions are ponderous and unreliable, a problem that is compounded by the uncertain lags in the impact of discretionary fiscal actions on the economy itself.

4. Fiscal policy decisions are biased toward deficits during recessions, without the discipline of surpluses during periods of excess demand, and toward expenditure increases rather than tax reductions to provide stimulus.

For all these reasons, countercyclical fiscal policy, though it has been—and remains—a valid tool for improving the performance of the economy, has limitations that are becoming increasingly apparent. Moreover, lagging productivity and a somber budget outlook for the next five years (see chapter 2) make budget discipline imperative. Consequently, a widespread search is on for some means of correcting the political biases that have resulted in sixteen deficits in the past seventeen years. But it is a long and perilous leap from this conclusion to a demand that there be no more deficits except in declared national emergencies.

The Balanced Budget Amendment

The most radical suggestion proposed in the name of fiscal responsibility is that deficits in the federal budget be prohibited by constitutional amendment. Only by incorporating this requirement in the fundamental law of the land, it is argued, can the pressures toward excessive federal spending and deficits be held in check.[2]

Analogies are sometimes drawn with similar requirements in state constitutions and city charters. However, such analogies frequently fail to point out that (1) the requirement for federal budget balance usually applies to receipts and outlays in the unified budget—which includes all types of purchases—while state and local governments usually balance the current account and finance capital outlays through borrowing; (2) individual states, unlike the federal government, have neither the responsibility for influencing nor the capability to influence the performance of the national economy through budget policy; and (3) despite such requirements, the state-local sector has grown faster than the federal sector since World War II, and some state and local governments have recently encountered substantial fiscal difficulties.

Article 5 of the Constitution stipulates that amendments can be initiated in one of two ways: by a two-thirds vote in both houses of Congress or by a constitutional convention called by Congress on application of the legislatures of two-thirds (thirty-four) of the states. In either case, a ratification of proposed amendments requires votes by three-quarters (thirty-eight) of the states. In fact, all the existing amendments were proposed by the Congress rather than through a constitutional convention. No definitive precedents exist, therefore, for the terms of reference of such a convention. Under the circumstances, there is considerable debate about the wisdom of calling a convention whose delegates might seek to revise other elements of the Constitution as well.

2. A requirement for balanced budgets does not automatically imply curbed expenditures, since taxes could be raised to match expanded outlays. The presumption is, however, that Congress would find it harder to raise expenditures if it had to vote matching tax increases.

If Congress were to propose an amendment, the ambiguities and risks of a constitutional convention would not arise. And in fact many such proposals have been introduced. Typical of the ones calling for a balanced budget was Senate Joint Resolution 38, introduced by Senator Harry F. Byrd of Virginia. That resolution said that "the Congress shall assure that total outlays of the Government during any fiscal year do not exceed the total receipts of the Government during such fiscal year,"[3] with an escape clause activated by a two-thirds vote in both houses in the case of a national emergency. The simplicity of the language masks innumerable complexities and uncertainties that would be encountered in implementation. These complexities arise because of (1) the length of time between budget preparation and completion of the fiscal year, (2) the sensitivity of receipts and expenditures to changes in the performance of the economy, and (3) the joint responsibility of the executive and legislative branches for budgetary decisions.

Presumably, the President would have to propose a balanced budget in his budget message in January for the fiscal year ending twenty-one months later, unless he decided to ask Congress to declare a national emergency. The economic assumptions underlying his budget estimates would be critical, since a one percentage point difference in real GNP can translate into an $8 billion change in the budget surplus or deficit. It is true that the President faces the same forecasting difficulties today in making up the budget. But when the forecasts go awry, as they almost inevitably have done (see table A-1), at least the President is not in jeopardy of violating the Constitution.

Since Congress always makes changes in the President's proposed budget, the onus for assuring balance would presumably pass to them. The first and second concurrent budget resolutions (in May and September) would have to show a balance or surplus.[4] But such resolutions—and, indeed, budgets in general—are *plans* for spending and taxing. What would be the remedy if the final budget accounting after the end of the fiscal year showed a deficit because of changes in the economy, despite the earlier plan to balance the

3. *Congressional Record,* daily edition (February 8, 1979), p. S1306.
4. Some amendments seek to limit *appropriations* to current receipts. These proposals fail to take into account that spending in any given year is (and must be) affected by appropriations of previous years and that appropriations of a given year influence future spending.

Table A-1. Comparison of Budget Estimates with Actual Outcomes, Fiscal Years 1969–78
Billions of dollars

Fiscal year[a]	Receipts		Outlays		Surplus or deficit	
	Estimate[b]	Actual	Estimate[b]	Actual	Estimate[b]	Actual
1969	178.1	187.8	186.1	184.5	−8.0	3.2
1970	198.7	193.7	195.3	196.6	3.4	−2.8
1971	202.1	188.4	200.8	211.4	1.3	−23.0
1972	217.6	208.6	229.2	232.0	−11.6	−23.4
1973	220.8	232.2	246.3	247.1	−25.5	−14.8
1974	256.0	264.9	268.7	269.6	−12.7	−4.7
1975	295.0	281.0	304.4	326.2	−9.4	−45.2
1976	297.5	300.0	349.4	366.4	−51.9	−66.4
1977	351.3	357.8	394.2	402.7	−43.0	−45.0
1978	393.0	402.0	440.0	450.8	−47.0	−48.8

Source: *The Budget of the United States Government,* various issues.
a. Ending June 30 for 1969–76 and September 30 for 1977–79.
b. First estimate made when budget for the fiscal year was submitted to Congress.

budget?[5] Senator Byrd's resolution says simply that "the Congress shall have power to enforce this article by appropriate legislation."

Aside from questions of mechanics and enforcement, one should ponder what new incentives would be set up by such an amendment. Would the amendment really instill the fiscal discipline intended by its sponsors, or would it lead to new and unimagined ingenuity in redefining the budget and restructuring modes of expenditures to comply with the mandate? The federal budget is a living document. To provide a more comprehensive accounting of the impact of federal transactions on the economy, the unified budget adopted in 1969 combined the earlier administrative budget with the operations of the important trust funds.[6] But there have been many shifts in the other direction. Federally sponsored lending institutions, such as the Federal National Mortgage Association and the Federal Intermediate Credit Banks (for agriculture), were "privatized" to remove them

5. One possibility might be to instruct the secretary of the treasury to stop issuing checks whenever the receipts fell short of expenditures during a fiscal year, an action that would grind the government to a halt, particularly when receipts were at a seasonal low. Probably for this reason, the typical proposal requires a balance between receipts and expenditures for an entire fiscal year.

6. In the aggregate, these trust funds are currently accruing annual surpluses. Under a balanced budget amendment, supporters of trust fund–financed programs (for example, social security and highways) would almost surely try to have the trust funds removed from the budget to protect spending for these programs, thus reversing the 1969 advance in budgetary accounting.

Table A-2. Outlays for the Budget, Off-Budget Federal Entities, and Government-Sponsored Enterprises, Fiscal Years 1969–80

Billions of dollars

| | Federal government | | | Government-sponsored enterprises[b] |
Fiscal year[a]	Budget	Off-budget federal entities[b]	Total	
1969	184.5	...	184.5	4.3
1970	196.6	...	196.6	9.6
1971	211.4	...	211.4	c
1972	232.0	...	232.0	4.4
1973	247.1	0.1	247.1	11.4
1974	269.6	1.4	271.1	14.5
1975	326.2	8.1	334.2	7.0
1976	366.4	7.3	373.7	4.6
1977	402.7	8.7	411.4	10.2
1978	450.8	10.3	461.2	25.6
1979[d]	493.4	12.0	505.4	15.2
1980[d]	531.6	12.0	543.5	19.1

Source: *The Budget of the United States Government, Fiscal Year 1980*, p. 313.
a. Ending June 30 for 1969–76 and September 30 for 1977–79.
b. The off-budget federal entities and the privately owned, government-sponsored enterprises primarily carry out loan programs. To prevent double counting, outlays of government-sponsored enterprises exclude loans to other government-sponsored enterprises and loans to or from federal agencies and off-budget federal entities.
c. $50 million or less.
d. Estimated.

from the budget. Subsequently, Congress created the Federal Home Loan Mortgage Corporation and the Student Loan Marketing Association outside the budget. The Export-Import Bank was removed from the budget in 1971, only to be reinstated in 1976. In total, outlays of off-budget federal entities are expected to amount to $12 billion in fiscal 1980 and those of government-sponsored agencies to $19.1 billion. The total of $31.1 billion is 6 percent of the $531.6 billion proposed by the President for 1980 (table A-2). Loan guarantees are another important means of allocating resources that escape current budget accounting. Guaranteed and insured loans outstanding are projected to be almost $284 billion in 1980.

The room for maneuver is by no means limited to moving specific agencies or programs into and out of the budget totals. There are any number of ways in which Congress can structure programs to serve similar public purposes but to have very different impacts on the budget. Instead of direct expenditures on behalf of, say, housing or agriculture, Congress can create subsidized loan programs, or loan guarantees, or special tax credits and deductions, or crop support prices and acreage allotments. In the environmental, health, and safety areas, Congress has mandated that companies in the private sector spend funds to assure compliance with the relevant standards, funds that otherwise might have shown up as budget outlays. Federal agencies could be instructed to defer payment of bills for extended periods, thereby creating a kind of under-the-table authority to run a deficit. Senator Gary W. Hart of Colorado recently renewed an old suggestion that would separate current expenses from long-term capital investments in the budget, supposedly to bring it into closer conformity with practices followed by state and local governments and by business. With a capital budget option, a strictly limited current budget would create incentives to (1) define many current outlays as capital outlays (for example, grants to students might be so defined because they build human capital), and (2) provide more federal stimulus through bricks, mortar, and steel rather than make a careful assessment of alternatives (for example, public housing would be favored over rent subsidies and more buses over fare subsidies).[7]

The tougher the constraints on spending budget dollars, the greater the incentive for finding off-budget means of accomplishing public purposes. Such pressures exist today. They could become irresistible if the alternative were violation of the Constitution. The ultimate irony would be that these off-budget devices would increase costs and promote inefficiency.

Federal Spending Amendment

A different sort of proposed constitutional amendment would not prohibit deficits but would limit federal spending "to protect the people against excessive governmental burdens and to promote sound fiscal and monetary policies." More specifically, the amended Constitution would read in part:

Total outlays in any fiscal year shall not increase by a percentage greater than the percentage increase in nominal gross national product in the last calendar year ending prior to the beginning of said fiscal year. . . .

If inflation for the last calendar year ending prior to the beginning of

7. See Maynard S. Comiez, *A Capital Budget Statement for the U.S. Government* (Brookings Institution, 1966).

any fiscal year is more than three percent, the permissible percentage increase in total outlays for that fiscal year shall be reduced by one-fourth of the excess of inflation over three per cent. . . .

This article may be enforced by one or more members of the Congress in an action brought in the United States District Court for the District of Columbia. . . . The action shall name as defendant the Treasurer of the United States, who shall have authority over outlays by any unit or agency of the Government of the United States when required by a court order.[8]

This proposal is the work of the National Tax Limitation Committee, of which Milton Friedman is a prominent member. Among other things, it covers both budget and off-budget outlays, incorporates an escape clause for national emergencies, and provides some protection for grants to state and local governments. This more elaborate drafting spells out more details but carries its own costs. As Senator Edmund S. Muskie of Maine said, "Our Constitution does only two things. It blueprints the structures by which we govern ourselves. And it defines the human rights we respect. Do we really want to devalue that currency with algebra and bar graphs?"[9]

Apart from constitutional aesthetics, the spending limitation amendment raises many of the same practical difficulties in implementation that the balanced budget amendment does. Especially attractive would be the conversion of existing spending programs into tax credits, thereby removing them from the outlay limit and from annual congressional budget review.[10] Since certain categories of expenditures (for example, unemployment insurance) rise automatically during recessions, expenditure reductions presumably would have to be made in other, noncyclical categories, with uncertain programmatic consequences. More fundamentally, in a changing society the Constitution should not specify a static relationship between the size of the federal government sector (with the inherent problems in determining which off-budget accounts to include) and the economy as measured by GNP.

Despite these questions, an amendment limiting outlays would have fewer capricious and adverse effects on the performance of the

8. *Congressional Record*, daily edition (February 1, 1979), p. S1022.

9. Address to the National Press Club, February 13, 1979. Reprinted in *Congressional Record*, daily edition (February 15, 1979), p. H632. Most economists would object to the introduction into the Constitution of such technical terms as gross national product. They fear that there would be pressure to redefine these terms if constitutional requirements had to be met.

10. See appendix B.

national economy than the proposal for perpetually balanced budgets. In particular, it would not necessarily require the federal government to cut total expenditures during cyclical downturns, a step that could only intensify a recession. It would also allow the use of tax policy as a tool for countercyclical adjustment.

Alternative Approaches

There have been a number of suggestions for greater fiscal restraint that involve taking less drastic steps. Senator William Proxmire and others, for example, have proposed a bill (S.331)—not an amendment—that would mandate a balanced budget whenever real economic growth was at or above 3 percent, an approximation of the long-term growth potential of the economy. Although this bill suffers from many of the measurement, incentive, and enforcement difficulties mentioned in connection with the balanced budget amendment, it does allow deficits in periods of economic slack. And as a law rather than a constitutional amendment, it could be changed with less delay if found to be unworkable or perverse in its effects.

A more modest but nevertheless important suggestion, designed to meet taxpayer concerns, has been put forward by Robert W. Hartman of the Brookings Institution. He would build on the improvements already introduced in the congressional budget process by the Congressional Budget and Impoundment Control Act of 1974. That act for the first time required—through the newly created budget committees in both houses—a comprehensive review of expenditures and revenues, and concurrent binding resolutions on the following year's budget.

Hartman's suggestion, which parallels similar proposals by the Congressional Budget Office, is that the concurrent resolutions include spending and taxing limits for the two years following the budget year, as well as for the budget year itself.[11] This kind of budget blueprint would (1) focus debate on longer-term trends in the budget and their implications for the trade-off between public and private needs (rather than on countercyclical fiscal policy, as is now the case), (2) require congressional committees to face up to the out-year trade-offs between federal programs and predetermined

11. Robert W. Hartman, "Kemp-Roth and All That," *Taxing and Spending*, vol. 2 (February 1979), pp. 12–18.

expenditure targets, (3) highlight rising expenditures before they became "uncontrollable," and (4) reduce the incentive for tax committees to load the effect of tax cuts into years beyond the concurrent resolution.[12]

The congressional budget process has already generated tension among members and committees as its constraints have taken hold. Out-year limits would add new pressures. However, it is much more appropriate to nudge Congress toward greater fiscal responsibility in this orderly way than to create a straitjacket that renders fiscal policy impotent as an economic policy tool or encourages subterfuge that would make a mockery of a constitutional amendment.

12. On April 2, 1979, Congress added to the annual debt-ceiling bill an amendment along the lines of the Hartman proposal. The amendment required the congressional budget committees to present to the Congress by April 15, 1979, alternative methods of balancing the federal budget in fiscal years 1981 and 1982 as well as the implications of these plans for the 1980 budget. In 1980 the President is required to present an alternative balanced budget plan if his proposals will result in a deficit in 1981 or 1982. Aside from requiring informational reports on the consequences of balanced budgets, this amendment does nothing to integrate future year considerations into the budget process itself, as Hartman proposed.

Tax Expenditures

JOSEPH A. PECHMAN

THE TERM "tax expenditures" is often applied to the special provisions of the income tax laws that reduce the tax liability of those who make payments or receive incomes in certain designated forms. Many of these tax subsidies are the equivalent of direct federal expenditures. But direct expenditures are shown in the budget as outlays, whereas tax subsidies are reflected in lower income tax receipts. The term "tax expenditures" emphasizes the similarity between tax subsidies and direct outlays. The Congressional Budget Act of 1974 requires a listing of tax expenditures in each budget and directs all congressional committees to identify any changes made in them by new legislation.

The 1974 act defines tax expenditures as "revenue losses attributable to provisions of the federal tax laws which allow a special exclusion, exemption, or deduction from gross income or which provide a special credit, a preferential rate of tax, or a deferral of tax liability." A tax expenditure, then, is a result of any deviation from the normal tax structure. The law does not define the normal tax structure, but it is generally regarded as being as close to economic income as practical measurement permits. (Thus capital gains are included in full, but imputed incomes such as rental values of owned homes are not because they are difficult to measure.) The normal

Amy E. Kessler and Andrew Winokur provided research assistance.

Table B-1. Effect of Tax Expenditures on the Federal Budget, Fiscal Year 1980
Billions of dollars

Item	Outlays	Receipts	Deficit
Official 1980 budget	531.6	502.6	−29.0
Tax expenditures[a]	169.0	169.0	...
Revised total	700.6	671.6	−29.0

Sources: *The Budget of the United States Government, Fiscal Year 1980*, p. 14; and *Special Analyses, Budget of the United States Government, Fiscal Year 1980*, pp. 207–11.

a. See table B-2. The totals of the tax expenditures are the sum of the revenue effects of the individual items, each computed separately and assuming no other changes in the tax laws. They probably understate the total revenue effects because individuals would be pushed into higher brackets if all or a group of tax expenditures were removed simultaneously.

individual income tax structure includes the personal exemption, the standard deduction, and the rate schedules.

Tax expenditures in fiscal 1980 are estimated at $169.0 billion. If they were replaced by direct expenditures of the same value to taxpayers, both outlays and receipts would be raised by $169.0 billion; thus outlays in 1978 would be $700.6 billion instead of the $531.6 billion reported in the budget, and receipts would be $671.6 billion, so that the deficit would remain at $29.0 billion (table B-1). (Total tax expenditures are the sum of the revenue effects of the individual items, each computed separately and assuming no other changes in the tax laws. They probably understate the total revenue effects because individuals would be pushed into higher brackets if all or a group of tax expenditures were removed simultaneously.)

The major tax expenditures are (1) personal deductions under the individual income tax (for state and local income, sales, and property taxes, charitable contributions, medical expenses, and interest paid); (2) exclusions from taxable income (state and local government bond interest, employee benefits, and transfer payments such as social security, unemployment compensation, and welfare); (3) preferential treatment of long-term capital gains; and (4) tax credits and accelerated depreciation for investment. The Energy Tax Act of 1978 introduced a number of new tax credits to encourage home insulation and the use of solar energy. A list of the major tax expenditures is given in table B-2.

Including estimates of tax expenditures in the budget encourages the administration and the Congress to take them into account in

Table B-2. Major Tax Expenditures, Fiscal Year 1980

Millions of dollars

Tax expenditure	Individuals	Corporations	Total
Deduction of state and local nonbusiness taxes	19,065	0	19,065
Deduction of charitable contributions	7,955	1,015	8,970
Deduction of mortgage interest and interest on consumer credit	12,235	0	12,235
Deduction of medical expenses	3,120	0	3,120
Deductibility of casualty losses	475	0	475
Exclusion of employer contributions to pension, health, and welfare plans[a]	25,750	0	25,750
Exclusion of benefits and allowances to armed forces personnel	1,470	0	1,470
Exemptions for age and blindness and tax credit for the elderly	2,050	0	2,050
Exclusion of transfer payments	13,305	0	13,305
Earned income credit	740	0	740
Residential, conservation, and new technology energy credits	435	390	825
Job credits	135	560	695
Dividend exclusion	450	0	450
Exemption for parents of students aged nineteen and over	1,020	0	1,020
Credit for child and dependent care expenses	705	0	705
Preferential treatment of capital gains	22,270[b]	1,010	23,280[b]
Maximum tax on personal service income	1,625	0	1,625
Exclusion and deferral of interest payments[c]	6,395	4,695	11,090
Tax credits or exclusions for income from abroad	555	730	1,285
Investment tax credit[d]	3,150	15,940	19,090
Asset depreciation range[e]	580	2,955	3,535
Excess of first-year depreciation and depreciation on buildings and rental housing over straight-line	540	250	790
Excess of percentage over cost depletion and expensing of exploration and development costs	990	2,425	3,415
Expensing of construction period interest and taxes	145	555	700
Expensing of research and development expenditures	35	1,745	1,780

Table B-2 (*continued*)

Tax expenditure	Individuals	Corporations	Total
Deferral of income of domestic international sales corporations and controlled foreign corporations	0	1,705	1,705
Deduction of excess bad debt reserves of financial institutions	0	855	855
Reduced rates on first $100,000 of corporate income[f]	0	7,075	7,075
Other	1,035	855	1,890
Total[g]	126,230	42,760	168,990

Source: *Special Analyses, Budget of the United States Government, Fiscal Year 1980*, pp. 207–11.

a. Includes contributions to individual retirement accounts and prepaid legal services and Keogh plans for the self-employed.

b. Includes revenue effect of deferral of tax on capital gains transferred by gift or at death.

c. Includes exclusion of interest on state and local government debt and life insurance savings and deferral of interest on federal savings bonds.

d. Includes credit for rehabilitation of structures and employee stock ownership plans.

e. Includes expensing of certain capital outlays.

f. Includes exemption for corporate surtax.

g. See table B-1, note a.

budget decisions. Tax expenditures constitute 31 percent of budget outlays (see table B-3), and in recent years they have grown faster than outlays. For some budget functions, tax expenditures (for example, aid for housing and to state and local governments) exceed direct outlays. The distributional effects of tax expenditures are often quite different from those of direct expenditures. For example, the deductibility of mortgage interest is of little benefit to the poor, whereas outlays for rent subsidies do help them.

There is a continual tug-of-war between proponents of tax credits and budget and tax experts who resist the proliferation of special tax provisions because they complicate the tax laws and are frequently less efficient than direct expenditures. Congressional appropriations committees prefer direct outlays, and the tax committees prefer tax credits. The budget committees, recognizing both the similarities of and the differences between the two approaches, are trying to focus the attention of Congress on the merits of alternative approaches rather than on the choice of the committee that originates the legislation. Only when it is understood and accepted that a vote for a tax expenditure is in many ways the same as a vote for a direct expenditure can the budget process be said to work.

Table B-3. Estimated Federal Budget Outlays and Tax Expenditures, by Function, Fiscal Year 1980

Amounts in billions of dollars

		Tax expenditures	
Budget function	Outlay[a]	Amount	Percent of outlay
National defense	125.8	1.6	1.3
International affairs	8.2	2.3	28.0
General science, space, and technology	5.5	1.8	32.7
Energy	7.9	4.3	54.4
Natural resources and environment	11.5	1.0	8.7
Agriculture	4.3	1.3	30.2
Commerce and housing credit	3.4	72.9	2,144.1
Transportation	17.6	[b]	0.2
Community and regional development	7.3	[b]	0.2
Education, training, employment, and social services	30.2	13.0	43.0
Health	53.4	14.1	26.4
Income security	179.1	35.7	19.9
Veterans' benefits and services	20.5	1.2	5.9
Administration of justice	4.4	...	...
Interest	46.1	0.6	1.3
General government	4.4	0.1	2.3
General purpose fiscal assistance	8.8	19.1	217.0
Total[c]	538.4	169.0	31.4

Sources: *The Budget of the United States Government, Fiscal Year 1980*, p. 85; and *Special Analyses, Budget of the United States Government, Fiscal Year 1980*, pp. 207–11. Figures are rounded.
a. Excluding undistributed offsetting receipts and allowances.
b. Less than $50 million.
c. See table B-1, note a.

TYPESETTING *Monotype Composition Company, Inc., Baltimore*
PRINTING & BINDING *R. R. Donnelley & Sons Company, Chicago*